Beyond the Mosque

Other books by the author:

The Fortress and the Fire
New Paths in Muslim Evangelism (Baker)
Bridges to Islam (Baker)

1986

Beyond the Mosque

Christians Within Muslim Communit

Phil Parshal

BAKER BOOK HOUSE
Grand Rapids, Michigan 49506

pyright 1985 by
ker Book House Company

3N: 0-8010-7089-9

rary of Congress Catalog Card Number: 85-70508

nted in the United States of America

ripture references are from the New American Standard Bible. Quranic
otations are from *The Meaning of the Glorious Koran* by Mohammed Mar-
duke Pickthall.

In Appreciation

Ed Welch
one who has traversed "the Way" with me,
in the valleys with sorrowful tears,
on the mountaintops with joyous laughter

Habel
formerly a Muslim, now a beloved brother in Christ

Dr. Ali
my confidant, teacher, and intimate Muslim friend

A friend is one soul abiding in two bodies.

—Aristotle

Contents

Contents

Foreword

There is built into all of humanity a deep desire for fellowship, a oneness with other human beings. At different times and different places in history this has worked itself out in many ways. The current American trend away from a culture of narcissism to what one author describes as "an ethic of commitment" is but a fresh example of our desire to be at one with one another.

Such oneness is fundamental to Christianity. Where we were once alienated from God and one another, the gospel declares us to be one in Christ. The intimacy of this relationship is so profound that Paul can only describe it as the kind of intimacy found among the various parts of the human body (Eph. 4). In some way too mysterious to fathom we are related to that special local body of Christians called the church and to all members of Christ's body everywhere. This oneness, this unity, is something that requires a constant search on our part. History indicates that just when we think we have attained it, it slips through our fingers. But the concept of unity, of oneness in Christ, is fundamental to all Christian thinking.

And so with Islam. The *ummah,* the total community of Islam, is a concept which dominates Muslim thinking and practice. Like Christianity, Isalm struggles with both the meaning and the practice. But as Phil Parshall so aptly demonstrates, there is little understanding on the part of Christians of this dominant feature of Islam, and there is equal ignorance on the part of Muslims about our concept of oneness in Christ.

Phil Parshall loves Christ. He also loves Muslims. In his writings he has attempted to give us a deeper understanding of not only the pillars of Islam, but also how Muslims think and respond and *why* they think and respond the way that they do. Islam is second only to Christianity in its claimed membership. It is militantly attempting to convert the world because it has a deeply held faith about the rightness of what it believes and the power of Islam to bring a new God-directed order to the world.

Parshall helps us to see not only the concept of *ummah* that is at the core of Islam, but also the internal struggles that exist as Muslims in their wide diversity seek to make it work. His intent is not only that we should *know* more, but also that God might use our understanding to bring us a deeper love for these seekers after God who have not yet found Christ. Rather than have us attack Islam, Parshall would have us appreciate that which is good within it so that with thoughtfulness and love we may frame the message of the gospel in a way that the Holy Spirit can touch hearts and lives.

As he has in his previous work, Parshall discusses the implication of Muslim thought and practice for the formation of churches of Muslim converts. He helps us work our way through the thicket of what is cultural and what is basically religious.

For those whom God has called to win Muslims to Christ this book is required reading. For those of us who want to know ourselves better in the light of how others see us, this book presents some challenges that cannot be ignored.

Edward R. Dayton
Vice President
World Vision

Acknowledgments

Introductory books on Islam continue to flow forth from Christian presses. I find this to be a bit distressing. It seems to me that we should leave the rudiments of Islam and press on to examine the weightier matters of Muslim life: theology, ethics, sociology, and ethnic distinctives. Our efforts should be directed toward exploring the potential to bridge differences between Islam and Christianity. Let us develop a meaningful theological statement on the Trinity that can clear away some of the fog in Muslim minds . . . and perhaps in Christian minds as well! What about a creative book on how radio and literature can be effectively contextualized for a Muslim audience? It is sad indeed to document the types of American cultural Christian programing that are currently being broadcast into Muslim countries.

In light of this feeling of frustration, I was pleased to receive a letter from David W. Shenk in which he mentioned his concern for a book dealing with the *ummah* (community) aspects of Islam. This area of study is particularly relevant to me, as I have worked in a Muslim country with a team that has sought to enter deeply into the general principles of Muslim sociological patterns. Thus, I embarked on this study with a high sense of expectation. It has been a stimulating experience, one that I trust has transferable value.

My mission society has been a model of supportive love and encouragement. It is my theory that few missions would have allowed me the freedom to study, write, and travel as I have over these past twenty-two years. Therefore, I gratefully acknowledge their input in all areas of my ministry—from top leadership to the very special team of missionaries with whom I have labored.

During these past few years the Lord has allowed new opportunities for me to forge deep and meaningful relationships with Muslims. Without this dimension of recent experience I would not have been emboldened to attempt this task of research and writing on the *ummah* of Islam.

In the fall of 1983, I was invited to spend a semester as a Fellow at Harvard University. During that stimulating period of time I was enabled to focus on the actual writing of this book. My gratitude is extended to William Graham, professor of Near Eastern languages and civilization at Harvard, for helpfully critiquing the first three chapters of this book. Other friendly critics who have influenced my work in a positive sense are Merle Inniger, David W. Shenk, and Ed Welch. Ed Dayton, vice president of World Vision, has taken time from his busy schedule to write the Foreword. Missionaries to Islam are grateful to Ed for his involvements with us during these past years of breaking new ground in Muslim evangelism.

One of the essential ingredients of a writer's "profile" is a supportive family. I have been blessed above measure in having a wife and daughter who unselfishly defer to a husband and father who is so frequently pen- and paper-bound. My books would never have been more than cerebral waves without their gracious and wholehearted support. To Julie and Lindy I extend my love and devotion.

The dedication of this book is directed toward three special people. One is an American missionary, one an Asian convert from Islam, and the one is a devout Muslim who has greatly endeared himself to me. These three are representative rather than exhaustive. How grateful to the Lord I am for those unnamed persons who have graciously overlooked my inadequacies and have been a great source of strength and encouragement to me over the years.

Introduction

Dr. Ali is a highly esteemed middle-aged Muslim college professor in an Asian country. His Ph.D is in the area of Sufism or folk Islam. Ali has appeared numerous times on national television and is a regular correspondent for the largest English-language newspaper in the country. He has published five books about Islamic-related subjects.

It has been my privilege to be an intimate friend of Ali. His family is comprised of his wife, who is a professor at the local girls' college, two teen-age boys in high school, and a lovely, talented daughter who is completing her university studies. Ali's father is a retired government officer. His mother is a devout and gracious Muslim lady. Both parents live with Ali's family. It is not unusual to find fifteen to twenty people gathered around the dinner table in the Ali home.

Over a period of two and a half years, my wife, daughter, and I integrated into the Ali household. In a psychological sense, we formed an extended family. At least twice a week we shared hospitality and gourmet delicacies. His burdens, heartaches, and joys were mine. My periods of despondency as well as times of elation were accepted by Ali as his very own. What delights were ours as we walked through the lush countryside and assimilated the beauty of God's creation. At times Ali would break forth into poetry or song. His liberated spirit would soar as he soaked in the smell of the budding roses. A gathering storm of billowing, ferocious clouds would send Ali into ecstasy as he lifted his arms and proclaimed the might and majesty of an almighty God.

Religiously, Ali is a convinced Muslim. Without fail, he prays five times a day. The month of Ramadan finds him refusing all food and water during the long hot days of fasting. Ali's family consistently exercises a practical concern for people who are in need. This involvement extends beyond Islam to those who are Hindus as well as those of the Christian faith.

It was interesting to me to observe Ali's concern for the spiritual welfare of his family. He forbade movie attendance. Observing the commencement of rebellion in his children, Ali purchased a television set as a regulated alternative to what he regarded as the more worldly entertainment of the cinema.

Through the Ali family I was able to enter into the flow of community life within Islam. It was a challenge to observe the sense of *ummah* within the extended family as well as to see how it rippled out to others, particularly those of the household of Islam. What a unique opportunity I received for entering into the mainstream of Islamic sociological and religious experience.

Overall, I give Muslims very high marks for a sense of solidarity. This is emphatically true of their own nuclear and extended families. It is applicable to the broader community of Muslims as well, but to a lesser extent. Regrettably, I find that most followers of the Prophet consider *ummah* to be limited to those within the Islamic fold.

The Influence of *Ummah*

Badru D. Kateregga comments on the initial small Muslim Arabic community which has grown to embrace one-sixth of the world's population:

> As Islam spread, the *Ummah*, which was essentially based on Islamic law, was quickly transformed from an Arab *Ummah* into a universal Muslim *Ummah*. It is not surprising that the *Ummah* extended very quickly, after the Prophet's death, far beyond the confines of the Arabian Peninsula. In the process, it brought together peoples of different cultures, races, and nations to form one great *Ummah*. Today the *Ummah* is still spreading.[1]

1. Badru D. Kateregga and David W. Shenk, *Islam and Christianity: A Muslim and a Christian in Dialogue* (Grand Rapids: Eerdmans, 1980), p. 52.

It is difficult, if not impossible, to postulate an accurate population figure for Muslims throughout the world. A current educated guess would be about 850 million. Only Christians (approximately one billion of them) outnumber Muslims. However, "Islam is larger than any single expression of Christianity, there being more Muslims than Roman Catholics, twice as many Muslims as Protestants, and perhaps three times as many Muslims as there are Orthodox and Oriental Christians."[2]

Muslims like Inamullah Khan receive spiritual satisfaction from noting the significance of Islam in the contemporary world:

> East to West from Indonesia to Morocco, and South to North from Tanzania to Turkey, there lies across the globe the Muslim belt consisting today of 38 independent countries. Apart from the sovereign Muslim States, there are Muslim minorities in other countries of the world, some big, like the Muslim minority of over 50 million in China, 60 million in India and nearly 50 million in the Soviet Union, others small and of varying sizes. During the nearly fourteen centuries since its inception the ideology of Islam has spread to all corners of the world. Today there is no country in the world where there does not exist a community of Muslims, big or small, with its mosques from where the Mu'addhin proclaims *Allahu Akbar* (God is Great) day in and day out.[3]

Equality Within *Ummah*

Often I am questioned concerning the equality among Muslims who are living in various cultural and ethnic settings. Is it true that no barriers of race or social standing exist among followers of the Prophet? Have they really reached an advanced stage of internal sociological acceptance of one another?

Many Muslims unhesitatingly will respond affirmatively. They will laud the fact that a beggar and the president will line up in the mosque and pray together. Quranic verses will be cited that definitively teach the oneness of mankind. On several

2. C. George Fry and James R. King, *Islam: A Survey of the Muslim Faith* (Grand Rapids: Baker, 1980), p. 20.

3. Inamullah Khan, "Islam in the Contemporary World," in *God and Man in Contemporary Islamic Thought,* ed. Charles Malik (Beirut: American University of Beirut), p. 1.

occasions Muslim friends have related an interesting story
about Muhammad in order to prove this point. The Prophet had
an overnight guest who was of low social standing. During the
evening, the guest became violently ill. The result was that he
defecated all over his bed. In shame and embarrassment he quietly left the house early the next morning. The Prophet, upon
arising, discovered the soiled bed. He quickly proceeded to
clean the bedclothes. The point is that Muhammad's home was
open to all. Also the Prophet would engage in even the most me-
nial and distasteful tasks.

This makes a good story, but often such an ideal is marred by
the reality of informal class distinctions. The coolie can be
harassed by the overbearing master. Servants are frequently
beaten for trivial mistakes. Lower-class people are denied ac-
cess to government officials.

Throughout this book I will quote extensively from Muslim
scholars. Only as we listen to these men will we as Christians
enter into an Islamic perspective on this subject. It is also important for us to see how Muslims perceive Christians in regard
to *ummah*.

> Another principle of Unity which manifests itself is that of hu-
> manity. According to Islam, all human beings, whether white
> or black, red or yellow, Europeans or Africans, Westerners or
> Orientals, form one Family. And here Islam has laid the founda-
> tions of the Fundamental Human Rights which is Islam's ma-
> jor contribution in the field of social relations. We might, by
> way of contrast, refer here to the racial superiority-complex
> which has been perpetrated by the Christians, the Jews and the
> Hindus.[4]

Consider the last sentence. Did not the Protestant Adolf
Hitler postulate Germans as the "master race"? In spite of all
their horrible sufferings, have not the Jews always perceived
themselves to be those who are uniquely chosen of God? Within
Hinduism, caste consciousness prevails to the point where a
Brahman Hindu will not allow the shadow of an outcaste to fall
upon his body.

4. F. R. Ansari, *Islam and Western Civilisation* (Karachi: World Federation
of Islamic Missions, 1975), p. 14.

Islam, therefore, is a strong reaction to such violations of the realization of the common roots and "humanness" of mankind. It is, however, appropriate to point out the embarrassment caused to orthodox Muslims by the rise of American Black Islam. On one hand, Muslims worldwide enthusiastically welcomed a widespread bridgehead for Islam in the United States. But it soon became evident that Black Muslims were racist in the sense that they were antiwhite. Elijah Muhammed was simply using Islam as a power base to build his own kingdom. In recent years there has been a concerted effort by many Black Muslims in America to overcome racism and bring Black Islam more into conformity with the norms of international Islamic doctrine and practice.

James L. Barton illustrates the principle of Muslim equality with a reference to the spread of Islam in India:

> The abolition of caste in India wherever the Mohammedan faith spread is evidence of the sense of brotherhood permeating the entire body. This fraternity does not extend to those outside the faith. Islam recognizes no race, no color, no rank, and no caste; whoever is a true follower of the Prophet is a brother of every other follower and as such can claim his protection and hospitality.[5]

During a tour of Africa, Malcolm X made this observation on the *ummah* of Islam: "I saw all races, all colors—blue-eyed blondes to black-skinned Africans—in true brotherhood! In unity! Living as one! Worshipping as one!"[6] Admittedly, this is a superficial analysis based on a brief visit to the African continent. One purpose of this book is to highlight the surface commitment of Muslims to brotherhood in contrast to the deep divisive issues which create dissonance within the community.

The Ethos of Unity

Is not the image of unity within Islam simply a good public-relations job? In reality, is Islam any more united than Christianity?

5. James L. Barton, *The Christian Approach to Islam* (Boston: Pilgrim, 1918), pp. 160–61.
6. Richard V. Weekes, ed., *Muslim Peoples: A World Ethnographic Survey* (Westport, Conn.: Greenwood, 1978), p. xxxiv.

The image that the Western observer could take away from his contemplation of this vast, turbulent unsettled area is one of precarious unease and violence—of strange, bearded men with burning eyes, hieratic figures in robes and turbans, of blood dripping from the stumps of amputated hands and from the striped backs of malefactors, and piles of stones barely concealing the battered bodies of adulterous couples.[7]

Although these emotive words are at best a caricature, yet there is documented truth within them. Ayatullah Khomeini has thrust violence to the forefront of Shia Islam. Muammar Gaddafi is an advocate of religious revolution in the name of fundamentalist Islam. Saudi Arabia has sanctioned beheading as a penalty for adultery. In Pakistan there has been public flogging of thieves. Muslim Filipinos have kidnaped American missionaries in order to publicize their cause.

So there is always to be found a gap between the theoretical and actual. The desirable is not always attainable, at least not in the fullest sense. Abul A'la Maududi makes his case in strong advocacy of Islamic unity:

It must be squarely stated that there is and was no ideology except Islam that can unite the world and serve as a basis for a world state. Islam is the only religion in the world that considers all of mankind to be one family and proclaims that all human beings have descended from the same parents: "O Mankind, We created you from a single male and a female," declares the Quran (49:13). Then it asserts that God has grouped them into nations and tribes not that they may fight with each other but that they may identify each other more easily for promoting co-operation among themselves. This so-called division into groups is to facilitate reference or identification rather than to set one against the other: "And We made you into nations and tribes that ye may know each other." Not that ye may despise each other![8]

Unification of mankind, to Muslims, always carries with it a political connotation. Maududi's "world state" is an international system of law governed by the Quran and Islamic

7. G. H. Jansen, *Militant Islam* (New York: Harper and Row, 1979), p. 12.

8. Abul A'la Maududi, *Unity of the Muslim World* (Lahore: Islamic Publications, 1967), p. 11.

Traditions. It would appear to the dispassionate observer that Islam has not been able to bring political unity to the Muslim world, much less to non-Islamic countries. Iranians and Iraqis are locked in conflict. Many Muslim countries denounce Egypt. Libya is an anomaly to all that is commendable in Islam. Rival factions among Muslims in Lebanon fuel internal hatred and political instability. There is no real affinity between the 250 million Muslims of Pakistan, Bangladesh, and India. Politically, there is not the slightest chance for the unification of the Muslim world. But Muslims will continue to articulate its desirability and practicality. However, the most that the world of Islam can hope for is an enhanced level of consciousness of *spiritual* unity.

Even though there exist rivalries and conflicts within Islam, Christians who desire to share their faith with Muslims must recognize the factors of homogeneity and community that give cohesion to Muslims. In the pages that follow I desire to explore in greater depth these issues of *ummah* as well as how Christ can be most effectively communicated within Islamic society. After dealing with these problems, I want to focus on how converts can continue to live and interact within their own Muslim society and culture. My major thesis is that extraction evangelism is an erroneous methodology and should immediately cease. We must see the light and salt of Christianity expressed through converts' lives within their own sociological milieu of relatives, friends, and acquaintances.

It is necessary at times to use pseudonyms and to disguise actual happenings. There are many sensitive situations throughout the Muslim world. I do not want to jeopardize any type of Christian ministry.

My request to the reader as he or she peruses these next pages is twofold. One must realize that Islam is as difficult to define as is Christianity. How amazing that the word *Christian* describes Roman Catholics, Mormons, Jehovah's Witnesses, Pentecostals, High Anglicans, Baptists, and snake-handling cultists. To a non-Christian onlooker this is an almost indefinable hodgepodge of loosely related bits and pieces. As we proceed to dissect Islam, we too will be confronted with continuity as well as contradiction. Islam is dynamic and in process. We will find that two Muslim scholars may vary as much as Harry Emerson Fosdick and Jerry Falwell, although this is not as likely in Islam as it is in Christianity! We also must seek to enter into the study of Islam in a deep and meaningful manner. Empathy is a key to understanding. We desperately need to "sit where they sit." It is only then that we can comprehend why the Islamic interpretation of the term *Son of God* is so offensive to the average Muslim. In fact, recently my empathy on this subject took a leap forward as I negatively reacted to an article in *Time* which reported on the pope's extolling of the Virgin Mary as the "Mother of God"! I was not comfortable with the concept of God having a mother, but I am completely relaxed with him having a Son! How carefully we need to consider perspectives and presuppositions.

The chasm that separates Islam and Christianity can be bridged only with empathetic love. Recently, I met with an author whose book will soon be published. The book is an overview of Christian ministry in a rather "closed" Muslim country. After completing ten years as a tentmaker, the author felt he wanted to share the challenge of ministry in that particular Muslim land with the Christian public. I was shocked to learn that the planned cover of the book is to depict an angry Muslim with an uplifted sword in the process of beheading a docile national Christian. I asked the author how we would react if a Muslim published a well-documented book on the horrible excesses of the Crusades. On the cover would be pictured the pious Crusaders with crosses on their breastplates, in the process of violating Muslims by looting, burning, and murdering men, women, and children. My suggestion evoked only a response of embarrassed silence.

My prayer is that this book might assist us in an understanding and a balanced appreciation of Islamic *ummah*. I hope this process will lead us to where we are in a better position to counsel the convert from Islam on how to remain within Muslim society and at the same time share his newfound faith in Christ.

The Foundation of Islamic Community

The population of Arabia, apart from a few settled communities, historically has been so constituted as to form a number of tribes, very loosely held together either by loyalty to a particular leader or by belief in the group's descent from a common ancestor. Within each such tribe, the independence of individual units is a matter of course. In the hands of the heads of these units lies the power to elect the tribal chief. The elected leaders and their families have traditionally wielded great influence, both militarily and politically.[1]

At the time of Muhammad's ascendancy these tribes were known for their fierce independence. There was little cooperation and interchange among Arabs in sixth-century Arabia. Often trade wars erupted that led to plunder and murder. Inamullah Khan has written of this period of history:

> What was the position of the world when Mohammad began his Mission? There were at that time two world powers contending with each other, the Byzantines and the Persians. In the Arabian peninsula, Syria was a colony of the Byzantines, while Iraq and Yemen were under the tutelage of the Persian Empire. The desert tribes were sunk in illiteracy and ignorance and lived a primitive life, in which the priestly class of the Quraish,

1. Reuben Levy, *The Social Structure of Islam* (Cambridge: At the University Press, 1969), p. 53.

as custodians of the 360 deities then worshipped by the different tribes, was exploiting the ignorant Bedouins. Within a span of two decades the Holy Prophet created a veritable revolution in Arabia. All people had become one nation, loyal to the one God, and believing in the brotherhood of man and enjoying social justice of the highest order.[2]

Before examining the causes for such a radical sociological transformation, let us lay the foundation for Islamic *ummah* by seeking to define the word *community* in both a secular academic and a religious sense.

Definitions of Community

Jessie Bernard sees a community as a "territorially bounded social system or set of interlocking or integrated functional subsystems (economic, political, religious, ethical, educational, legal, socializing, reproductive, etc.) serving a resident population, plus the material culture or physical plant through which the subsystems operate."[3] This definition emphasizes the integration of human activity. By contrast, Hammudah Abd-al Ati focuses on the psychological or symbolic aspects of community:

> In one basic sense, the concept community means an idea, an ideal, a symbol. As such, it symbolizes all forms of relationship that are characterized by a high degree of personal intimacy, emotional depth, moral commitment, social cohesion, and continuity in time. It may be found in locality, religion, nation, race, occupation, or common cause. Its archetype is the family.[4]

Muhammad was able to utilize all of these components of *ummah* when he founded Islam in Arabia. Nation and race

2. Inamullah Khan, "Islam in the Contemporary World," in *God and Man in Contemporary Islamic Thought*, ed. Charles Malik (Beirut: American University of Beirut, 1972), p. 68.
3. Jessie Bernard, "Community Disorganization," in *International Encyclopedia of the Social Sciences*, ed. David L. Sills (New York: Free Press, 1977), p. 163.
4. Hammudah Abd-al Ati, *Establishment of Islamic Communities* (Plainfield, Ind.: The Muslim Students' Association of the U.S. and Canada, 1974), p. 5.

were geographically fixed in a relatively small area. Occupation was normally that of a farmer or a merchant. Religious revelation and command became common cause. The family was, from the beginning, the core of community.

Carl C. Zimmerman has identified four characteristic elements which are found in any community. These are social fact and action, definite specification (each community is unique), association, and limited area (a relatively definite and compact geographic base).[5]

George Peter Murdock gives an excellent synopsis which highlights the emotional aspects of community:

> United by reciprocal relationship and bound by a common culture, the members of a community form an "in group," characterized by internal peace, law, order, and cooperative effort. Since they assist one another in the activities which gratify basic drives, and provide one another with certain derivative satisfactions obtainable only in social life, there develops among them a collective sentiment of group solidarity and loyalty which has been variously termed synercism, we-feeling, *esprit de corps*, and consciousness of kind.[6]

We will only inadequately understand Islam if we underestimate the powerful impact of the emotional solidarity that provides the esprit de corps for the tremendously diverse Muslim world. Emotional unity is an intangible component of Islam. It cannot be put under a microscope and scientifically analyzed. Yet an amazing allegiance is engendered among Muslims of all races by the emotional recitation of Quranic stories. I have watched a group of intellectual Muslims break forth into sobbing upon hearing a powerful telling of the story of Abraham's willingness to slay his son in obedience to the command of God.

Kenneth Cragg in his inimitable manner succinctly juxtaposes academic Muslim belief with the more emotional aspects of the community-engendered sense of belonging. "Community, then, tends strongly towards an externalized concept of

5. Carl C. Zimmerman, *The Changing Community* (New York: Harper and Brothers, 1938), p. 15.

6. George Peter Murdock, *Social Structure* (New York: Macmillan, 1949), p. 83.

faith in which allegiance takes precedence over conviction. Belonging dominates believing."[7]

The Arabic word *ummah* is said to be derived from *umm*, which means "mother." It is also believed to be related to the Hebrew word *ummah*, which is defined as "nation."[8] "In classical [Arabic] it [*ummah*] is used of both ethnic and religious entities and even of groups of men linked by some common quality or attribute. . . . In a contemporary document preserved in the traditional biography of Muhammad, the community of Medina is described as *umma dun al-nas*—a community apart or distinct from other men."[9]

The apartness or distinctiveness of Islamic community became an important foundational doctrine early in Muslim history. It was only at the commencement of the nineteenth century that Muslims had to possess visas to visit other Islamic countries. The "open-border" policy greatly contributed to a sense of continuity and coherence among the worldwide community of Muslims. Conversely, political realities of the twentieth century have been a deterrent to the free flow of Muslim travel and subsequent building up of an international realization of Islamic brotherhood.

The development of Muhammad's philosophy of *ummah* is summarized as follows:

In the first period of his prophetic activity Muhammad regarded the Arabs in general or his Meccan countrymen as a closed *ummah*. Just as the earlier messengers and admonishers of God had been sent to the *ummahs* of the past, so he had now been given the task of transmitting the divine message to the Arab *ummah* which had hitherto been neglected, in order to show it the way to salvation. Like the earlier messengers, he also was fiercely attacked by his *ummah* and accused of lying. After he had finally broken off relations with the pagan Meccans and migrated with his followers to Madina, he created a new community there. He went beyond the circle of Muslims

7. Kenneth Cragg, *The Dome and the Rock: Jerusalem Studies in Islam* (London: S.P.C.K., 1964), pp. 222–23.

8. Louis Gardet, *Mohammedanism*, ed. Henri Daniel-Rops, trans. William Burridge (New York: Hawthorn, 1961), pp. 65–66.

9. Bernard Lewis, "Politics and War," in *The Legacy of Islam*, ed. Joseph Schacht, 2d ed. (Oxford: Clarendon, 1974), p. 157.

proper and included those citizens of Madina who had not yet
heeded his religious appeal in one political combination. "The
constitution of the community of Madina," in which this unification is laid down in writing, expressly states that the citizens
of the town, including the Jews, now form an *ummah*. The predominantly political character of this new *ummah* was however only a makeshift. As soon as Muhammad felt himself
firmly established and had successfully attacked the pagan
Meccans, he was able to exclude from his politico-religious
community the Madinese (especially the Jews) who had not yet
adopted his religion. As time went on, his *ummah* came more
and more to consist only of his proper followers, the Muslims.[10]

It is important for us as Western Christians to listen carefully to Muslim scholars as they seek to interpret the ethos of
Islamic community to the non-Muslim world. Pure history is
objective. Historians, however, have introduced their presuppositions and biases in their record, thus creating accounts of
historical events clothed in the garb of (for the most part) unin-
tentional prejudices. Going to primary sources does not ensure
scholastic objectivity but it at least permits the involved parties
to state their case. Christians would affirm it is the Muslim's
right and duty to speak—and the Christian's obligation to listen.

Mohammad Muslehuddin, one of these Muslim voices, defines society in Islam as "an association, formed according to
Divine Law, for the purpose of harmonious and peaceful coex-
istence." He goes on to state that "Islamic society is neither sectarian, nor racial but universal, for it is just submission to the
Law of God who is One and the Only One. Thus belief in One
God is to transform all mankind into one brotherhood."[11]

The point here, by implication, is that Islam will be the transforming agent by which all mankind will be forged into one
great worldwide *ummah*. One can easily compare these sentiments with those of a segment of Christianity which is eagerly
awaiting a "last-days" revival in which multitudes from every
tribe, tongue, and nation will be swept into the Christian *ummah*.

    10. H. A. R. Gibb and J. H. Kramers, eds., *Shorter Encyclopedia of Islam*
(Leiden: Brill, 1953), pp. 603–4.
    11. Mohammad Muslehuddin, *Sociology and Islam* (Lahore: Islamic
Publications, 1977), p. 75.

Badru D. Kateregga is an East African Muslim university professor who eloquently defines *ummah* in terms of historical Quranic as well as contemporary societal perspectives:

> The *umma* is different from any other community. It is not centered on tribe, nationality, race, or linguistic grouping. The *umma* does not take its name from the founder or an event. The *umma* is the community of Allah. He is the Absolute Truth to which the Muslim community owes its life and existence. The life and activities of the *umma* are all under His legislative direction. Equally, the life of the individual member of the *umma*, both private and public, is under God's legal command. It is Allah's Law which must be supreme within legal command. It is Allah's Law which must be supreme within the *umma*. What God has recommended as good for the community, shall always remain good, and what He has forbidden shall always be denied. The *umma* cannot authorize negation, deletion, or abrogation of Allah's supreme Law and scheme of values.
>
> The *umma* is divinely established by God, as the Quran witnesses: "And there may spring from you a nation who invites to goodness, and enjoins right conduct and forbids indecency. Such are they who are successful" (Quran 3:104). In another Quranic verse Allah praises the *umma* in the following words: "Ye are the best community that hath been raised up for mankind. Ye enjoin right conduct and forbid indecency; and ye believe in Allah" (Quran 3:110).[12]

These paragraphs allow the reader to step inside the world view of a sincere, articulate follower of the Islamic religion. It is easy to grasp the comprehensiveness of *ummah* in Kateregga's life. His faith is not just one small compartment of life. Rather, it is the integrating force of every facet of his total being.

Abd-al Ati has written that "the community in Islam is not founded on race, nationality, locality, occupation, kinship, or special interests. . . . It transcends national borders and political boundaries."[13] The universality of the Quranic message is repeatedly emphasized by Muslims. A worldwide *ummah* of

12. Badru D. Kateregga and David W. Shenk, *Islam and Christianity: A Muslim and a Christian in Dialogue* (Grand Rapids: Eerdmans, 1981), p. 48.

13. Hammudah Abd-al Ati, *Islam in Focus* (Indianapolis: American Trust Publications, 1975), p. 38.

devout Muslims is to be regarded not as an unachievable ideal but rather as a potentially realizable goal.

Quranic Teaching about Community

The Quran, Muslims believe, is the very Word of God given directly by Allah to the prophet Muhammad. Quranic revelation is without error. Muslims almost universally subscribe to the dictation theory of inspiration. Therefore there is little scope for historical or redaction criticism of the Quran. Fazlur Rahman, a professor at the University of Chicago, has been severely criticized by persons high in the Pakistani government because of his more liberal and critical investigation of Quranic scriptures. He stands as a scholar unique in the contemporary Muslim world.

> The common possession of the *umma* and its pre-eminent bond of union is a book, the Koran, looked on as the very word of God and, according to the most authoritative teaching, the uncreated word of God. . . . This reverence for the Koran and the Arabic of its text offers a tentative basis for unity through a common language among Muslims throughout the world, whether Arabic speaking or not.[14]

The Quran is said to "concern itself with all aspects of life, be it economics, politics, sex and others, and lays great stress on sincerity of faith and mutual help."[15] These words point to the integrative world view of the Muslim. The Quran is the authoritative primary agent of integration which defines the basis and foundation of a unified community. "It is clear that the Quran expresses no racial or color prejudice. What is perhaps most significant is that the Quran does not even reveal any awareness of such prejudice. . . . In the Quran the question of race is obviously not a burning issue."[16]

I would agree that the Quran lacks serious prejudice as regards race and color. Yet one cannot help but detect the limited view of *ummah* which caused Muhammad to go to war against

14. Gardet, *Mohammedanism*, p. 67.
15. Muslehuddin, *Sociology and Islam*, p. 124.
16. Bernard Lewis, *Race and Color in Islam* (New York: Harper and Row, 1971), p. 7.

those who disagreed with him. *Ummah* became restricted during the time of the Prophet. This quite naturally affected all subsequent Muslim interpretations of Islamic *ummah*.

> The passages in the Kuran in which the word *umma* occurs are so varied that its meaning cannot be rigidly defined. This much however seems to be certain, that it always refers to ethnic, linguistic or religious bodies of people who are the objects of the divine plan of salvation. Even in passages like Sura 7:164 and 28:21, where *umma* is used in quite a colourless fashion, there is a hint of this significance. The term is in isolated cases applied to the Djinn, indeed to all living creatures (Surah 6:38) but always with the implication that these creatures are to be included in the divine scheme of salvation and are liable to judgment. *Umma* is exceptionally applied in one passage (Sura 16:12) to an individual, Abraham. Here the term either has the meaning of *imam* or Abraham is so called in his capacity as head of the community founded by him. Otherwise *umma* always refers to whole groups or at least to groups within large communities.[17]

The following are key Quranic verses on *ummah*:

> And hold fast, all of you together, to the cable of Allah and do not separate. And remember Allah's favour unto you: how ye were enemies and He made friendship between your hearts so that ye became as brothers by His grace; and how ye were upon the brink of an abyss of fire, and He did save you from it. Thus Allah maketh clear His revelations unto you, that haply ye may be guided, and there may spring from you a nation who invite to goodness, and enjoin right conduct and forbid indecency. Such are they who are successful. And be ye not as those who separated and disputed after the clear proofs had come unto them. For such there is an awful doom. [3:103–5]

There is a lot of Islamic theology in these few short verses. How picturesque is the symbolism of Muslims unitedly grasping the rope of God. The believers are acting in concert as they make a unified community of faith in Allah. There is linkage among members of the *ummah* as well as between God and the corporate group of believers.

17. Gibb and Kramers, *Shorter Encyclopedia of Islam*, p. 603.

While visiting a Sufi meeting, I observed the induction of one hundred devotees into the *tarika* (path) of an aged *pir* (Muslim popular mystical teacher). At one point a long narrow cloth was folded to resemble a rope. It was then passed out among the initiates. Each of the one hundred men soberly grasped a portion of the cloth. The *pir* took hold of the two ends and connected them in his hands. All present raised their heads and fervently prayed to Allah for his bestowal of mercy and blessing upon their lives. This brief ceremony beautifully symbolized the community making an act of commitment to one another and to God.

> Ye became as brothers by His grace; and how ye were upon the brink of an abyss of fire and He did save you from it. [3:103]

What powerful imagery! Muslims are gripped by Quranic authority that assures them that, whereas once they were tottering on the precipice of hell itself, now they are delivered by the grace of God and knit into a close brotherhood of believers committed to the true path. Needless to say, there are close parallels here with New Testament teaching. *Ummah*, Muslims believe, is being forged in the common experience of deliverance from the terrible reality of eternal damnation. Such spiritual roots of community go deep into the social fabric of Islam. This sense of comaraderie in the pilgrimage of life forms an almost impregnable spiritual kinship.

"And there may spring from you a nation . . ." (3:104). Here is the perpetuating role of members of the *ummah*. Faith will be handed down through the generations. The bonds of community will be continued in unbroken succession. Nations will evolve that are simply communities of the faithful.

"And be ye not as those who separated . . ." (3:105). The cable is not to be broken. The links of *ummah* are to be forever sealed. In light of such clear Quranic injunction, one can understand the dissonance created when a Muslim dares to break the strands of community by becoming a Christian.

The most frequently quoted verse relating to the *ummah* of Islam is 3:110: "Ye are the best community that hath been raised up for mankind. Ye enjoin right conduct and forbid indecency; and ye believe in Allah. And if the people of the Scripture had believed, it would have been better for them. Some of them are believers; but most of them are evil-livers."

Muslims point with pride to the fact that their scriptures identify them as the "best community." The basis for such an assertion rests upon their correct conduct, the fact that they forbid indecency, and their belief in Allah. These three qualifiers often are not noted in conversations. The statement stands as a sociological reality which has the effect of bonding Muslims together in a sort of mystical *ummah*. There is also a sense of purpose to be noted in this verse. The community has been raised up for the good of mankind. It is to be a model of righteousness.

In the Quran the phrase *people of Scripture* is to be understood as referring to Jews and Christians. Muhammad was ambivalent toward them. This verse declares some of them to be true believers and others to be evil. He, of course, consistently denounced those who "ascribed a partner to Allah." In his mind this would include most if not all of the Christian community.

"O ye who believe! Take not for intimates others than your own folk" (3:118). Here again we see the basic foundation of Islamic *ummah*. Confidence can be reposed only in those who share a similar belief in Allah, the Quran, and the prophet Muhammad. I once quoted this verse to Dr. Ali and asked how he, a devout Muslim, could reconcile our intimate friendship with his Quranic belief. His rationale was that I am a seeker of God, one who attempts to avoid evil and to practice righteousness. Therefore, a Christian in such a category is a special exception. For the sake of our friendship, I was grateful that such an explanation was adequate for him.

"And lo! this your religion is one religion and I am your Lord, so keep your duty unto Me. But they [mankind] have broken their religion among them into sects, each sect rejoicing in its tenets" (23:52–53). Islam is presented as the one religion. The focus is on Islam having exclusive rights to ultimate truth. It is others who have broken religion into various sects. *Ummah*, then, is the rightful domain of those who follow the true path of Islam.

> O mankind! Lo! We have created you male and female, and have made you nations and tribes that ye may know one another. Lo! the noblest of you, in the sight of Allah, is the best in conduct.

[49:13] [The "we" in this and other Quranic verses refers to Allah. Arabic uses the plural to indicate high honor and respect.]

The [true] believers are those only who believe in Allah and His messenger and afterward doubt not, but strive with their wealth and their lives for the cause of Allah. Such are the sincere. [49:15]

God is the master designer and creator of the human race. He has formed people into social structures. But his purpose is clearly defined as creating a society in which "ye may know one another." The ideal community is that which is made up of people who care for each other as well as believe in God and the Prophet.

Therefore, every one of the community is considered as a brother unto every other and this has found expression in the sayings of the Prophet (peace and blessing of Allah be upon him) who speaks of each member as a brother unto the other and enjoins him to wish for his brother what he wishes for himself. This is explained by Kant in a maxim: "Treat everyone as an end and never as a means to gain your end."[18]

So the *ummah* of Islam emerges as a loosely knit brotherhood. A similar relationship within the Christian community is described in 1 Corinthians 12. All are members of one body, but each has varying gifts.

The Hadith (Traditions) of Islam speak of the concept of Muslim community. "A large body of traditions survives, the general purport of which is to deplore racial prejudice and to insist on the primacy of piety. One of the commonest is the phrase ascribed to the Prophet. 'I was sent to the red and the black'—an expression taken to embrace the whole of mankind."[19]

Nothing in Islam carries more credence or authority than the Quran and Hadith. Almost all Muslims know by rote some of the Arabic scripture. I have watched four- or five-year-old children in non-Arabic-speaking countries hard at work early in the morning on their Arabic alphabet. Throughout the vast Muslim world one can hear the recited Arabic prayers which are taken directly from the Quran. There is a powerful sense of

18. Muslehuddin, *Sociology and Islam*, p. 231.
19. Lewis, *Race and Color in Islam*, p. 19.

community inherent in such a common allegiance to holy scriptures.

An Overview of Community

W. Montgomery Watt outlines the interaction between the individual and collective components of *ummah*:

> In one respect the *ummah* was a community of individuals, for Islam accepted the tendency towards individualism, and even encouraged it (as in the new family structure). The ultimate moral sanction in Islam, punishment in Hell, applies to the individual for his conduct as an individual. On the other hand, the individual was taken out of his isolation and insecurity and made to feel that he belonged to the *ummah*. The early practice of "brothering" may seem artificial, but the sense of brotherhood between Muslims has become very deep; witness such a title in our own days as "the Muslim Brotherhood."
>
> ... The *ummah* was a closely-knit community, thought of on the lines of a tribe, and much of the old mystique attaching to the kinship group has become attached to it.[20]

Watt accurately refers to the individual's sense of isolation and insecurity that occurs if he or she is excluded from a group. This is common not only to Muslims but to all mankind. For example, my daughter recently took the big plunge into college life. All summer she expressed a deep anxiety about the upcoming separation from her secure home base. She had convinced herself that the college would be inhabited by autonomous human units walking about in lofty isolation one from another. In fact, within a few hours of arrival on the campus, Lindy was in happy and intimate discourse with other eighteen-year-old girls who had harbored similar fears throughout the long summer.

Islam, then, is the sociological webbing agent that brings individual Muslims into a cohesive unit of brotherhood. No longer is isolation a societal threat. The warmth of like-minded individuals who seek God forms the basis for Muslim *ummah*.

20. W. Montgomery Watt, *Islam and the Integration of Society* (Great Britain: Northwestern University Press, 1961), pp. 301–2.

Philip K. Hitti has written of Muhammad's instituting a *Pax Islamica:*

> These are the words of the Prophet in his noble sermon at the "farewell pilgrimage." "O ye men! harken unto my words and take ye them to heart! Know ye that every Moslem is a brother to every other Moslem, and that ye are now one brotherhood. It is not legitimate for any one of you, therefore, to appropriate unto himself anything that belongs to his brother unless it is willingly given him by that brother."

> Thus by one stroke the most vital bond of Arab relationship, that of tribal kinship, was replaced by a new bond, that of faith. Herein lies one of the chief claims of Muhammad to originality. A sort of *Pax Islamica* was instituted for Arabia. The new community was to have no priesthood, no hierarchy, no central see.[21]

Here we see the focus shifting to theological considerations. The bond of faith became the integrating force behind the unification of disparate tribal groups. Islam is one of the most theocentric religions of the world. God is totally central to all activity of the faithful.

Muslims in Africa are aware of a pervasive *ummah* that affects their world view. "Islamic law governs (more or less) the worship, the belief, the customs, the trade, and even the politics. Everyone adopts a certain style of politeness and cleanliness, everyone has an Arabic name, everyone joins in the fast and festivals, and often everyone wears the same style of clothes, all these things show the solidarity of the community."[22]

Solidarity is a high-value sociological concept among Muslims. It is, however, an elusive reality. From time to time Libya has been able to sign pacts with neighboring Muslim countries based on the lofty principles of Islamic solidarity. The paperbound commitments have, without exception, been disregarded in times of stress when self-interest has triumphed.

21. Philip K. Hitti, *The Arabs: A Short History* (Chicago: Henry Regnery, 1943), p. 40.
22. *Christian Witness among Muslims* (Accra, Ghana: Africa Christian Press, 1971), p. 78.

Still, it is important to be aware of the commonly recognized desirability of a cohesive Islamic community.

One Muslim has written of the responsibility incumbent upon each individual who is a participant in the brotherhood of the faithful:

> The historic role of the Islamic community is to be the true embodiment of the virtuous, the wholesome, and the noble. A truly Islamic community is the alert guardian of virtue and the bitter enemy of vice. What is required of the community at large is likewise required of every individual member. This is because the whole community is an organic entity and every individual is accountable to Allah.[23]

A few years ago the world was shocked to see pictures of the execution of an Arabian princess and her boyfriend. She was charged with committing adultery. Even her position within the royal family did not exempt her from the ultimate punishment of death. The princess was guilty of bringing disgrace to her family, community, and the name of Allah.

In one Muslim country a young poet who was a bit of a rebel wrote a satire about the Prophet. Within days the whole nation was incensed. There were demands for the man's execution. In the end he was jailed for his unsavory writings about Muhammad. He had dared to break the religious continuity of Islamic community.

In 1962, my wife and I had just arrived in a Muslim country for the purpose of commencing our missionary career. We were resident in a small town in the interior of the country. One afternoon I heard the distant shouts of a large procession. A young boy came running up and advised my wife and me not to go outside the house until the group had passed. Soon the jeering demonstrators filed by our house, chanting anti-American slogans. Later I determined the cause of the outbreak to be centered around an article on Islam that had been printed in the United States. Accompanying the article was a drawing of the prophet Muhammad. This was interpreted by students thousands of miles away to be an intentional and government-orchestrated attack on Islam. No pictorial representations of the Prophet are allowed within many sectors of Sunni Islam. A

23. Abd-al Ati, *Establishment of Islamic Communities*, p. 8.

deep emotional and spiritual allegiance to Isalm permeates the community and actively resists any external attack.

One of the great strengths of the Muslim faith is its emphasis on racial harmony.

Undoubtedly one of the outstanding successes of Islam has been its creation of a great community of many races, in which there has been a genuine sense of brotherhood. The brotherhood of different races may never have been perfect, for there are occasional traces of race consciousness in medieval writings; but there was certainly never any of the racial animosity which is found in occidental countries in the present century.[24]

Abul A'la Maududi boldly states that "there is no religion apart from Islam that has succeeded in obliterating distinctions of race, colour, language, place of origin and nationality in the establishing of a universal brotherhood of men." He goes on to assert that "as far as Muslim society is concerned the entire human race has in fact become one *ummah*."[25]

Perhaps Watt is closer to the mark with his more equivocal assessment than is Maududi with his assertions. We live in a world of imperfect people. To say that a group of 850 million people has succeeded in obliterating anything would stretch the limit of credibility. On numerous occasions I have been called "red monkey," "foreign dog," and "pig" in a Muslim country in which I was resident. My wife has been spat upon in a ricksha as we were being transported down a main road of a town. Our antagonists did not know us personally. Their hostility was directed toward a white face that symbolized a foreign "power-hungry, imperialistic, inordinately wealthy nation."

I would, however, be quick to affirm that usually Muslims do seek to overcome natural racial prejudices. For most of my missionary career I have been accorded great respect and honor from my Muslim friends. My negative experiences with a certain small minority of people does not impinge upon my love and esteem for Muslims.

24. W. Montgomery Watt, *What Is Islam?* (New York: Longman Group, 1968), p. 233.

25. Abul A'la Maududi, *Unity of the Muslim World* (Lahore: Islamic Publications, 1967), p. 13.

Some Western scholars have been highly critical of an *ummah* that is religiously dictated:

> There is no phase or interest of the Muslim's life which his religion leaves untouched. . . . There are detailed instructions for his use of the tooth-stick, for his marriage and marital life, for the payment of his income-tax and for the division of his estate. . . . There is nothing that the Muslim dreams or thinks or says or does that is outside the scope of the interest of his religion. . . . The system under which the Muslim lives is totalitarian; it undertakes to regulate all his beliefs and acts.[26]

Webster defines the word *totalitarian* as "subordination of the individual to the state . . . by coercive measures." The majority of Muslims live in states heavily influenced by Islamic law and tradition. However, I do not agree that most Muslims live under totalitarian oppression. The Westerner may choose to evaluate it thusly, but many, if not most, Muslims consider it a privilege to be a citizen of a country that so integrates Islam into the warp and woof of life. There is usually no sense of coercion, but rather a voluntary submission to a pervasive Islamic world view. The word *totalitarian*, to a Muslim, speaks of the totality of life—a life that is lived thoroughly within the orbit of Islamic regulation. This lifestyle is regarded as liberating rather than restraining. The American with his bias toward separation of church and state is caught in a web of ethnocentrism that inhibits, if not prohibits, an empathetic understanding of Islam.

Bert DeVries puts it this way: "Informally, too, religion is accepted as inseparable from all aspects of life. Whether one is at the plow, in the market, or in the bath, what one does is religious. In this sense there is no formal Islamic religion: all that one does is a religious act."[27] I would certainly agree that, for the devout believer, it is true that there is no dichotomy between secular and sacred. Life is a kaleidoscope of activity worked out within the orbit of religious devotion.

Ritual strengthens the communal life of Muslims. It is im-

26. Edwin E. Calverley, *Islam: An Introduction* (Cairo: The American University at Cairo, 1958), p. 12.

27. Bert DeVries, "Islamic Renewal in the Twentieth Century," *The Reformed Journal*, vol. 30 (July 1980), p. 10.

portant to understand the role of certain rituals that are regularly practiced within Islam. Muslims love to engage in obligatory Islamic ritual in communal settings. All of this deeply contributes to an outworking of *ummah*. The next section will touch briefly on how the experience of Islamic community is enhanced through the rituals of prayer, fasting, pilgrimage, and almsgiving.

The Means of Experiencing *Ummah*

Prayer

Psychologically prayer heightens the religious fervor, it is an aid toward the spirit of brotherhood. As one Christian religious writer once remarked, "to pray together, in whatever tongue or ritual, is the most tender brotherhood of hope and sympathy that man can contract in this life."

Islamic prayer can be called a discipline in democracy. There is complete equality before God when men pray in the mosque. Rich and poor, the wise and the ignorant, stand shoulder to shoulder just as they enter, there are no privileged seats, all are equally humble before God. In the mosque, the Muslims become a classless society. There is no clergy, there is only the *Imam*, the one who leads the prayer, standing in front of the congregation, facing like them towards Mecca.

There is another important element of unification in Muslim prayer. Whenever Muslims pray all over the globe, they turn their faces toward the Kaaba in Mecca, which strengthens the sense of unity in a world wide brotherhood.[28]

I personally am deeply impressed with the observance of Muslim community prayers. The onlooker can almost feel the reality of *ummah* as Muslims line up in proximity one to another and bow to the floor in synchronized movement. They conclude their ritual by looking to the persons on the left and the right, greeting these fellow members of Islamic community with the words *Salam alaikum* (Peace be upon you).

Syed Abdul Latif describes the cultural dimension of com-

---

28. Erich W. Bethmann, *Steps Toward Understanding Islam*, Kohinur series, no. 4 (Washington, D.C.: American Friends of the Middle East, 1966), pp. 23–24.

munal prayers: "This sense of equality, this standing shoulder to shoulder without regard for colour or race or station in life, this standing and kneeling and sitting together in a common worship before one common language of devotion, expressing one common wish, this sense of equality or its manifestation is the culture of the Musalmans."[29]

One writer has claimed that the Muslim prayer ritual "has reconciled the claims of rich and poor, the governor and the governed, slave and free."[30] That may be a lofty ideal, but unfortunately, it is not a reality. The *ummah* of prayer does perform much the same function as the statement of Christians who affirm that "the ground at the foot of the cross is level." That is, there are no sociological distinctions in the sight of God. All sinners who approach the cross of Christ for cleansing and forgiveness are equal. There can be no considerations of status as one humbly seeks God. However, as the worshiper moves out of the mosque or away from the cross, the old barriers of race and caste often reassert themselves.

Prayer is frequently performed by Muslims in the mosque. This is not obligatory. I have been on buses that have pulled off the road at sunset so that Muslim passengers could go off into a field and pray together. My friend, Dr. Ali, unashamedly goes through the ritual wherever he happens to be at the prescribed times. Women throughout the Islamic world infrequently attend the mosque. They pray at home.

Yet the mosque is important in regard to prayer. It is that unique place where the devout can gather and worship within the visible *ummah* of Islam.

The mosque is exclusively the meeting place of the faithful. The non-Muslim may admire its architectural glories and study its meaning at any time other than the weekly assembling. In some countries it is true, prevailing conditions make it impolitic to visit mosques even for this purpose. At the Friday noon hour the outsider is only present on very rare occasions and under unusual circumstances. Nevertheless, the mosque remains a gatherer: the minaret proclaims an invitation that has no limits of race or background. If one cannot become an habitué of the

29. Syed Abdul Latif, *Islamic Cultural Studies* (Lahore: Shaikh Muhammad Ashraf, 1947), p. 42.
30. Mohammed Marmaduke Pickthall, *The Cultural Side of Islam* (Delhi: Islamic Book Trust, 1982), p. 59.

mosque without being first a Muslim, the latter is a possibility which is always open. The muezin means to be taken seriously when he calls to worship and to good. If his summons is primarily an interior exhortation and not an exterior evangel, the whole impact of his faith and culture he symbolizes is certainly open to adherence. Mosques, then, are for meeting in the ultimate as well as the immediate sense.[31]

Prayer, then, in its communal observance is a function of the *ummah* of Islam. It provides a foundation of togetherness. Islam teaches that it is considerably more meritorious to pray in a mosque than in other locations.

Erich W. Bethmann has enlarged on the community-enhancing functions of the mosque:

> The primary function of the mosque is, of course, religious, but it serves also to house religious schools of an advanced type and occasionally even primary Koran schools. It is also an inn where any belated traveler may rest for the night, where the poor who must beg for their living can sleep, and where any man who is sick may rest till he recovers, if he has no better place to go. This function of the mosques as philanthropic institutions is very important. No beggar, no traveler, no stranded sick man need lack of shelter, at least, in any Mohammedan city.
>
> The mosque has become the center of community life. And here probably lies the secret of that marvelous influence of Islam, the mosque, the place of worship, where the faithful join in prayer five times a day, and the simple *"kuttab"* school attached to every mosque, where the Quran was taught exclusively, have welded the heterogeneous elements of so many alien nations into one big fraternity—the fraternity of Islam.[32]

The centrality of the mosque to Islamic *ummah* must not be underestimated. It is a haven for the spiritually and physically needy. Many times I have observed Muslims eating and sleeping in mosques. It is an embarrassment to Muslims that, in comparatively recent times, some unattended mosques have had to remain under lock and key. They are opened only for

31. Kenneth Cragg, *The Call of the Minaret* (New York: Oxford University Press, 1956), pp. 176–77.
32. Erich W. Bethmann, *Bridge to Islam* (Nashville: Southern Publishing Association, 1950), pp. 98–99.

times of worship or communal gatherings. That has been in response to increasing incidents of vandalism.

The mosque school is attended by many Muslim children between the ages of five and seven. They are taught the basics of
Arabic (in non-Arabic-speaking countries), the prayer forms,
and the meaning of Islamic festivals. Memorization of vast seg-
ments of the Quran is also encouraged. In these religious
schools a sense of brotherhood with other Muslim children is
fostered at an early age.

Fasting

Fasting during the daylight hours of the month of Ramadan
is obligatory for all faithful Muslims. They are to refrain from
eating, drinking, smoking, and sexual intercourse from half an
hour before sunrise until half an hour after sunset. It is extremely difficult for Muslims to keep the fast in the long, hot
days of the summer. "Yet the very effort of endurance promotes
the solidarity of the community, for men know that they are in
this together. The fast, like the pilgrimage, may also be said to
help to extend the control of the Islamic vision over all spheres
of life, since both are undertaken out of a desire to obey God's
commands."[33]

Abd-al Ati exalts the practice of fasting as an exemplary ritual which promotes *ummah*:

> The fast originates in man the real Spirit of Social Belonging,
> of Unity and Brotherhood, of Equality before God as well as be-
> fore the Law. This spirit is the natural product of the fact that
> when man fasts, he feels that he is joining the whole Muslim
> society in observing the same duty in the same manner at the
> same time for the same motives to the same end. No sociologist
> can say that there has been at any period of history anything
> comparable to this fine institution of Islam. People have been
> crying throughout the ages for acceptable belonging, for unity,
> for brotherhood, for equality, but how echoless their voice has
> been, and how very little success they have met. Where can they
> find their goals without the guiding light of Islam?[34]

One cannot read these words without entering into the deep
emotional dimension of *ummah* which is resident within the

33. Watt, *What Is Islam?*, p. 187.
34. Abd-al Ati, *Islam in Focus*, p. 88.

rigorous ritual of keeping the annual fast. Muslims who dare to break the sociological and religious strictures of the fast are subject to legal and communal penalties. I have seen windows of restaurants which have been shattered by rocks thrown as a spontaneous punishment because the owners dared to remain open for business during daylight hours of Ramadan.

I have asked Muslims if spirituality can be legislated. They do not have the same presuppositions concerning spirituality that the Western Christian does. Muslims believe that the life submitted to God is a total experience and must embrace law as well as spirit. Therefore, it is not inconsistent to use law to enforce that which is Islamic. So the fast, Muslims will affirm, must be an external as well as an internal ritual. The physical body must be purified as well as the heart. Muslims declare that governmental legislation can actually assist the believer in his spiritual journey.

Cragg comments on the fast and the sense of belonging:

> Belonging in Ramadan can be a figure of men's involvement with each other. The whole power and theme of the fast is communal. Men in Islam participate because they are "in Islam." This is a form of their membership and the fact that others, with strong communal sanction, are fulfilling it also both commands and fosters the individuals' conformity. In a sense the realization that we live among fellows, among a common humanity, can become a force in the conquest of self-will. There is clearly an intimate connection between what the individual ought to do and the fact that he is part of a whole, a human whole.[35]

Here one sees society acting in concert. The fast becomes "easy" because everyone is doing it. Celebrations of communal eating at the end of the day have a powerful bonding effect. Islam is much the more homogeneous because of the fast.

Pilgrimage

The Hajj (pilgrimage) is the largest multinational annual gathering of people on earth. It is estimated that three million people went to Mecca during the Hajj of 1983. They represented almost every ethnic group, political entity, economic strata,

---

35. Cragg, *The Dome and the Rock*, p. 29.

and skin color known to the human race. "The skin colours are every shade of black, brown and pinkish white, but the simple uniform enjoined on the pilgrims makes of them a sea of white, until the main rites are performed. Then, like a butterfly emerging from its chrysalis, national costumes of every sort and colour re-emerge and the unity before God fragments into an international kaleidoscope."[36]

If it is at all financially and physically possible, every Muslim is to make the pilgrimage to Mecca once in a lifetime. This is the goal and aspiration of all Muslims worldwide. Mecca is uniquely an Islamic holy center. No non-Muslims are allowed within the city limits. This prohibition in itself strengthens the concept of Islamic *ummah*.

All normal differences of the human race are to be minimized by the common white cloth worn by all pilgrims. Each rite is to be meticulously performed by the devotees. Upon his return to his own country, the Muslim is in a privileged category of religious people. He precedes his name with the descriptive term *hajji*. In certain cultures the pilgrim dyes his beard red. Often the *hajji* will paint the fence around his house or the walls of the house with colorful depictions of significant events that occurred on his journey. He is afterward expected to live a life above reproach. Never is he to tell a lie or engage in any type of immoral or unethical activity. For this reason alone many Muslims delay going on the Hajj until they reach an advanced age. Added to this is the strong Islamic belief that any Muslim dying while on pilgrimage will go directly to paradise. Relatively few Muslim women go on the Hajj. It is my personal opinion that this fact is an outgrowth of the male Muslim's chauvinistic world view. Another consideration would be financial limitations.

Professor M. N. Karim from Bangladesh writes enthusiastically of the sense of Islamic community which is to be found at Mecca during the time of the pilgrimage:

> The social significance of the Hajj is a glorious testimony of the social equality and universal brotherhood of Islam. Dressed in two white pieces of cloth men and women of different countries of the Muslim world; irrespective of rich and poor; high and

36. G. H. Jansen, *Militant Islam* (New York: Harper and Row, 1979), pp. 32–33.

low; assemble together at Kaaba testifying to their very presence there and to the unity of Allah and also glorifying Him and expressing their gratitude to Him in the same breath at the top of their voices. They stand shoulder to shoulder as no distinction exists between the rich and poor, high and low. They are all humble creatures of Allah forming one fraternity of true believers and having the common idea of the same Allah; the same Kaaba; the same Quran; and the same Prophet. Such a spectacle of social equality and brotherhood is nowhere to be seen in the world.[37]

A. K. Brohi refers to the Hajj as being supraracial, supralinguistic, and supranational. He then goes on to give a symbolic interpretation of the pilgrimage. "Mankind as visualized by Islam, is to be pictured as marching in huge formations on its way to God—common aspirations, common realization that we are from God and to God we return, enable mankind to go forward as one compact and organized fraternity."[38]

Almsgiving

Islam mandates that all true believers give two and a half percent of their income to needy people. This can be designated for family members, neighbors, acquaintances, or for the beggar on the street. Almsgiving is stated to be an extension of the principle of brotherhood. Sharing one's abundance with the poor is theoretically an act of great piety. Gifts in excess of the two and a half percent are encouraged as well. For instance, subscriptions are solicited for mosque maintenance and construction.

The Quran lays great stress on kindness toward neighbors (4:37). The Prophet emphasized on many occasions the duty owed to a neighbor saying: "So repeatedly and so much has God impressed upon me the duty owed to a neighbor that I began to think that a neighbor might perhaps be named an heir." On one occasion while urging his companions to keep constantly in mind the need of kindliness toward their neighbors, he said: "This is not at all difficult; all that is necessary is that one should be willing at all times to share with one's neighbor; even

37. M. N. Karim, "Hajj and Muslim Fraternity," *The Bangladesh Observer*, 27 September 1982, p. 8.
38. A. K. Brohi, *Islam in the Modern World* (Lahore: Publishers United, 1975), p. 36.

if you have only broth for a meal, it is easy to add an extra cup of
water and share the broth with your neighbor."[39]

How do Muslims deal with the overwhelming numbers of
beggars in extremely poor countries? I have personally observed hundreds if not thousands of Muslim beggars soliciting
alms. Many of these men, women, and children had legitimate
needs. Others had chosen beggary as a way of life. It was difficult if not impossible to distinguish the two categories. My observation is that most Muslims give or refuse to give on the
basis of emotional reaction. A few of the factors that influence
the decision are the physical condition of the beggar; how cog-
nitively convincing is his story; whether his plea generates an
emotional response; how many onlookers are there; whether
others are giving; the extent of available financial resources;
and whether the donor is in a benevolent mood.

On an international scale, it would seem appropriate, for instance, for wealthy Saudi Arabia to give massive economic aid
to desperately impoverished Bangladesh. Unfortunately, this
does not occur. Petrol in Bangladesh is more than three dollars
per gallon. The assistance from oil-rich Muslim countries to
many poor Islamic nations is but a trickle.

One could make a case that the teaching of Islam on the subject of almsgiving creates a dependency syndrome. Muslims receive merit for giving to the poor. Therefore, the needy at times
seem to feel they are doing the donor a favor by soliciting his
gifts. Many times I have seen beggars become angry when they
are refused alms.

In its purest sense, community is worked out by Muslims
sharing their possessions with the needy and oppressed. In
practice, a great deal more could be done to make one of the
pillars of Islam, that of almsgiving, a more viable and effective
expression of the *ummah* of Muslims. Still, even with this
qualification, I would give Muslims due credit for emphasizing
and to some extent fulfilling the Quranic ideal of Islamic
ummah. The next chapter, however, will investigate some of
the distintegrative forces within and without Islam that are
affecting its sense of community.

39. Muhammad Zafrullah Khan, *Islam: Its Meaning for Modern Man*
(New York: Harper and Row, 1962), p. 145.

2

Diversity Within Muslim Community

The Prophet foresaw the schisms that would arise among his disciples. In one of the most famous Traditions, Muhammad is reported to have said, "Verily, it will happen to my people even as it did to the children of Israel. The children of Israel were divided into seventy-two sects, and my people will be divided into seventy-three. Every one of these sects will go to hell, except one sect."[1]

The assumption by Muhammad was that heresy would be easily identifiable. All deviants would be consigned to hell by the *ummah*. Only true Muslims would be privileged to enter paradise. In reality, heresy in a religion or ideology has never been easy to identify. There are many admixtures of doctrine, interpretation, and practice within any group. Purity is relative.

Islam has literally thousands of sects and subsects. Some of these deviations are based more on personalities than on significant doctrinal aberrations. Others are as major as that of the Ahmadiyya, who have proclaimed Mirza Ghulam Ahmad their surpreme prophet. Marshall Hodgson, the late professor of history at the University of Chicago, documented in his excellent three-volume survey of Islam, *The Venture of Islam*, the diverse currents of leadership as well as theological discord among Muslims over the past thirteen hundred years. One cannot help

1. *Mishkatul-Misabih*, bk. 1, chap. 6, pt. 2.

but assume that Islam probably has experienced as much internal conflict and dissonance as has Christianity during comparable historical periods.

> The tendency of Mohammedanism was to break up into sects
> often openly antagonistic to each other. Since the followers of
> the Prophet lived under so many different governments, spoke
> such a variety of tongues and represented so many divergent
> interests, it was but natural that even with the common creed
> and ritual and the pilgrimage to Mecca, there should be a ten-
> dency to draw apart. The ideal Moslem state was a theocracy in
> which the leader was both the civil and religious head. So long
> as Mohammed lived, and until Islam had extended beyond the
> borders of the caliphate a unity was maintained through the
> state. This was not difficult while wars of conquest were waged
> and the entire Moslem body was called upon to fight the battles
> of their faith. When, however, allegiance to different and even
> hostile chiefs was demanded, and the caliph no longer ruled
> over all Moslems, the traditional unity was broken. When to
> this we add the fact of some 150 different sects, we have a
> heterogeneous mass of religionists whose chief unity lies in
> the name, the repetition of the creed, the fast of Ramazan, the
> Book, and the pilgrimage to Mecca.[2]

Within Islam homogeneity and heterogeneity, unity and discord, love and hate all merge into that which is at once a religion, a world view, a community, a ritual, and a code. For all, an
overriding unity is a sought-after but elusive phenomenon. Perhaps the word *faith* best describes the reality of universal oneness. Most Muslims experience frustration that the *ummah* of
Islam falls short of the ideal of unity set forth by the Prophet.

There are four schools of Sunni law that have retained their
influence over the centuries. Because of legal interpretations
which vary with the schools, a certain tension arises among
devotees as they make claim to the correctness of their own particular position. Muslims are conditioned to think in absolute
terms; thus variances of opinion lead to some measure of confusion and discord.

The most widespread school is the Hanifi, which is traced to
the teaching of Hanifa (died 767). In this school, a relatively liberal interpretation is placed on the Quran. Reason and analogy

---

2. James L. Barton, *The Christian Approach to Islam* (Boston: Pilgrim,
1918), p. 82.

are stressed. Hanifi judges permit marriage of a Muslim male to a Christian or a Jew. Their numerical strength lies in Turkey and Asia.

Al-Shafi (died 820) stressed consensus and the rights of the community under its religious leaders. Muslims and non-Muslims are not permitted to marry. Followers of the school associated with his students are clustered in lower Egypt, western and southern Arabia, East Africa, and Indonesia.

A judicial system based heavily on the Hadith grew up under the aegis of the pupils of Malik Ibn Anas (died 795). The adherents of this relatively small school are found in North and West Africa, upper Egypt, and the Sudan.

The smallest and most conservative of the schools, the Hanbali, was founded by Ahmad Ibn Hanbal (died 855). Its teaching is followed only in central Arabia. Most innovation beyond the literal Quran and Sunna is rejected.[3]

Surah 6:159 states, "You have nothing to do with those who divide over religion and make parties." It is slightly incongruous yet true that many of the divisions within Islam started out in theological and political discussions within the holy precincts of the mosque. Here men sat together to discuss points of interpretation concerning law and ritual observances. Differences of opinion led to a hardening of positions. The result of this process was the engendering of sectarian feelings which led to the formation of a variety of schools of thought.

A. K. M. Aminul Islam, in a doctoral dissertation on the conflicts current among Muslims in a village of Bangladesh, writes:

> Within a home, different family members may choose different mosques. In fact, over the slightest misunderstanding between two family members, one may for some time attend a different mosque. However, as soon as the misunderstanding is over, he may come back to his original mosque. . . . Muslim religious leaders, who lead prayers, always try to differentiate between the villagers in terms of their affiliation with different sects; these leaders often accuse sects other than their own of being sacrilegious and un-Islamic.[4]

3. Richard V. Weekes, ed., *Muslim Peoples: A World Ethnographic Survey* (Westport, Conn.: Greenwood, 1978), p. xxv.
4. A. K. M. Aminul Islam, *A Bangladesh Village: Conflict and Cohesion* (Cambridge, Mass.: Schenkman, 1973), p. 85.

The condemnation of being "un-Islamic" does seem to be used rather frivolously among some Muslims. I have heard devout Muslims issue this charge at various times against Saudi Arabia, Iran, Iraq, Turkey, and Pakistan. Sufis are a constant target of these verbal attacks. Such internal bickering has led one Islamic leader to observe that "the worst enemies of the Muslims are Muslims themselves."[5]

Sects Within Islam

It would be impossible to document all of the Islamic sects which are to be found throughout the world. Their number and variety are simply incalculable. In this section I have chosen to comment on a few of the sects which are highly visible and, to some degree, significant. The Shiis, Ismailis, Wahhabis, and Ahmadiyyas will be examined as being somewhat illustrative of the diversity within twentieth-century Islam.

Shiis

The torches and weirdly lit banners, the bunch of black chains in the right hand of every man, the black garments, the glazed and exhausted eyes of the performers, and their drenched, sweating bodies signified a religious experience with which I was totally unfamiliar. Intense yet deliberate, the rhythm of the slow, liturgical chant never varied, its tempo ruled by the downward sweep of the chains, by the long, sustained cries of the leaders, by the thud of metal on flesh. In ancient and dignified figures, these young men were spelling out once more for a million pilgrims the renunciation, the humility, and penitence which lie at the heart of Shiite Islam.

"Ohhhh—Hussein, most great, most honored, we grieve for thee," called the leader, walking backward, step after measured step down the cleared aisle of the street. At this signal the chains were swung like incense burners, across the body, out to the side; a silent half beat, marked by the thump of bare feet marching in unison, passed before the score of chains swung back to thud on the bared shoulders.

5. Amir Shakib Arsalan, *Our Decline and Its Causes*, trans. M. A. Shakoor (Lahore: Shaikh Muhammad Ashraf, 1944), p. 39.

"Yaaaa—Hussein," answered the young men. Their shoulders were bruised blue from the ritual beatings, the kerchiefs around their heads blotched from perspiration. Still they kept up the sustained note, the measured beat, and the chains swung again like censers. The chains thudded and the chant swelling higher from a score of throats, from a hundred, as the taaziyas awaiting their turn inside the mosque were heard in the distance, in the silent half beats of the continuing ritual.

"Ohhhhhh—Hussein, our beloved martyr, we grieve for thee," cried the leader.

Tears streamed down the faces of sobbing men standing near me, and the piercing wailing cries of the women spoke of loss and pain and grief and lamentation.[6]

Such was the experience of Elizabeth W. Fernea as she visited Hussein's tomb at the huge Shiite pilgrimage center in Karbala, Iraq. A similar ritual occurs among Shiite Muslims throughout the Islamic world on the anniversary of the death of Hussein, their leader, hero, and most importantly, martyr.

It is important to realize that the initial and fundamental split between Sunnis and Shiis was over the question of succession. The issue was of a political nature. Today approximately 90 percent of all Muslims are Sunnis while 10 percent are Shiis.

Muhammad made no provision for his successor. This created the climate for Islam's first major crisis as it tried to constitute itself as a major political cum religious force following the decease of its autocratic and charismatic leader.

Abu Bakr, Umar, and Uthman followed Muhammad successively in leadership. Upon the assassination of Uthman, Ali became the caliph. He was a first cousin of Muhammad's as well as a son-in-law of the Prophet through his marriage to Fatimah. Immediately, Ali came into conflict with Muawiyah, the governor of Syria, who was also a relative of Uthman. It is at this point the divergence between Sunnis and Shiis takes place. Ali is recognized by Shiis as the first legitimate caliph. Ali's son, Hasan, according to Shiis, should have been the rightful leader, followed by Ali's other son, Hussein. In the critical historical moment when Hussein might actually have assumed such

6. Elizabeth W. Fernea, *Guests of the Sheik* (Garden City, N.Y.: Anchor, 1965), pp. 242–43.

leadership, Muawiyah's loyalists killed Hussein and seventy of his followers at the battle of Karbala.

Shiis take up their line from Ali the father and Hussein the martyred son. Sunnis, on the other hand, recognize the line of Abu Bakr, Umar, Uthman, Ali, and Muawiya.

Shiis give the successors of Muhammad the title *imam* rather than *caliph*. These *imams* are historically regarded as infallible guides to all truth. The largest group of Shiis believes that there were twelve of these *imams*. The last one in the lineage was Muhammad al-Mutazar, who was also known as al-Mahdi (the guided one). He was reputed to have disappeared into the mosque of Samarra, Iraq, in 878. The "Twelver" Shiis believe him to be still alive and actively engaged in guiding the believers. At the end of the age he will reappear and convert the world to Islam. Allegiance to him is a cardinal doctrine among those Shiis who are specifically called the "Twelvers."

Over the years of Islamic history there developed a number of Shiite distinctives that have put some distance between them and other Muslim traditions. For instance, their Quran contains a few variants when compared to the Quran used by the rest of the Islamic world.[7] Also the Shiis "have their own collections of hadith, composed during the tenth century, at a time when the Buyid amirs were masters of Bagdad."[8] A practice that separates some Shiis from Sunnis has been that of *muta* or temporary marriage. This has particularly taken place among soldiers who were fighting a war far from family and home. A contract was drawn up and a stipulated sum of money exchanged hands. The period of time for which the marriage would be valid was written into the contract. Orthodox Sunni leaders have condemned the practice as tantamount to adultery.[9] The Quranic citation of 4:28 has been interpreted as supporting the practice of *muta*.

It is appropriate to give equal time to Ayatullah Khomeini, the most famous of all contemporary Twelver Shiis, to present his case for the necessity of brotherhood among all Muslims as

7. Maurice Gaudefroy-Demombynes, *Muslim Institutions*, trans. John P. Macgregor (London: George Allen and Unwin, 1950), p. 38.

8. Ibid., p. 39.

9. L. Bevan Jones, *The People of the Mosque* (Calcutta: Baptist Mission Press, 1932), p. 135.

they together wage war against the "agents of America and Zionism."

> More saddening and dangerous than nationalism is the creation of dissension between Sunnis and Shiis and diffusion of mischievous propaganda among brother Muslims. Praise and thanks be to God that no difference exists in our Revolution between these two groups. All are living side by side in friendship and brotherhood. The Sunnis, who are numerous in Iran and live all over the country, have their own *ulama* and *shaykhs;* they are our brothers and equal with us, and are opposed to the attempts at creating dissension that certain criminals, agents of America and Zionism, are currently engaged in. Our Sunni brothers in the Muslim world must know that the agents of the satanic superpowers do not desire the welfare of Islam and the Muslims. The Muslims must disassociate themselves from them, and pay no heed to their diverse propaganda. I extend the hand of brotherhood to all committed Muslims in the world and ask them to regard the Shiis as cherished brothers and thereby frustrate the sinister plans of foreigners.[10]

It could be stated that Khomeini is an advocate of pragmatic *ummah*. He is looking on it as a unifying force to further his revolutionary goals. In actuality, current political alienations in the Muslim world contribute to religious divisiveness. In 1983, I visited a Shiite mosque in Detroit. A huge portrait of Khomeini was hung in the outer room. Revolutionary literature was spread over a large table. It is obvious that no Iraqi Muslim would feel comfortable worshiping in the mosque, even though he has religious affinity on most doctrinal issues with his Iranian coreligionists. I could not help but contrast this with the spirit of brotherhood I observed during the 1974 Lausanne Congress on Evangelism. At the conference Bangladeshis and Pakistanis, South Africans and Zimbabweans, East and West Germans, all believers in Christ, transcended normal political antagonisms and freely demonstrated the reality of the oneness of Christ that is commanded in John 17.

One further quote from a Muslim who minimizes Sunni and Shiite differences is shared with the aim of investigating primary sources and allowing Muslims of varying traditions to speak to the issues under consideration:

10. Imam Khomeini, *Islam and Revolution: Writings and Declarations of Imam Khomeini,* trans. Hamid Algar (Berkeley, Calif.: Mizan, 1980), p. 302.

Sunnism and Shiism, belonging both to the total orthodoxy of Islam, do not in any way destroy its unity. The unity of a tradition is not destroyed by different applications of it but by the destruction of its principles and forms as well as its continuity. Being "the religion of unity" Islam, in fact, displays more homogeneity and less religious diversity than other worldwide religions. Sunnism and Shiism are dimensions within Islam placed there not to destroy its unity but to enable a larger humanity and differing spiritual types to participate in it. Both Sunnism and Shiism are the assertion of the *Shahadah, La il-aha ill Allah* expressed in different climates and with a somewhat different spiritual fragrance.[11]

Ismailis

Out of Shiism flowed innumerable splinter sects, one of which is the Ismaili community. These people are also known as "Seveners." Ismailis honored the traditional Shiite belief of succession down to the sixth *imam*, Jafar al-Siddiq (died 765). Then they designated Jafar's eldest son Ismail (died 760) as the seventh *imam*. Thus their identity as "Seveners" became popularly accepted.

Other Shiis point out that al-Siddiq's father, upon learning of Ismail's addiction to strong drink, appointed his second son Musa as his successor. These Shiis therefore take the line on to the twelfth *imam* through Musa.

In their cosmogony and religious belief Ismailis reflect a distinct influence from Greek philosophy. The Pythagorean system with its stress on the number seven was consecrated by the Ismailis, who have used it interpretatively in regard to cosmic and historical developments. "Neo-Platonism imparted to them the conception of gnostic knowledge through emanation in seven stages: (1) God; (2) the universal mind; (3) the universal soul; (4) primeval matter; (5) space; (6) time; (7) the world of earth and man."[12]

The two basic entities are space and time. The appearance of man is explained by the need which the soul feels to attain to perfect knowledge. From knowledge there is progression to

11. Seyyed Hossein Nasr, *Ideals and Realities of Islam* (New York: Praeger, 1967), pp. 147–48.
12. Caesar E. Farah, *Islam: Beliefs and Observances* (Woodbury, N.Y.: Barron's Education Series, 1968), pp. 178–79.

universal reason. When man reaches this stage all movement will cease. Man has then attained salvation.

The Ismailis have been propagation conscious, as indicated in this conversion scenerio:

> The Ismaili missionary began by putting embarrassing questions to the neophyte on knotty points of Muslim theology and led him quite gradually to admit that these difficulties were easily solved by the allegorical and symbolical interpretation of the Kuran. Calculations made from numerical value of letters played an important part. When the proselyte had acknowledged the force of his arguments, the missionary made him take an oath not to reveal any of the mysteries which were going to be entrusted to him and taught him that in order to be saved it was necessary to submit blindly to the spiritual and temporal guidance of the Imam. The majority of the adepts did not pass beyond the first or second stages of initiation; the missionaries hardly reached the sixth. Only a few superior individuals could hope to reach the higher degree.[13]

Ismailis look beyond the external or obvious. The esoteric or inner reality is what captivates them. The apparent is a camouflage which veils the true meaning from the noninitiates. All words, even those of the holy Quran and Hadith, must be examined for their secret meanings.

The Druze community in the mountains of Lebanon is an offshoot of Ismailism. It is, however, important to realize that the Druzes have so altered basic doctrine and practice that they are no longer considered to be in the mainstream of Ismailism or for that matter Islam itself. The Druzes are extremely esoteric and sealed off religiously from the rest of the world.

The Ismailis do accept the basic tenets of Islam. They affirm an unshakable belief in the unity of God, the divine mission of the Prophet, and the authority of the holy Quran. "There is no doubt that the only aim of the authors [early Ismaili formulators of doctrine] was to develop and to refine the primitive principles of Islam, making them acceptable and attractive to the critical and sophisticated mind of a cultured man, who had

---

13. M. Houtsma, A. J. Wensinck, T. W. Arnold, W. Heffening, and E. Levi-Provencal, *The Encyclopedia of Islam* (London: Luzac, 1927), vol. 2, p. 552.

gone a long way from the crude mentality of the Arabs of the first century."[14]

The question then arises as to the compatibility of Sunni Islam with the Greek philosophic, Neo-Platonic, Gnostic, and astrological emphases of Ismaili doctrine. This issue will be dealt with later when I seek to irreducibly define who is a Muslim. It can be clearly stated that Ismailism is considered a definite component within the Islamic mosaic. It is a small group of sects (the largest being led by the Agha Khan) spread throughout the Muslim world. But it is a movement of significance.

Wahhabis

Muhammad Ibn Abdal-Wahhab was born at Ayinah in North Arabia in 1691. He was carefully instructed in Islamic doctrine according to the Hanbali school, the strictest of the four schools of law. Ibn Abdal-Wahhab traveled extensively and studied at Mecca, Baghdad, and Medina. For a year he was recognized as an exponent of Sufism. In the end he became a disciple of the ideas of Ibn Taimiyya, a fourteenth-century Hanbalite theologian who was a proponent of meticulously observing Islamic law and ritual.

Ibn Abdal-Wahhab was expelled from his hometown. He then took refuge in the village of Dariya under the patronage of the local chief, Muhammad bin Saud.

This association was to determine the whole course of Arabian history. The Wahhabis, with the patronage of the Saud family, began to attack neighbouring towns and tribes and as each town was reduced, Wahhabi doctrines were imposed upon it. By the end of the nineteenth century the Wahhabis controlled most of what is now called Saudi Arabia. The name itself is suggestive: "The Arabia belonging to the Saud family." The Saudi family have controlled important parts of Arabia ever since, with two important interruptions. The first was the Turkish occupation (1818–33), the second was Muhammad bin Rashid's reign between 1891 and 1901.[15]

The aim of Ibn Abdal-Wahhab was to purge Islam of any ac-

14. H. A. R. Gibb and J. H. Kramers, eds., *Shorter Encyclopedia of Islam* (Leiden: Brill, 1953), p. 181.
15. Michael Nazir-Ali, *Islam: A Christian Perspective* (Exeter: Paternoster, 1983), p. 96.

cretions which were added later then the third century of the Muslim calendar. He was horrified to note in his travels the aberrant practices of Muslims. The following list of rituals, beliefs, and prohibitions set forth by Ibn Abdal-Wahhab indicates his concerns regarding the Islam he observed.

The four schools of law and six books of Hadith must be acknowledged.

All objects of worship other than Allah are false, and all who worship other gods are worthy of death.

To visit the tombs of Muslim saints in order to seek to please God and win his favor is prohibited.

Introduction of the name of a prophet, saint, or angel into a prayer is an act of polytheism.

Intercession may be made only to Allah.

No vows may be made to any human being.

It is unbelief to profess knowledge which is not based on the Quran and Sunna.

Attendance at public prayers is mandatory.

Smoking of tobacco is forbidden and can be punishable by up to forty lashes.

The shaving of one's beard and the use of abusive language are prohibited.

Alms are to be paid on all income.

The use of the rosary is forbidden. Names of God are to be counted on the knuckles of one hand.

Wahhabi mosques are built with great simplicity; no minarets or ornaments are allowed.

Muhammad's birthday is not celebrated.

The use of silk, gold, and silver is forbidden. Music is also disallowed.

Anthropomorphic concepts of God are believed. Quranic texts about God's hand, his hearing and seeing, along with his ascent to the throne are literally interpreted.

Jihad or religious war is regarded as an obligation to be engaged in when necessary.

Use of tombstones is not allowed.[16]

Wahhabis are dedicated to the strict interpretation and application of Islamic law. At times Wahhabis have gone beyond the Quran in seeking to implement strict social codes. An illustration of this is the before-mentioned execution of the Arabian princess and her boyfriend for the sin of adultery. Such a stern and extreme punishment is not prescribed in the Quran.

It would be accurate to perceive present-day Wahhabism as most of all a movement that favors conservative legal interpretation. Libya, Iran, Saudi Arabia, and Pakistan are a few examples of states in which radical Islamic fundamentalism has been dominant. These countries are seeking to return to the original purity of early Islam. Oil funds are pouring out of Libya and Saudi Arabia for the support of Muslim missionaries. The worldwide program of building mosques is unprecedented in the modern era. If Ibn Abdal-Wahhab himself were alive today and could observe the "Islamic Revolution," he indeed would be pleased.

Ahmadiyyas

The founder of the Ahmadiyya movement, Mirza Ghulam Ahmad, was born in 1839 at Qadian in Punjab, India. The title *mirza* indicates his ancestors came into India with the conquering Mughals. Ahmad received a good education in Arabic and Persian. He also meditated and pursued religious study. He was said to have frequently had a mystical experience of hearing voices which came from an unknown source. About 1880 he concluded that he was called of God for a special mission in life. Shortly thereafter, he published *Barahini Ahmadiyya* which, in the initial instance, was well received by fellow Muslims.

On March 4, 1889, Ahmad announced he was the recipient of a divine revelation that authorized him to initiate disciples of his own. From that time forth, he began to expound a series of new doctrines. Soon he had attracted a very able group of followers.

Opposition to Ahmad was quickly generated by traditional Muslims. This controversy raged until his death in 1908.

The Ahmadiyyas teach several distinctive doctrines:

16. Samuel M. Zwemer, *Islam: A Challenge to Faith* (New York: Student Volunteer Movement for Foreign Missions, 1907), pp. 150–51.

No verse in the Quran is or can be abrogated. If one verse appears to be inconsistent with another, that is due to faulty exegesis.

Jihad or "holy war" has lapsed, and coercion in religion is condemned.

To say that Muhammad is the "seal of the prophets" does not mean that he is the last of them. A seal is a hallmark and he embodies the perfection of prophethood; but a prophet or apostle can come after him as did the Hebrew prophets after Moses.

Jesus is dead, as are the rest of the prophets, and he did not ascend bodily into heaven.

Hell is not everlasting.

Apostasy is not punishable by death.

Any innovation in religious practice is culpable. The worship of saints is an invasion of the prerogative of God.

Ijma or catholic consent is generally limited to the Prophet's companions.

Revelation will always remain a privilege of the true believer.

Belief in Mirza Ghulam Ahmad al Qadiani as the Messiah-Mahdi is an article of faith. Faith is incomplete without it.

Spirituality in religion is more important than legalism. An Ahmadi need not belong to any particular *madhhab* or school of law.

The mediaeval *ulama* need not be followed in the interpretation of Quran and Hadith.[17]

Within this set of doctrinal belief is to be found the most controversial of all of Ahmad's claims. In reflecting on the Muslim teaching of the Imam-Mahdi, he noted that the scriptures of Zoroastrians, Hindus, and Buddhists all prophesied the coming of a great Teacher. Over a period of time Ahmad came to feel that he was the *mujaddid* sent by God for the purpose of restoring the true faith of Islam. He thus professed to be both the promised Messiah and the Mahdi. "Likewise, on the ground that God, at intervals, sends 'renewers' of religion, he claimed that in his capacity of Mahdi no other than Muhammad had

17. Alfred Guillaume, *Islam* (Baltimore: Penguin, 1954), pp. 126–27.

made his 'second advent'. He was, in fact, an 'image of the Holy Prophet.'"[18]

As Kenneth Cragg has observed, Ahmad's "most serious potential heresy was the precise import of his claims to Islamic revelation."[19] But what was Ahmad really saying regarding his prophethood or messiahship? Muhammad Ali postulates that Ahmad never claimed prophethood in the technical sense. Ali saw Ahmad's usage of words like *prophethood, revelation,* and *disbelief* in Sufi allegorical and metaphorical terms.[20] Once Sufi esoteric language is introduced into the controversy, we have moved into an area that prohibits any type of specificity. Sufi words can carry many different meanings. The main issue is that present-day Ahmadiyyas firmly perceive Mirza Ghulam Ahmad as a prophet of God.

The Ahmadiyyas thus proceeded to raise up a new structure of religious beliefs and practices outside of the mainstream of Islam. They developed a new prophet, a new focus of devotion, a new mission, a new spiritual center, new rituals, and new religious leadership. These are the features which raise Ahmadiyyaism to the level of a new religion. Muslims who choose to convert to the Ahmadiyya fold must reject old institutions and personalities.

> Moreover, it is also to be noted that the Mirza raised the standard of the prophethood and declared all those who did not accept his claim as *Kafirs* in a Muslim world which was already torn by dissensions. By so doing, however, the Mirza raised an iron wall between himself and the Muslims. On the one side of this wall there are a few thousand followers of the Mirza, and on the other side is the rest of the Muslim world which stretches from Morocco to China and has great personalities, virtuous movements of reform and valuable institutions. They stand isolated from and opposed to the whole of this world. Thus he unnecessarily added to the difficulties of Muslims, further aggravated their disunity and added a new complication to the problems facing them.[21]

18. L. Bevan Jones, *Christianity Explained to Muslims* (1937; Calcutta: Baptist Mission Press, 1964), p. 169.

19. Kenneth Cragg, *Islamic Surveys 3: Counsels in Contemporary Islam* (Edinburgh: University Press, 1965), p. 156.

20. Abul Hasan Ali Nadwi, *Qadianism: A Critical Study,* trans. Zafar Ishaq Anseri (Lahore: Shaikh Muhammad Ashraf, 1965), p. 121.

21. Ibid. pp. 136–37.

Ahmad was said to be a severe and unyielding person. The overwhelming force of his personality and sense of mission seemed to draw disciples. He had a magnetic quality about him that would cause men in significant numbers to forsake all and follow him. He is said to have performed many miracles. He was also able to "will" evil upon his detractors through imprecation and curses. A documented sample of his violent attacks upon traditional Muslim leaders has been preserved: "Of all animals, the filthiest and most repellent is the pig. But filthier than pigs are those, who owing to their base desires conceal the evidence of reality. O corpse-eating Maulvis! O filthy spirits! Pity on you that you concealed the true evidence of Islam out of hostility. O worms of darkness! how can you hide the radiant rays of truth."[22]

As a result of such inflammatory rhetoric, Ahmad was branded a heretic, blasphemer, enemy of the faith, and imposter. He was ostracized and was forbidden the use of mosques. Subsequently, a number of Ahmadiyyas in Afghanistan have suffered the penalty of death for their heresy. In Pakistan in 1953, there were riots between Sunni Muslims and the Ahmadiyyas. The campaign of mutual antagonism continued to be waged until 1974 when the Ahmadiyyas were formally declared non-Muslims by an act of the Pakistan Parliament. An article in *Arabia* updates the situation in Pakistan:

> The Pakistani government has banned the use of Muslim nomenclatures by the Qadianis. The new ordinance, passed in April, 1984, provides a punishment of three years imprisonment and a fine for a person of the Qadiani group or the Lahori group who, by words either spoken or written, or by visible representation, refers to the successors or companions of Mirza Ghulam Ahmed or Sahaba, his wife as an ummul-Momineen, or a member of his family as "Ahle-Bait" or calls his place of worship a Masjid.

> The same penalty is provided for any Qadiani who directly or indirectly poses himself as a Muslim or refers to his faith as Islam or preaches or propagates his faith or invites others to accept his faith. The ordinance empowers the provincial government to confiscate any newspaper, book or other document printed by the Qadianis.[23]

22. Ibid., p. 86.
23. "Qadianis—Non-Muslim," *Arabia*, June 1984, p. 72.

According to their own figures there are five hundred thousand members of this group, half of them living in Pakistan. The headquarters of the movement is in Rabwah, Pakistan, where there is a strong ruling secretariat. Ahmadiyyas give very generously through expected gifts and donations. They have a strong publishing program that disseminates their propaganda throughout the Muslim world. In addition, they have emphasized the establishment of schools and colleges. The people of their former center, Kadiyan, are some of the most educated in all of India.

There is a sect of the Ahmadiyya in Lahore that is relatively small. The group accepts Ghulam Ahmad as *mudjaddid* but not as a prophet. It too has emphasized the publication of tracts and books in its outreach program.

Ahmadiyyas are extremely anti-Christian in orientation. They believe that Jesus journeyed to Kashmir and today they can point to his grave in Srinagar. I spent some time seeking to trace down another of their claims by searching for the reputed grave of Mary, the mother of Jesus. It is said to be located on a mountainside near Murree, Pakistan. I was, however, unsuccessful in my quest.

There was a small, fanatical group of Ahmadiyyas living in the town where I was resident for several years in one particular Muslim country. They were not a significant force in the community. But they were able to give our small group of missionaries a difficult time. Once their leaders went to talk to one of our new missionaries who was engaged in language study. He, not knowing of their identity, was gracious to them and sought to answer honestly their many queries. A few days after that visit an article in the district newspaper accused our missionary of being an agent of the Central Intelligence Agency. It was evident that his Ahmadiyyan guests had been the "informants."

In that town the Ahmadiyyas had their own small mosque exclusively for their own use. They did not participate in any Muslim ritual with Sunni Muslims.

The zeal of this sect amazes me. They are highly motivated people who are willing to endure even death for their beliefs. In fact, they seem to thrive on persecution. Are they members of the *ummah* of Islam? That is a question of persisting irritation throughout the Muslim world. It is important to note that they consider themselves to be Muslims.

Sufism

In *Bridges to Islam*, I delved deeply into the history and practices of Sufis. The material I will present in this section has been gleaned, in most instances, from new sources. Also, the focus here is on tensions within the Islamic community that have been caused by what Muslims perceive as Sufi departures from the path of orthodoxy.

It is instructive to observe the aspects of *ummah* within Sufism that are found in this account of Albert W. Sadler's participation in a Sufi meeting. Toward the conclusion of an emotionally charged worship service, one of the devotees had reached a high level of ecstasy.

All the while he moaned, he shouted "oh!", and he beat on his temples with his fists. When he staggered into the *pir* [Sufi holy man], himself a giant of a man and now obviously a father to all, the *pir* held and patted his shoulder as one would comfort one's own child. This was a moment of intense fellowship for the whole group. Those for whom the Christian experience of *koinonia* has deep personal experience will, I think, understand this. The music, the devotional words of the song, but above all the ecstasy of this man had transformed this deeply religious gathering into an intensely loving community, and had brought out the role of the *pir* as father to his community.

After fifteen or twenty minutes the man fell at the feet of the orange-robed disciple seated to the left of the *pir*, and lay there inert, like a physically exhausted child in sleep. All sat down, and the song went on. One of the disciples kissed the *pir's* feet.

Toward the end of the song one of the disciples began to spread a white cloth on the floor. On it he placed two dishes of sweets wrapped in paper, and a brass container of water. At his direction, two boys in embroidered caps went and emptied whole boxes of incense sticks into the charcoal burners in the four corners of the porch. The roof being low, the heavy fumes quickly closed over us. Now a selection from the Quran was recited. We all stood. The officiating disciple took the brass container and sprinkled water on us all. Now he uncovered the two dishes and passed them around; we each took a white sugar bonbon. Some shook hands with those around them, as at the end of a Quaker meeting. This was a double handshake with both hands enclosing the hand of the other. Taking our leave along with the others now, we shook hands with the *pir* in this manner, and thanked him. He was warmly gracious to everyone.[24]

J. Spencer Trimingham, the famous Islamist, has defined Sufism "in wide terms by applying it to anyone who believes that it is possible to have direct experience of God and who is prepared to go out of his way to put himself in a state whereby he may be enabled to do this."[25] It would appear to me that this definition is adequate for mysticism but not for Sufism. There is a more specific quality about Sufism than is contained in Trimingham's definition.

The Arabic word *suf* means "wool" and was originally applied to the Muslim ascetics who, in imitation of Christian hermits, clothed themselves in a type of coarse woolen garb which was a visible sign of their renunciation of the world. In the early days of Sufism, the doctrinal emphasis was on the fear of God. Simplicity of lifestyle was enjoined on the devotees as a means of ensuring acceptance by God on the great day of judgment.

The oldest major Persian treatise on Sufism is the *Kashf Al Mahjub* written by Ali Bin Uthman Al-Hujwiri. This book, written in 1040, documents the hundreds of Sufi sects which were current in the Islamic world by the eleventh century.

In the eleventh century the greatest Sufi of all times came on the scene. Al-Ghazzali was a gifted professor at the University of Baghdad. He came to feel totally unworthy before God. At age thirty-seven, after a severe inner struggle, he left Baghdad and for a time became a wandering ascetic. This crisis experience of conversion was to have a profound effect on the future course of Sufism. Al-Ghazzali became a prolific writer, thus establishing an academic and philosophical base for Islamic mysticism. Other mystical poets—Faridud-Din, Jalud-Din Rumi, and Shaykh Sadi—followed.

24. Albert W. Sadler, "Visit to a Chishti Qawwadi," *The Muslim World,* vol. 53, no. 4, pp. 291–92.
25. J. Spencer Trimingham, *The Sufi Orders in Islam* (London: Oxford University Press, 1971), p. 1.

The emphasis on Sufism had shifted early on from the fear of God to the all-embracing concept of love. Persian Sufi poetry is pregnant with mystical symbolism which employs worldly terminology to express divine truths. The word *wine* is a metaphor for divine love. The lover longs for his beloved. A tavern is depicted as a place where one encounters God. The bird which flees the cage is the soul in search of God.

Over the centuries, Sufism has expanded into literally thousands of sects. These sects are known as *tarikas*. "The *tarika* is the way of sanctity in Islam and it is the *tarika* that has produced saints over the centuries to the present day, saints who keep society together and rejuvenate its religious life by vitalizing it with the spiritual forces which have brought the religion itself into being."[26]

Few world religions have succeeded in teaching mysticism to the masses. In Sufism this was done by the devotee's taking membership in one of the *tarikas*. In the early days of Sufism every workers' guild was affiliated with a *tarika* and most villages supported some resident *pir*.

The Sufis have been the great missionaries of Islam. Their mystical, heartfelt interpretation of Islam has proved attractive to people from Morocco to the Philippines. In many countries Sufis syncretized their own beliefs with the religious ritual which was already prevalent among the people. A specific example would be the incorporation of Hindu philosophy and practices into Sufism in the Indian subcontinent. Ishak M. Husaini cites an illustration from Africa where "daily recitations, the gathering around the Shaikh, belief in spiritual powers and communal living" are commonalities between African traditional religious practices and Sufism.[27]

Sufi Practices

Ritual is the point where Sufis most dramatically come into conflict with orthodox Islam. Fundamentalist Muslims cannot countenance what they consider to be severe departures from Quranic teaching. The Sufis, on the other hand, like to make their own orthodox apologetic.

---

26. Nasr, *Ideals and Realities of Islam*, p. 144.
27. Ishak M. Husaini, "Islamic Culture in Arab and African Countries," in *Islam: The Straight Path*, ed. Kenneth W. Morgan (New York: Ronald Press, 1958), p. 248.

There are two texts which have inspired Muslim mystics on countless occasions, namely, "We are nearer to him [i.e. man] than the vein of his neck" and "Wherever ye turn there is the face of God." In the hearts of men longing for a deep and intimate knowledge of God, discussions of anthropomorphism and pantheism found no place. They concentrated on the text, "A people whom He loveth and who love Him" (5:59). It was this text above all others which appealed to the Sufis, who sought to lose themselves in the divine love.[28]

Unfortunately, many Sufis do not attain such a high level of mystical questing for the reality of union with the Divine. One needs only to think of specific practices like the exaltation of a *pir* to a point where he is very nearly worshiped. This spiritual guide, usually through performing some supernatural act, is elevated to the position of master teacher. Soon he gathers a large number of devotees who blindly follow his every direction. These *pirs* are recipients of large donations. Their sphere of influence often spills over into the political arena. Politicians make obsequious visits to the *pir* ostensibly to seek his blessing but in reality to have their photos taken with him and released in major newspapers.

When a *pir* dies, his tomb becomes a sacred object of veneration and pilgrimage. Devotees are convinced his power still remains within the general area of the gravesite. Offerings are given by the disciples to the keepers of the tomb. "These celebrations attract pilgrims from neighbouring villages and tribes, or depending upon their fame, from a still wider area. Special concerts of *mawlids* are held, animals sacrificed, and offerings made. They are generally associated with a fair attended by traders and peddlars, mountebanks, and story-tellers."[29]

The Dervish orders are another Sufi distinctive. These Sufi mystics are committed in initiatory rites to be absolutely obedient to their spiritual leaders *(shaikhs)*. Their initiation binds them together by secret oaths and symbolism.

Jalal ad-Din ar-Rumi (died 1273) is the celebrated founder of the whirling dervishes. He invented a mystical dance, a sort of waltz in six-time with an orchestra consisting of the German

28. Guillaume, *Islam*, p. 143.
29. Trimingham, *The Sufi Orders in Islam*, p. 180.

flute, the lute, and the violin. His biographers stated that he was capable of whirling for hours and days.

> The dancer crosses his arms over his breast and clasps his shoulders. A singer chants, to the accompaniment of flutes and drums and sometimes of other instruments. Then at a given moment the Shaykh takes up his position for the folded-up figures to file solemnly past him; and each dancer, as he enters the orbit of the Shaykh's presence, begins to unfold his arms and turn his body round, slowly at first but soon more quickly with his arms now stretched out on either side to their full extent, the right palm upwards as receptacle of Heaven and the left palm downwards to transmit Heaven to earth and so the whirling continues.[30]

This dancing in circles is the reproduction of celestial orbits which lead to the realization of the forms of the universe. Through this dance one can reach the Form who is God. At the moment of attainment when the trance is total, the music and dancing cease.

In order to further understand orthodox Islam's rejection of this form of mystical expression it will be helpful to consider a selection written by Rumi and performed by the whirling dervishes:

> What is to be done, O Moslems? For I do not recognize myself.
> I am neither Christian nor Jew nor Gabr nor Moslem.
> I am not of the East, nor of the West, nor of the land, nor of the sea;
> One I seek, One I know, One I see, One I call.
> He is the first, He is the last, He is the outward, He is the inward.
> I know none other except "Ya Hu" (O He!) and "Ya man Hu".
> I am intoxicated with Love's cup; the two worlds have passed out of my ken.
> I have no business save in carouse and revelry.
> If once in my life I spent a moment without Thee,
> From that time and from that hour I repent of my life.
> If once in this world I win a moment with Thee;
> I will trample on both worlds, I will dance in triumph forever,
> Up, O ye lovers, and away! Tis time to leave the world for aye.

---

30. Martin Lings, *What Is Sufism?* (Berkeley: University of California Press, 1975), p. 84.

Hark, loud and clear from heaven the drum of parting
  calls—Let none delay![31]

To a Sufi, such poetry is divine; to a fundamentalist Muslim,
it is heresy!

In *Modern Egyptians*, there is an account of dervishes jump-
ing and leaping in the air. One devotee rushed away from the
dancers and put pieces of red-hot charcoal into his mouth,
chewing them and finally swallowing them. Another put a live
coal into his mouth. As he released his breath sparks flew out
from between his lips. Neither man showed any indication of
pain or harmful aftereffects.[32]

Another favorite Sufi ritual is the *dhikr* (remembrance). This
ceremony centers around the continual repetition of the word
Allah or of certain other attributes of God. Men sit in a circle
and jerk their heads back and forth as they emotionally recite
spiritual terms. If the emotion gets to a very high pitch, some
men may stand and start dancing in circles. It has even been
documented that men in a great frenzy of abandonment to God
have discarded their clothes and danced in the nude.

One Sufi sect called the Bektashiya has syncretized its belief
in the twelve Shiite *imams* with a trinity of God, Muhammad,
and Ali. In Albania this sect, at the time of receiving new members, celebrates with wine, bread, and cheese. Members also
confess their sins to their spiritual guides, who grant them ab-
solution.[33]

These practices of Sufis have quite naturally created a great
deal of dissonance in the Muslim *ummah*.

Reaction to Sufism

One of the first crises in the Islamic community with a Sufi
of stature was the alleged heresy of the popular teacher, Hu-
sayn ibn Mansur al-Hallaj (died 922). Al-Hallaj believed in "uni-
tive life," the idea that God manifests himself on earth in the
lives of his devotees. This doctrine in itself was acceptable but
al-Hallaj took it one step further by saying that a seeker after
God could receive an ultimate mystical experience by which he
could merge into a union with the Divine. *Ana Al-Haqq* (I am the

31. John Alden Williams, *Islam* (New York: Braziller, 1963), pp. 150–51.

32. Guillaume, *Islam*, p. 153.

33. Fazlur Rahman, *Islam*, 2d ed. (Chicago: University of Chicago Press,
1979), pp. 163–64.

truth) was a claim made by al-Hallaj. He had so sought the Divine that as a result of his union with God, he felt he could now appropriate one of the names of God for himself.

This proclamation scandalized the orthodox. As a result of refusing to recant, al-Hallaj was crucified. A wave of persecution against the Sufis of Baghdad ensued. The image of al-Hallaj among later Sufis is that of a holy martyr.

It is difficult to be definitive concerning the history of Sufism. Ghazzali lifted Sufi philosophy to its highest peaks. Few Muslim scholars attack him. But through the centuries Sufism has fragmented into so many thousands of sects that it is inevitable that there would be much that is undesirable and even repugnant. The members of one sect ritually drink the menstrual blood of women. Another group engages in heavy drug use in order to induce a more powerful experience with the cosmic entity. Yet another has so integrated Hindu philosophy into its belief structure that it gives only passing acknowledgment to its Islamic roots. Mysticism at its highest level of quest for God is commendatory. But by its very nature it tends toward becoming freewheeling and libertarian. Every person is a free agent, unhindered and unshackled in his pursuit of ultimate reality. This can, and often does, lead the mystic into deviations of behavior and denials of doctrine that anger his nonmystical peers.

> Some Sufis like the Qalandars, Islamic beatniks, violated all the norms of Islamic society. With the passing of time and the social decline of the eighteenth and nineteenth centuries, almost every pervert entered a Sufi order, and almost every madman was accounted a saint. This was partly because Islam lacks ecclesiastical machinery for defining dogma or casting out heretics; in any case, these abuses have little to do with the intrinsic value of the religious ideas of the Sufis.[34]

The Indian subcontinent is a fertile breeding ground for innumerable Sufi sects. *Pirs* have emerged in every village and town. "The result of all this was that the Muslim masses had developed an uncommon relish for things esoteric, for miracles, for supernatural performances, for inspired dreams and prophesies. The more a person had to offer people by way of

---

34. John Alden Williams, ed., *Islam* (New York: Washington Square, 1961), pp. 137–38.

these things, the greater was his popularity."[35] All of this has caused great distress to the legalists of the Middle East. In Bangladesh, the Saudi Arabian ambassador spends a significant amount of time exhorting the Muslim masses to leave the path of the *pirs* and to return to the more orthodox fold.

It should be noted that Sufis are present everywhere in the Middle East except for Saudi Arabia, where Wahhabis strongly oppose Sufism. The Sufis, however, maintain a low profile in Arab countries. It is east of Iran that the more deviant forms of Sufism find expression.

Fundamentalist Muslims oppose mystical dancing. Most also condemn the chanting of poems to the accompaniment of musical instruments. They see this as an aid to emotional excesses. "Theologicans and doctors of law feared the emotive power of music, the incontrollable magic of which is capable of striking most subtle chords in man's heart, but also of unleashing the most confused passions and of leading him into the worst of moral disturbances."[36]

The orthodox are not pleased with the integration of the sexes at Sufi gatherings. Women are not allowed to mingle with men in mosques. They either do not attend or are seated behind partitions. Valerie J. Hoffman, a doctoral candidate at the University of Chicago, was a Fellow at the American Research Center in Egypt in 1980. While there she researched various Sufi sects.

> I became acquainted with some illiterate and poorly educated Sufis, among whom were women considered to possess an unusual spiritual intuition, and who exercise authority in a spiritual and practical sense even over men. In this group there appeared to be no barriers of sexual segregation, which is a cause of great horror among other Muslim groups which believe sexual segregation to be essential for moral purity. But in this world, where spiritual authority is conferred by God-given power rather than man-given certification, there can be no exclusion of women.[37]

Sufis, with few exceptions, have remained within Muslim

35. Nadwi, *Qadianism*, p. 4.
36. Haider Bammate, *Muslim Contributions to Civilization* (Brentwood, Md.: American Trust Publications, 1962), p. 60.
37. Valerie J. Hoffman, "Researching the Religious Life of Muslim Women in Modern Egypt" (paper submitted to the American Research Center, Egypt, 1981), p. 4.

ummah. They have regarded themselves as part of orthodoxy. Indeed, they believed they were the very core of the community. This is expressed in the famous Sufi saying, "The most excellent of Muslim community, who keep their respiration with God and safeguard their heart from the intrusions of heedlessness, have singled themselves out with the name of Sufism."[38]

Traditionalist Muslims cannot agree. Yet they are not ready for a head-on confrontation. Perhaps the relationship of Sufis to the fundamentalists can be summed up in these words by R. A. Nicholson, "It is the nature of mystics to soar just as it is the business of legalists to imitate the old woman who clipped the wings and cut the talons of the king's falcon that fell into her hands."[39]

Political Factors

In order to understand the tight cohesion between religion and state within Islam, it is necessary to retrace history to the time of Muhammad. From 622, the Prophet reigned as the head of the *ummah.* He was no longer the persecuted Prophet. Muhammad ruled by absolute religious prerogative. His source of guidance was Allah. A theocracy had been created. There was no distinction between the religious and the political. All social norms, collective or individual, were to conform to Islamic law as prescribed in the Quran. The Muslim army was regarded as the army of God. The wealth of the community was in reality owned by Allah.[40]

The early years of Islam were overwhelmingly successful. There was massive geographic expansion within an unbelievably short time. Soon followed significant achievements in science, philosophy, medicine, and astronomy. Builders, designers, and craftsmen created a wealth of architectural beauty. I have been thrilled to see Muslim art in the great mosques of Damascus, Istanbul, and Jerusalem. The Taj Mahal simply overwhelmed my family and me as we stood in awe be-

38. Menahem Milson, trans., *A Sufi Rule for Novices,* being a translation of *Kitab Adab al-Muri-din* by Abu al-Najib al-Suhrawardi (Cambridge: Harvard University Press, 1975), p. 6

39. R. A. Nicholson, "Mysticism," in *The Legacy of Islam,* ed. T. W. Arnold and Alfred Guillaume (London: Oxford University Press), p. 237.

40. Badru D. Kateregga and David W. Shenk, *Islam and Christianity: A Muslim and a Christian in Dialogue* (Grand Rapids: Eerdmans, 1981), pp. 50–51.

fore one of the most powerful artistic expressions ever created
by man. Muslims can point with justifiable pride to their superior accomplishments in a number of important areas.

> But in later times it seemed that God in general history had half
> forsaken Islam. The Caliphate fell on evil days. At times there
> were at least three competing Caliphs. It was true that conquer-
> ors of Muslim heartlands coming out of Asia, Seljuk, Turks,
> Mongols, Tartars, Ottoman Turks, sooner or later became Mus-
> lims. The Islamic heritage might change its political masters
> but it always emerged religiously and culturally dominant. In
> modern times even this comfort became dubious. In the eigh-
> teenth and nineteenth Christian centuries the historic lands of
> Islam came increasingly under the domination, if not political
> certainly economic and cultural, of Western powers represent-
> ing a non-Islamic faith. India fell from a position of hegemony
> in Islam to be the "vassal" of the East India Company and then
> of the British Crown. Victoria occupied the heritage of Akbar
> and Aurangzib, while Ottoman rule, looked at from the West,
> was the sick man of Europe. It seemed as if the course of Is-
> lamic history had gone awry, as if the God of the Prophet had
> forsaken His people, as if the Divine election had miscalcu-
> lated.[41]

Muslims have been politically humiliated. It is quite understandable to find a spirit of vindictiveness in acts like hostage
taking, oil embargoes, and inflationary prices for their "black
gold." Muslims long to regain the political supremacy they enjoyed centuries ago. At last, Muslims believe, God is bringing
forth his children from the dark night of oppression and suffering. Inamullah Khan has summarized the mood of many contemporary Muslims: "We the Muslims of the modern world are
also students of history, trying to walk in the footsteps of Ibn
Khaldun. We admit that the ideal of the *umma* which was
shown by the Prophet by precept and example has not yet been
realized on a world scale, but Muslim history is not yet over; it
is continuing its unfoldment."[42]

Current Islam affirms that God is the absolute ruler of all

41. Kenneth Cragg, *The Call of the Minaret* (New York: Oxford University
Press, 1956), p. 205.
42. Inamullah Khan, "Islam in the Contemporary World," in *God and Man
in Contemporary Islamic Thought*, ed. Charles Malik (Beirut: American University of Beirut, 1972), p. 7.

mankind. He is sovereign and nothing can occur outside of his will. The state too is part of the realm of God. The political structure of the people cannot be conceived of as an isolated entity. Integration between religion and state is regarded as an achievable ideal. "To have separate religious and political organizations would be an unimaginable disjuncture in the religious organization of society."[43]

Abul A'la Maududi distinguishes between the theocracy of Islam and the theocracy which he perceives in the Roman Catholic Church. He accuses the Catholic priesthood of being isolated from the rest of society. The leadership reputedly makes laws of its own in the name of God, thus imposing its religious system on the common people. He regards such a hierarchical authoritarian system as satanic.

Maududi states in contrast that the theocracy of Islam is not ruled by any particular religious class but by the complete community of Muslims. The basis for societal government is the Quran and Hadith. He then states, "If I were permitted to coin a new term, I would describe this system of government, as a 'theo-democracy,' that is to say, a divine democratic government because under it the Muslims have been given a limited popular sovereignty under the suzerainty of God."[44]

It is helpful to consider a rather extensive quote from Ayatullah Khomeini. Even though he is an extreme fundamentalist, his sentiments expressed eloquently in this writing addressed in exile to his people who were still living under the Shah are at the very core of the Islamic resurgence. No one can properly understand the Islam of today unless he can enter deeply into the world view of this architect of the Iranian political and religious revolution.

> Present Islam to the people in its true form, so that our youth do not picture the *akhunds* as sitting in some corner in Najaf or Qum, studying the questions of menstruation and parturition instead of concerning themselves with politics, and draw the conclusion that religion must be separate from politics. This slogan of the separation of religion and politics and the demand that Islamic scholars not intervene in social and political

43. Bert DeVries, "Islamic Renewal in the Twentieth Century," *The Reformed Journal*, vol. 30 (July 1980), p. 10.

44. Abul A'la Maududi, *Political Theory of Islam* (Lahore: Islamic Publications, 1960), pp. 22–23.

affairs have been formulated and propagated by the imperialists; it is only the irreligious who repeat them. Were religion and politics separate in the time of the Prophet (peace and blessings be upon him)? Did there exist, on one side, a group of clerics, and opposite it, a group of politicians and leaders? Were religion and politics separate in the time of the caliphs— even if they were not legitimate—or in the time of the Commander of the Faithful (upon whom be peace)? Did two authorities exist? These slogans and claims have been advanced by the imperialists and their political agents in order to prevent religion from ordering the affairs of this world and shaping Muslim society, and at the same time to create a rift between the scholars of Islam, on the one hand, and the masses and those struggling for freedom and independence, on the other. They have thus been able to gain dominance over our people and plunder our resources, for such has always been their ultimate goal.

If we Muslims do nothing, but engage in the canonical prayer, petition God, and invoke His name, the imperialists and the oppressive governments allied with them will leave us alone. If we were to say, "Let us concentrate on calling the *azan* (call to prayer) and saying our prayers. Let them come rob us of everything we own—God will take care of them? There is no power or recourse except in Him, and God willing, we will be rewarded in the hereafter!"—if this were our logic, they would not disturb us. . . .

If you pay no attention to the policies of the imperialists, and consider Islam to be simply the few topics you are always studying and never go beyond them, then the imperialists will leave you alone. Pray as much as you like; it is your oil they are after—why should they worry about your prayers? They are after our minerals, and want to turn our country into a market for their goods. That is the reason the puppet governments they have installed prevent us from industrializing, and instead, establish only assembly plants and industry that is dependent on the outside world. . . .

Now the Prophet (peace and blessing be upon him) was also a political person. This evil propaganda is undertaken by the political agents of imperialism only to make you shun politics, to prevent you from intervening in the affairs of society and struggling against treacherous governments and their anti-national and anti-Islamic policies.[45]

45. Khomeini, *Islam and Revolution*, pp. 38–39.

It is essential to realize these words were not penned by a communist revolutionary who wants to destroy the capitalist system at any cost. Khomeini is a nationalist with a strong monotheistic world view. He is in a process of strong reaction against what he considers to have been a flagrant violation of the rights and sensitivities of the Muslim people. Islam, in response to aggression, does not turn the cheek. It never has and most likely never will. Politics and religion make strong bedfellows. Islam has proved this.

From the early days of Islam the world came to be seen as divided into two portions. *Dar-ul-Harb*, the territory of war, is the designation given to the lands of the infidels. *Dar-ul-Islam*, the territory of Islam, is where the people of the *ummah* dwell. Between the two is an active state of antagonism and belligerency. *Jihad* (striving; Islamic holy war) is regarded by many Muslims as an Islamic prerogative to use political and religious persuasion to bring nonbelievers into the *Dar-ul-Islam*. Historically, *jihad* has been invoked numerous times as the incentive for a holy war against infidels.

A few years ago, I met with a high government official of one Muslim country. I asked this dedicated Muslim what he considered the greatest obstacles to Muslim *ummah* were. Without hesitation, he identified "sects and political fragmentation" as the two outstanding problem areas. I then pushed him to comment on the Iranian revolution. He thoughtfully answered, "I do not approve of all of Khomeini's methods, but events in Iran have put the Islamic cause before the nations of the world . . . and that is good."

The crosscurrents of unity and disunity continue to buffet the Islamic world. Cragg has commented on the future of Islam:

> Certainly no concrete scheme of Muslim world-federalism is on the horizon. Whatever may be true ideally, centripetal forces are very potent in actuality. Even within the more homogeneous Arab world the forces of unity are compromised by personal and dynastic rivalries and suspicions, which the common hostility to Israel has some part at least in abating.[46]

46. Cragg, *The Call of the Minaret*, p. 191.

The Caliphate

Muhammad had served his community as minister, judge, and ruler. He had retained all power for himself. Upon his death believers elected the respected Abu Bakr as successor (caliph). Thus began the Islamic institution of the caliphate which lasted, in various forms, until 1924 when Mustafa Kemal of Turkey abolished it. The caliph was not only the ruler but also the commander of the faithful and the guide of the community. Beginning with the first Umayyad caliph Muawiyah (661–681), the caliphate became hereditary and remained that way until the end of the Abbasid caliphate in 1258.

The caliphate in its prime was a powerful instrument for promotion of Islamic solidarity. The caliph enforced legal decisions, safeguarded religious ordinances, maintained armies, enforced order, received and distributed the alms of the faithful, and generally attended to the welfare of Muslim people.

The Abbasid caliphs, successors to the Umayyads, under the influence of Persian advisors, began to emulate the worldly ways of the Persians. They were lavish in their way of life, incorporating much of the pomp and splendor that is familiar to the reader of the *Arabian Nights*. The caliph was no longer the religious leader who led by a personal example of godliness. He was rather a sovereign with considerable powers at his disposal.

By the ninth century a bureaucracy had effectively muted the powers of the caliph. Soon he was no more than a ceremonial figure, isolated and withdrawn from his followers. Only loose ties were maintained between the caliph and the growing community of Muslims.[47]

The boundaries of the caliphate are defined by Mahmud Shaltout:

> The caliphate or Imamate in Islam is not based on a heavenly sanction which gives the caliph power from God to rule the nation; he has no divine authority which makes it the duty of the people to obey him at any cost. The Caliph or Imam is only a member of the society whose actions are determined by divine laws and orders. The Caliph and the nation form an inseparable whole linked together by the strong tie of religious faith,

47. Farah, *Islam*, pp. 154–57.

worship of God, fair dealing, and interest in the public welfare. The Prophet (may God bless him), says, "The Muslims are equal before God." The first Caliph in Islam said, "Obey me so long as I obey God and the Prophet in dealing with you. Once I cease obeying them you are no longer obliged to obey me."[48]

In the early part of the sixteenth century, the sultans of Turkey laid claim to the office of the caliphate. For a period of time the caliphate was a powerful force because of the political and military influence of Turkey. But in 1924 an incident occurred which convulsed the entire Muslim world. Mustafa Kemal was dedicated to the cause of secularizing Turkey and bringing the country into a close relationship with the rest of Europe. By abolishing the caliphate, Kemal seriously undermined the prevailing sense of *ummah* among Muslims worldwide.

The loss of the Caliphate in 1924 threw a greater onus on community and at the time engendered a real, if indefinable, feeling of loss. The institution had endured, after all, from the immediate hours of the Prophet's death and through all, its fortunes had been taken as a *sine qua non* of Islamic life and order. When the Turks terminated, first the Imamate, and then the Caliphate, bewilderment, indeed a sense of outrage, took hold of Muslims everywhere. The religious efficacy of the duties and ritual of Islam were understood to depend upon the existence of the Caliphate, who was head of the faithful. The Khilafatist movement, until its sad disillusionments at the hands of Arab nationalism and Turkish secularity, was a passionate and intelligent expression of deep Islamic convictions.[49]

Kemal not only abolished the caliphate but also banned the call to prayer in Arabic. The Latin script was introduced in place of the Arabic, wearing of the fez was forbidden, and the word *Islam* was removed from the constitution of Turkey. Many mosques were forcibly closed.[50]

Gradually, Muslims came to accept the absence of the caliphate. The drive for unity became more of a dialogue between

48. Mahmud Shaltout, "Islamic Beliefs and Code of Laws," in *Islam: The Straight Path*, ed. Kenneth W. Morgan (New York: Ronald Press, 1958), p. 125.

49. Cragg, *Islamic Surveys 3*, pp. 68–69.

50. Kurshid Ahmad, *Fanaticism, Intolerance, and Islam* (Lahore: Islamic Publications, 1957), p. 9.

nations. A central symbol of *ummah* no longer existed. "The demand for the Caliphate, in the political sense, has greatly less-
ened in modern times. Pan-Islamism in our day is not a
movement for one super-government over all Muslims, but for
cooperation between Islamic nations."[51]

All is not well on the Islamic front. If Muslims are not politically united neither are they religiously integrated. The two are
totally interrelated. The Palestinian political conflict has de-
stabilized the entire Middle East. Countries like Lebanon,
Egypt, and Jordan have not known how to handle the Palestin-
ians. Lebanon today is but a broken, bleeding testimony to the
conflicts of all parties, Christian and Muslim alike, in the Middle East. Antagonisms of various types continue in such countries as Chad, Sudan, Somalia, Uganda, Afghanistan, Pakistan,
Bangladesh, and Indonesia.

While visiting the Moros in the southern Philippine island of
Mindanao I saw many evidences of Libyan involvement, militarily, politically, and religiously, in the unrest between Muslim
and Christian Filipinos. In the most remote areas of the island
there were signs in front of mosques that read, "A gift of the
Libyan Government." When the American principal of a school
was kidnaped by Muslim terrorists, the Libyan ambassador
was flown down from Manila to negotiate for his life. My wife
and I were conducted on a tour of a Muslim village in the interior of the island by Muslims carrying automatic weapons.
There is an atmosphere of fear and uncertainty in the area.

Libya is an enigma to much of the Muslim world. On one
hand Muammar Gaddafi portrays himself as the most pious of
all Muslims. He not only proclaims Islam in word but also personally seeks to obey all its laws and rituals. On the other hand,
he is a documented exporter of violence and terrorism. Most
Muslim rulers fear Libya's brand of fanatical Islam.

Malaysia is an increasingly troubled land.

> Haji Hadi Awang, 35, a charismatic *imam* uses his mosque as a
> pulpit for preaching Islamic fundamentalism. Hadi wants to
> make Malaysia into a theocratic state governed only by the Ko-
> ran. "This is not an Islamic country," Hadi proclaimed in one

---

51. Mohammad Rasjidi, "Unity and Diversity in Islam," in *Islam: The
Straight Path*, ed. Kenneth W. Morgan (New York: Ronald Press, 1958), p. 426.

sermon recently. "The authorities say they uphold Islam, but their Islam was learned from colonial masters. We have no Islamic constitution, no Islamic law. If the government refuses to abandon the constitution and set up an Islamic state with Islamic laws, it is our duty as good Muslims to topple the government."[52]

Dato Abdullah Ahmad Badawi, an Islamic scholar who advises Malaysian Prime Minister Dato Seri Mahathir Mohamad on religious affairs, expressed his fears thusly: "Bringing politics into the mosque already has divided many *kampongs*, and ultimately will destroy Malay unity. If partisan politics tears apart the largest and most active component of our population, how can the country remain stable?"[53]

Ayatullah Khomeini was asked if his movement were religious or political. He replied, "In Islam politics and religion are not two different things. Our Islamic Revolutionary Movement is gaining momentum day by day. It is working on both these fronts simultaneously."[54] Khomeini, like Gaddafi, is a feared Muslim ruler. His radical suppression of dissent has caused most of his antagonists to go underground. One such man is Ayatullah Jalal Ganjei, now in exile in Paris. Ganjei sees Khomeini as a "power-hungry reactionary and an archopportunist."[55]

Khomeini sincerely believes he is only following closely the dictates of the Quran. However, his ongoing battle with Iraq is a serious blow to the *ummah* of Islam. Most Muslims are deeply embarrassed by this cleavage which has brothers killing brothers while screaming at the top of their lungs, "God is great, God is great!" Both sides are convinced that Allah is on their side.

It is indeed sad to observe the politically fractured world of Islam. Yet, it is important to note that this reality has not been a serious deterrent to the Muslim resurgence which is rippling out through the Islamic world. Perhaps what is lacking in quality is being overwhelmed by the sheer force of quantity. Even

52. Mayo Mohs, "Muslims Against Muslims," *Time*, 6 September 1982, p. 14.

53. Ibid.

54. Mohiuddin Ayyubi, ed., *Khumeini Speaks Revolution*, trans. N. M. Shaikh (Karachi: International Islamic Publishers, 1981), p. 44.

55. "Battle of Two Islams," *Time*, 7 March 1983, p. 58.

within dissonance, there are to be found overarching ideals and commitments.

Western Influence

The reality of human existence leaves little scope for isolationism. Societies are interrelated and interdependent. It is no longer possible for a country to avoid world concerns. One startling example of this truth came home to me as I listened to the esteemed cosmologist, Carl Sagan, lecture to an overflow crowd at a Kennedy School of Government forum at Harvard University. Sagan spoke gravely on the subject of nuclear holocaust. One billion people would be killed in the first hours. Another billion would die within a few weeks. Clouds of dust would envelop the planet, causing a continuous winter of subfreezing temperatures. Daylight would become months of dim twilight. Crops would be wiped out. Psychological damage to the survivors would be incalculable. Sagan forcefully pushed home his point that the consequences of such madness are global. There would be no winners. Because of interdependence, all countries would be affected.

Muslims have also accused the West of exporting degraded values to their cultures. In this section I will examine their claims. How tragic that, important as these issues are, they pale into insignificance when we rationally contemplate the potential influence the superpowers have over every country in the world at the moment the silos open and hell visits planet Earth!

Over the past century great changes have taken place in the world. Western countries in particular have leaped forward at a breathtaking pace. It has been interesting to note the role of Christianity in the midst of this technological boom. In Europe, Christianity has been edged out by the secularizing influence of materialism. Americans have generally accommodated Christianity as one of the components of culture. Massage parlors operate around the corner from the church. Nuclear scientists, if they are of the minority breed, attend a neighborhood Bible study. Presidents affirm the born-again Christian experience while threatening to wipe Russia off the map. Such are the contradictions between the sacred and secular that pluralistic Americans have learned to live with.

Muslims, with their emphasis on an integrated world view, simply cannot comprehend such segmentation. Allah, to them, is sovereign and Lord over all. Submission to God is a state of being that creates harmony in every area of life. Thus the stage is set for a cataclysmic rift between the Muslim world and the West. "The Arab measures the vital essence of culture quite differently from the Westerner. A high standard of living and technological progress are vital to success in the West. The Arab claims superior cultural attainment by emphasizing social forms, attitudes, and religious beliefs. He reacts strongly to any suggestion of western cultural supremacy."[56]

Muslims work from an agenda distinct from that of Westerners. What is important to many Muslims are the hours upon hours of talking with one another about every conceivable subject under the sun. Spatial relationships are also meaningful. The closer one can be to a friend the better one feels. Ali, my Muslim friend, expressed his deep sense of warmth for me by holding my hand, sometimes for an hour at a time. This normal type of affectionate expression does not carry with it any sexual connotation. In light of such an emphasis on personal intimacy, how cold and barren the impersonal industrial milieu appears.

Erich W. Bethmann has written that "in some cases the Muslims arrived at the air age before going through the bicycle age."[57] In other words, the Islamic nations did not go through the process of internal technological development. If they had, change would have been on their own terms. The crisis of adaptation would have been muted. Instead, the West imposed on Muslims that which was helpful and meaningful to itself. This was during the colonial period of history when up to 90 percent of Muslim people were subjected to the humiliation of domination by Western nations, most of which were made up of predominantly Christian populations.

The great Muslim Mughal Empire which had ruled India was utterly defeated by the British. What is now Pakistan, India, and Bangladesh became part of the far outreaches of the British Empire. Indonesia, the world's most populous Muslim

56. Tim Matheny, *Reaching the Arabs: A Felt Need Approach* (Pasadena, Calif.: William Carey Library, 1981), p. 75.
57. Erich W. Bethmann, *Steps Toward Understanding Islam*, Kohinur series, no. 4 (Washington, D.C.: American Friends of the Middle East, 1966), p. 49.

country, was under Dutch domination. Malaysia, Egypt, and the Sudan were ruled by foreigners. North Africa and West Africa were subdued by the French. Persia was divided into British and Russian spheres of influence. All of the northern tier of Islamic peoples came under Russian domination.

Only inaccessible and inhospitable parts of the Muslim world, like Afghanistan, the Arabian Peninsula, and Yemen held out. The ultimate psychological low point was reached when the Ottoman Empire disintegrated and was occupied by Westerners. Turks, in their bid to become part of a secularized Europe, abolished the caliphate and thus destroyed the one remaining outward symbol of transnational Islamic *ummah*.[58]

Such an occupation set the stage for a massive cultural and religious confrontation.

> When the armies of Europe came to Egypt, they brought with them their laws, schools, languages, and sciences; but also their "wine, women and sin." The introduction of the traditions and values of the West has corrupted society, bred immorality and destroyed the inherited and traditional values of Muslim society. Social and family life is corrupted by the "cheap" cinema, stage, radio, and music. The moral and sex problems of youth are related to the "naked" women in the streets, the "dirty" films, the "suggestive" popular music, the "uncontrolled" press and its lewd pictures and the permissibility of wine.
>
> Indiscriminate mixing of the sexes has led to debauchery. Women have lost their Muslim virtues by their immodest participation in the partying and dancing which marks so many of the official and unofficial functions. Why? Because "European women do it and we want to be like Europe in all respects!" As a consequence, the nation is torn in its personal and home life between an Islamic and Western pattern; some have remained Muslim while others have "outwesternized the Westerners."[59]

Many devout Muslims have been deeply grieved by the incorporation of Western cultural values into their societal norms. Things permitted now would have caused public outrage a few

---

58. Ibid., p. 48.
59. Richard Mitchell, *The Society of the Muslim Brothers* (London: Oxford University Press, 1969), p. 223.

years previously. The media have been particularly influential in this ongoing process of cultural imperialism.

I have personally observed this process in one Muslim country. Billboards portray women in a state of seminudity to advertise everything from watches to cinemas. Western novels of the most degraded type are available in the marketplace. Covert wine drinking (legally prohibited) is on the rise. I have been offered pornography for a cheap price by a street vender in the capital city. Western prostitutes visit the large hotels to solicit Muslim businessmen. Programs like "Solid Gold," "Dallas," and "Charlie's Angels" are shown on national television . . . making a greater impact now than ever before, since the government has put a television set in the public halls of most towns and large villages.

My task as a conveyer of "good news" has been seriously hampered by my white skin and American passport. People often ask, "If your country is Christian, why does it allow such cultural filth to circulate freely? And why do you export it to our country so it can do its destructive work of degrading our impressionable young people?"

David Brown comments, "Thus the Muslim judges the western missionary in terms of the image of European and American culture which has been presented to him . . . by the 'glamour' of the cinema and the propaganda of the press."[60] It is not easy to be both an American and a missionary in a Muslim country!

Education

Colonialization of Islamic countries by the West brought a unique opportunity for imposing alien educational systems on Muslims. Many Westerners regarded this as a chance to uplift the degraded and ignorant. Muslims had other thoughts about the process.

The Muslim world is passing today through a crisis unprecedented in its history. This crisis has been created by the impact of Western civilization on the world of Islam. It began when, after enslaving the Muslim world politically, the Western impe-

---

60. David Brown, *The Way of the Prophet* (London: Highway, 1962), pp. 95–96.

rialist powers planned their subtle strategy of crushing the
spirit of cultural self-determination among the Muslims, on
the one hand, and of introducing a system of education which
aimed at enslaving the Muslim mind, on the other.[61]

The colonialist depicted his efforts as liberating and the
Muslim interpreted them as "enslaving." East-West relationships have repeatedly been shipwrecked on the shoals of misconceptions. The Muslim has perceived Westerners in several
ways: proud and arrogant; dominant and demanding; wealthy
and wasteful; secular and materialistic; degenerate and sick.
Westerners have perceived Muslims as backward and awk-
ward; fatalistic and fanatical; lazy and unmotivated; greedy
and ungrateful; corrupt and uncouth. No wonder there is so
much mistrust and alienation.

For many years, as an observer of the American foreign service, I have felt deeply the inadequate cultural and religious
sensitivity on the part of our career diplomats. They should be
immersed in language study and sociocultural orientation before they represent a superpower in countries where people are
easily offended.

In Egypt one area of Western influence has caused rather serious dissonance in society. Western educational methods have
been juxtaposed with the traditional religious system of Muslims.

> It is important for us to appreciate the width of this rift be-
> tween religious and secular education in Egypt and its far-
> reaching consequences. Not only has it ranged school against
> school and university against university; but it has contributed
> more than any other single factor to the division in Muslim so-
> ciety, which is to be seen especially in the larger towns, ranging
> orthodox against "Westernizer" in almost every department of
> social and intellectual activity, in manner of dress, living, so-
> cial habits, entertainment, literature and even speech.[62]

The two streams of education in the Muslim world are
clearly defined. One is modern, scientific, state-controlled, and

61. F. R. Ansari, *Islam and Western Civilization* (Karachi: World Federation of Islamic Missions, 1975), p. 1.
62. H. A. R. Gibb, *Modern Trends in Islam* (New York: Octagon, 1972),
p. 42.

professional. It has standards of critical scholarship, has no reservations of doctrine, is open to evidence, and is committed to scientific verification of hypotheses. Important disciplines include history, social studies, politics, and the natural sciences. It is internally regarded as progressive, empirical, and dynamic.

The alternative, and in many ways contradictory, stream is the mosque-centered, more traditional, and at all times dogmatic system of Islamic education. It is concerned with recitative ability, Quranic knowledge and exposition, and the review of Muslim scholars who have been the interpreters of Islamic law. Its perspective is historical. It is authoritarian, deductive, and often on the defensive.[63] There is also an economic issue at stake. The *imams* and teachers of Islam are dependent for their welfare on financial benefits derived from the exposition of Quran and Hadith. Their objections to Western styles of education are therefore somewhat influenced by pragmatic concerns.

Quite apart from all of the rhetoric, I would be prone to agree with H. A. R. Gibb, who observes that "the influence of secular education has done little to disturb at least outward acceptance of the basic theological doctrines of Islam."[64] But what counts most is how Muslims themselves view the threat of Western education.

Secularism

G. E. Von Grunebaum has described the ethos of "modernity" that so disturbs the Muslim: "The basic factor in modern Western mentality is the stress on science as the path to truth and consequently as the most powerful nonreligious means of amelioration of man and community. This mentality implies the belief in the power of man to evolve by his own volition and to transcend his (apparently) natural measure and his current phase. It is essentially the Greek heritage. And it is lacking in the East."[65]

Fazlur Rahman has written about one Muslim mindset re-

63. Kenneth Cragg, *Sandals at the Mosque: Christian Presence amid Islam* (New York: Oxford University Press, 1959), p. 50.

64. Gibb, *Modern Trends in Islam*, p. 49.

65. G. E. Von Grunebaum, *Modern Islam: The Search for Cultural Identity* (New York: Vintage, 1962), pp. 273–74.

garding the West, namely, the idea that the West is technologi-
cally superior to the East. Its concomitant idea is that the
Muslims are advanced in the spiritual arena. Therefore all Muslims have to do is adopt that which is helpful and reject the undesirable. Rahman states that this theory has been most
inadequate and has led to a de-emphasis on spiritual values and
a shift toward a "New Society" which is quite materialistic and
secular with only a surface veneer of Islam retained for purposes of popularization.[66]

Inamullah Khan forcefully states his concerns about the effects of secularism and materialism on Western religious values:

> The Holy Prophet foretold about the rise of the demon of Mate-
> rialism which will be the greatest danger ever faced by human-
> ity. Pure materialism is a threat not only to Islam but to all
> religious groups, big or small. This demon was born in the
> West. First came Humanism, the child of the Renaissance,
> which substituted belief in God by belief in Man. Then there
> was development in technology and industry which made man
> more dependent on material objects. Science and Religion then
> came to be considered in Europe as incompatible with one an-
> other. . . . Even Benjamin Franklin had to say "The way to see by
> Faith is to shut the Eye of Reason." Thus grew materialism till it
> gave birth to the materialistic conception of history pro-
> pounded by Karl Marx and Engels. Human life to them was
> nothing but the interplay of economic forces and Religion was
> pronounced to be the opium of the people. . . . Under the rising
> forces of Materialism, there were hardly any spiritual values
> left. Life became a mere quest for possession, position and
> power. Religion ceased to be a force in matters of the world and
> this quest for economic control and power brought about the
> clashes between powers culminating in two wars.[67]

This is a splendid and thoughtful analysis of where the materialistic orientation to life takes man. It fits Europe almost
completely. America seems to be on the same path, although as
yet religion remains a fairly strong force. But without doubt,
life has become a mere quest for possession, position, and
power for millions of Americans. Muslim religious leaders see

66. Rahman, *Islam*, pp. 252–53.
67. Khan, "Islam in the Contemporary World," p. 14.

the danger signals and desire above all to deal with the cancer of secularism before it affects the vital organs of the *ummah* of Islam.

Many of us see real beauty in Islamic culture. We have been humbled by the hospitality of the host, charmed by the dignity and grace of the Indian Muslim lady in a sari, and warmed by the embrace of an affectionate, God-questing Son of Ishmael.

> Finally we would desire that the young Muslim should not succeed in Americanising himself too completely, and that he should not lose all the charming qualities of the ancients: a kind of smiling resignation which was not without greatness; an attention to outward bearing that achieved dignity; a profound sense of the solidarity which brought forth goodness and the charity that conceals itself; the taste for the happy life, with a tender feeling for colour, nature, and the harmony of things.[68]

An Irreducible Definition of Community

Who is a Muslim? At what point is a professing Muslim declared unfaithful and expelled from the *ummah*? Where are the boundaries of the community? What about the Sufis with all their sects and subsects? Do the Ahmadiyyas deserve to be branded heretics and declared non-Muslims? These are questions which perplex the insider and frustrate the external observer.

Two Western scholars have sought to define the term *Muslim* in these specific terms: "In the strictest sense, a Muslim is one who can repeat the *Shahada* or confession of faith that is associated with Islam: "There is no god but God, and Muhammad is his prophet." A Muslim, then, is a monotheist who follows the teachings of Muhammad and who belongs to the community or *ummah* that he founded."[69]

This raises a legitimate question. What does it mean to follow the teachings of Muhammad? How broad are the perimeters? What is the *ummah*? Whose *ummah*? Is the Baul Sufi sect in Bangladesh a part of the Islamic community? As they sit in a circle and prepare to smoke marijuana, they cry out, *Bismilla-*

---

68. Gaudefroy-Demombynes, *Muslim Institutions*, pp. 215–16.
69. C. George Fry and James R. King, *Islam: A Survey of the Muslim Faith* (Grand Rapids: Baker, 1980), p. 18.

har Rahmanar Rahim (in the name of God, the merciful and
beneficient!). They affirm membership in the *ummah*. Fellow
Sunni Muslims accept them. But no legalist from Saudi Arabia
would consider them to be legitimate Muslims. Still, "the normal pattern in Muslim countries is to consider all born in the
land to be Muslim (except those who can readily be identified
as belonging to another faith)."[70] This is true because of the lack
of a formal ritual of initiation within Islam. There is no "born-
again" experience or baptism. Circumcision is the nearest
thing to a rite of acceptance into the *ummah*. There is, however,
no mention in the Quran of circumcision as an obligatory rite.
Also, with a few regional exceptions, it is not a rite followed by
Muslim women.

Cragg has summed up the confusion one encounters upon
seeking to define the word *Muslim:*

> There was once a recognisable boundary, even if only geo-
> graphical, by which the Islamic could be known for certain and
> the hostile identified unerringly. True, there arose very early a
> controversy about faith and works and whether conformity
> alone sufficed to designate the true Muslim and how that con-
> formity could be indisputably known. It is also true that here
> and there the Quran suggests a distinction between believing
> and belonging. But, these apart, the Quranic instinct is to see
> the discrimination plain between the faithful and the faithless,
> the *muminun* and the *kafirun*, the loyal and the hypocrites. It is
> just this quality of simplicity about the Quran's knowledge of
> the good and of the evil, the sheep and the goats, which is so
> great an item in its assurance and its guidance.

> Yet how is it ascertainable now—and how enforceable? Have
> we not here the deepest problem of the Islamic soul, in and be-
> yond all the questions of *sharia* and *fiqh*, *din* and *iman*, with
> which its modern analysts have to deal? Or who shall now say
> with the old clarity and ruthlessness where and when there is
> apostasy—that *irtidad* for which the faithless soul was cut off
> from the community? "Tis all confusion, all coherence gone,"
> one might almost say with Donne, echoing different bewilder-
> ments.[71]

70. Ibid., p. 20.
71. Cragg, *Islamic Surveys 3*, pp. 180–81.

A Muslim scholar postulates this rather broad view: "The Quran proclaims that whatever one's race or community or affiliation, he who offers sincere devotion to God and practices righteousness in accordance with that belief, he has attained salvation and no fear shall come upon him. Such is the noble view of universal humanity which the Quran advances."[72] Here the necessity of faith and works is clearly defined. But note the absence of the Prophet's role in the salvific process. I have found many Muslims who would agree with Azad's thinking. They are the universalists who emphasize the general rather than the specific. Yet, they are the minority.

In 1983, while I was teaching a course on Islam at Wheaton Graduate School in Wheaton, Illinois, I invited a Muslim scholar to come and lecture for an hour to my class. The gentleman is vice president of the newly formed American Islamic College, an institution which I cannot help but feel has been modeled after, or at least influenced by, Wheaton College. It is an Islamic liberal-arts college, the first of its kind in North America. In reading the catalog, I found the first "doctrinal statement" I have ever encountered (although I understand there are others) in my study of Islam. Perhaps this will assist us in determining the meaning of "Muslim."

1. We believe in the oneness of God (Allah), oneness of mankind, oneness of monotheistic faiths, oneness of the prophets, oneness of their divine revealed messages, oneness of life and the Hereafter, and oneness of sciences.
2. We believe that every human being has to exert efforts to attain eternal salvation.
3. We believe that God's creation is meaningful and that life has a sublime purpose beyond the physical needs and material activities of man.
4. We believe that God does not hold any person responsible until He has shown him the right way.
5. We believe that faith is not complete when it is followed blindly or accepted unquestioningly unless the believer is reasonably satisfied.

72. Abul Kalam Azad, *Basic Concepts of the Quran* (Hyderabad, India: Academy of Islamic Studies, 1958), p. 92.

6. We believe that in human nature, which God created, there is more good than evil, and the probability of successful reform is greater than the probability of hopeless failure.
7. We believe that the Quran is the Word of God revealed to Muhammad through the Angel Gabriel.
8. We believe in a clear distinction between the Quran and the traditions of Muhammad. The latter are the practical interpretations of the Quran.[73]

It would not be practical in this brief study to seek to analyze this Sunni mainline statement of faith. But it does assist us in understanding what these Muslim academicians consider essential in the definition of their faith.

Muslim brotherhood, then, is open to all who are willing to embrace Islam. The convert will be required only to affirm verbally his faith in the two basic tenents of Islam, "There is no God but God and Muhammad is His Apostle." "There is equality only after conversion. Other persons can claim at best only the status of guest or client."[74]

The distinction between orthopraxy and orthodoxy is important. Sects have differed more on questions of practice (orthopraxy) than on substantive issues of theology (orthodoxy). So, if basic theology is Islamically acceptable, then there can be a wide range of behavioral variance within the ranks. "The two propositions (belief in Allah and Muhammad as His Prophet) on which the conceptual structure of Islam is based are so simple that it makes heresy in the sense of turning the heretic outside the fold of Islam almost impossible."[75] Abu Hanifa, founder of the Hanifi school of law, stated that "if a man called himself a Muslim yet did not behave in an orthoprax or devout fashion, so long as there was any reasonable doubt that he had apostacized, he should be left to the judgment of God."[76] It is my belief

73. Ismail Al-Faruqi, "Statement of Faith," in the catalog of the American Islamic College, Chicago, 1983, pp. 2–3.

74. Jacques Jomier, *The Bible and the Koran,* trans. Edward P. Arbez (New York: Desclee, 1964), p. 99.

75. Muhammad Iqbal, *Islam and Ahmadism* (Lucknow: Academy of Islamic Research and Publications, 1974), p. 6.

76. Williams, *Islam,* p. 160.

that these statements define the broad perimeters of who is and who is not a Muslim.

A Quranic verse which, to me, promotes an excessively narrow and even bigoted (an extreme word, I acknowledge) view of the Islamic *ummah* is found in Surah 5:51:

> O ye who believe! Take not the Jews and Christians for friends. They are friends one to another. He among you who taketh them for friends is [one] of them. Lo! Allah guideth not wrong-doing folk.

Fortunately, millions of Muslims have a broader interpretation of Islamic acceptance and graciousness than is found in this verse of their holy scriptures.

Monolithic? Yes and no. Islam stands unyielding in its insistence on submission to Allah and acceptance of Muhammad as the unique and last prophet of God. It appears that all other areas are negotiable, depending in large part on local personalities and current conditions.

Diversity? Decidedly yes! This diversity at times leads to serious rifts within the *ummah* of Islam. But cracks are not severances. The great rock of Islam remains cohesive. One can safely conclude that Islam is going to be around for a very long time.

3

Muslim Community in the Islamic World

A sense of community is engendered by a degree of homogeneity. If there is no cohesion within society, then it is proper to question whether that society is functioning as an *ummah*. But homogeneity and heterogeneity are sociological terms and realities that cannot be rigidly defined. The definitions are always subjective.

An example would be the world of Sufism. The *ummah* of Atroshi Pir Sahib's following in Bangladesh is fairly definitive. This mystical Sufi expression of Islam has drawn several hundred thousand disciples into a circle of belief and ritual that centers around a charismatic spiritual leader. One either believes or does not believe in his spiritual authority. One submits to initiation or does not. Only the devotees make the pilgrimage to the *pir's* massive annual *urs*, which lasts for three days and resembles a camp meeting. Such a community is easily identifiable because of its size and unique features of internal structure.

But the next step outward, in sociological terms, would be to the broader and more inclusive world of Sufism in general. The *ummah* of Sufism would embrace millions of Muslims. Atroshi Pir Sahib is but a microscopic component in this brotherhood of the mystical. In fact, most other Sufis have never heard of him. Chishtis may not have encountered the Sufis of the Suhrawardi order. Qadiris could live in a world apart from Naqshbandis. Yet, all four of these significant groups of Sufis are to be found in the Indian subcontinent. Every subsect within each Sufi order has its own distinctive elements, and most importantly, its own revered leadership. The commonality of worldwide Sufism promotes a sense of brotherhood that defies the barriers of manmade divisions. These mystics are drawn together through their heartfelt quest for God. Prayer, *dhikr*, poetry, and visits to the shrines of departed saints all contribute to the feeling of universal brotherhood.

The outer rim of the Sufi world belongs to institutional Islam. The Quran and Traditions saturate the fibre of Sufi consciousness. Allah is the focal point of worship. Muhammad is often exalted even beyond that which traditional Islam allows. All recitations of *dhikr* are based on the Quran.

Are Sufis Muslims? Of course. Are they a homogeneous group? Yes, in the broadest sense. Do they have internal distinctions? Without question. Thus the dynamics of Islamic homogeneity and heterogeneity are well illustrated by the world of Sufism.

But there is more. The Muslim world is a complex of many contradictory and noncontradictory forces. Each political entity has a set of values and presuppositions that may well be rejected by other equally pious Muslims in a nation with a different political orientation. Ritual observances vary greatly from country to country. Female circumcision is carried on in some villages of Egypt and the Philippines, whereas it would be considered unthinkable in most other Muslim societies. Women are welcome in some mosques and prohibited in others. Pictures of the Prophet are allowed in Iran and disallowed in Pakistan. Wearing a head covering when praying is imperative in Bangladesh, whereas it is optional in the Middle East. A beard is a sign of religious piety in parts of the Muslim world, but is not an issue in other Islamic countries. Some Shiis have practiced temporary marriages, whereas many Sunnis regard such acts as immoral.

This chapter will seek to briefly highlight Islamic community as found in such diverse places as the Middle East, Bangladesh, Indonesia, China, and the Philippines. I will then give a critique of various strengths and weaknesses of the Muslim sense of community. Admittedly, I will bring to this analysis my own baggage of ethnocentrism. The reader must be aware of this and make the necessary allowances.

Islam in the Arab World

Stretching more than 4,000 miles across North Africa and the Middle East, all the way from the Atlantic to the Indian Ocean, a conglomerate of more than a dozen independent nations, protectorates, sheikdoms and other political units is encompassed in a simple phrase: "the Arab world." At first glance, however, that world seems to deny all semblance of unity. Much of it is pure wilderness. One part of this world, the Sudan, is larger than all of western Europe; yet the Sudan has a smaller population than the Netherlands. Saudi Arabia is bigger than Texas and Alaska combined and has fewer people than New York City. Egypt, the Arab state with the largest population, has less arable land for its 40 millions than West Virginia; about 95 percent of Egyptian territory is desert. A true map of the Arab world would show it as an archipelago: a scattering of fertile islands through a void of sand and sea, islands that stretch from Morocco through the Algerian coastal plain and the thin periphery of Libya to the slim island valley of the Nile, then on to the oases of Syria and Arabia and finally, the larger island of Iraq.[1]

This sweep of humanity embraces 220 million people, of whom 92 percent are Muslims. Most Westerners would speculate that this concentration of Arabs constitutes the heartland of the Islamic world, both spiritually and numerically. In actuality, only 25 percent of the world's Muslim population live in this area. The majority are spread throughout Europe, Central Africa, and especially the vast area of Asia.

Who is an Arab? A simplistic response would point toward one who lives in the Middle East or North Africa. Another answer would highlight the importance of speaking the Arabic language. Still another would state that 92 percent of all Arabs can be identified by their being Muslims. An anthropologist would emphasize tribal and societal links between Arabs. A political analyst would identify historical relationships between governments. Another observer may even see linkage through culinary preferences.

But do any or all of these really capture the essence of "Arabism": that unique sense of compelling personal identity? Do

---

1. Desmond Stewart, *The Arab World* (New York: Time-Life Books, 1962), p. 9.

Arabic-speaking Christians of the Middle East comfortably relate to being members of the Arab "race"? Is the Islamic factor
too overwhelming to allow Christians to have a sense of belonging within the Arab fold? Then there is the whole question of
where the Middle Eastern Jew fits in. Added to this is the complicated issue of the Palestinian's identity and his rights.

It is not wise to be dogmatic in regard to the criteria for the
determination of Arab self-understanding. Authenticating
one's identity is indeed a complicated process. Perhaps a brief
historical and linguistic survey will be helpful as we seek to
understand what constitutes the *ummah* of the Arabs.

Muhammad was born into an age of transition from a no-
madic existence to a more orderly urban life. Mecca was a financial and trading center which sent caravans to Syria and
Iraq. However, the city's social organization still reflected a no-
madic lifestyle. The city was ruled by a group of clans, many of
which were interrelated. These bands of kinsmen were collec-
tively responsible for keeping law and order within the community. An individual who belonged to no clan was deprived of
protection. Community was imperative in the rugged life of
sixth-century Arabia.

Unfortunately, these clans often engaged in violent attacks
against each other. The law of the desert could be summarized
in a simple maxim: The strong survive . . . the weak perish.
Raids on enemy caravans were commonplace. The subjugated
were turned into slaves and concubines.

Into this social milieu came an illiterate Arab with a strong
conviction that he was a prophet of God bearing a heavenly
communication. After establishing his military and political
base, Muhammad turned his attention to building a cohesive
sense of community among his followers.

> With the expansion of the new faith and with the manifold po-
> litical ties which Muhammad forged with the various existing
> tribal communities in the desert, in Mecca, and in Medina, the
> concept of the Community of Believers broadened and devel-
> oped into a sort of super-tribe. Communities, nomadic tribes
> and sub-tribes or urban "clans" could all join Muhammad's
> super-tribe. It appears that the conditions of admission were
> not always the same. Muhammad knew how to vary them ac-
> cording to the strength of the community seeking admission,

the circumstances of "joining" (whether by conquest or negotiated treaty) or the religion of the new community.[2]

Admission regulations may have varied in the initial instance, but soon all were being effectively forged into a community that was permeated with religious ideals, morals, rituals, and law. Islam, in those early days, became the all-important and powerful force for societal unification. "The community produced was one in which everyone acknowledged Muhammad as Messenger of God. Old forms had been observed, but the community was essentially founded on this common acknowledgement. Its basis was not kinship and alliance but religion."[3]

After the Prophet's death, there was an intense movement toward the expansion of Islamic *ummah*. It is of interest to note that this propagation effort knew no geographical or linguistic limitation. From the earliest period, Islam sought to forge an *ummah* which transcended normal societal and political boundaries.

Islam was eminently successful in its pursuits.

No other people made as important a contribution to human progress as did the Arabs. . . . For centuries, Arabic was the language of learning, culture and intellectual progress for the whole of the civilized world, with the exception of the Far East. From the IXth to the XIIth century there were more philosophical, medical, historical, religious, astronomical and geographical works written in Arabic than in any other human tongue.[4]

Arabic has always been an important unifying element among Muslim people. It, Muslims believe, is the very language of Allah. Of all of the languages of the world, God chose Arabic through which to convey his spiritual message to mankind. Only the Arabic Quran carries with it the divine imprimatur. Translations into other Muslim languages are not regarded as

2. Arnold Hottinger, *The Arabs* (Berkeley: University of California Press, 1963), p. 30.

3. W. Montgomery Watt, *Islam and the Integration of Society* (Great Britain: Northwestern University Press, 1961), p. 147.

4. Haider Bammate, *Muslim Contribution to Civilization* (Brentwood, Md.: American Trust Publications, 1962), pp. 1–2.

authoritative. Therefore, it is incumbent on Muslims worldwide to learn enough Arabic to be able to read and chant the
Quran. All ritual prayers are to be performed in Arabic. "The
Quran is learnt by heart, with a superb disregard of intelligibil-
ity. The virtue of its words lies in their form and sound rather
than in any sort of correspondence with the facts of every day."[5]

Arnold Hottinger interlinks the Quran, Arabic, and the Muslim community:

> If one wishes to understand it properly one must first of all
> take into account that the language of the Quran is not only
> good Arabic, but, in the opinion of nearly every Arab, it is the
> best Arabic that one could possibly imagine. As a model for
> every Arab writer it has never been equalled (nor, according to
> dogma, can it ever be equalled). There is one whole class of lit-
> erature, the books on Ijaz, which is wholly concerned with
> proving this point. It analyses the prose of the Quran and com-
> pares its beauties with those of the Arab poets and thereby
> reaches the conclusion that the Quran is unsurpassable. . . .
>
> Islam, in theory, recognizes no other community except the Be-
> lievers. All Muslims are the servants of God and their ethnic
> ties are of no importance. But the fact that the Quran was re-
> vealed in Arabic gave, in practice, a force and unity to the Arabs
> in the time of their expansion and, even in times of stagnation
> and decadence, an unshakeable conviction of their particular
> mission.[6]

Arab Life

There are many excellent books written about Arabs, although few internal critical studies have been made by Muslim
Arabs themselves. One then can fault Western academicians
for taking an alien situation and running it through a grid heavily laden with Christian, capitalistic, democratic, and materialistic presuppositions. It must be admitted, however, that any
scholar who undertakes an analysis of the Arab people takes on
a formidable task. Currents of change, contradiction, and confusion confound all but the most tenacious researcher.

Apart from their common language, Arabs express a sense of

5. Jacques Berque, *The Arabs: Their History and Future*, trans. Jean Steward (New York: Praeger, 1964), p. 191.
6. Hottinger, *The Arabs*, pp. 25–26.

unity in a variety of ways. An example cited by Greg Haleblian, a Christian Syrian, is seen in Muslim architecture. As one enters a mosque, he is submerged in an atmosphere of unity. Every element within the four walls is designed to avoid that which is conspicuous and particular. No individual part or pattern is highlighted. Another illustration relates to the uniformity which is found in the structure of houses. Without zoning laws or government control, Egyptian houses are often almost exact replicas of each other.[7] Such an appreciation for unity and continuity contributes considerably to the feel for and the desire to attain *ummah* within Muslim society.

Later in this chapter I will discuss family life within a broader Islamic context. Suffice it to say here that Arabs, particularly in recent years, have been a target of Western feminist wrath. A few liberated Arab women have joined the protest against male chauvinists who denigrate the role of women in society. Yet, without doubt, the family structure in the Middle East provides cohesion to society. Overall, I would confidently assert that Arab homes are as peaceful and contented as are Western ones.

Many Muslim women are confused. In Iran, under the Shah, they were told to discard the veil. Khomeini, on the other hand, has firmly legislated the wearing of very modest clothes. In the 1930s, Egyptian women were commanded to adopt Western dress. Presently, many women are reverting to wearing veils. They feel this brings them into closer harmony with Islamic teachings. This is true of young women as well. Such mixed signals are a deterrent to the building up of the broadest base for the *ummah*. Women are questioning their identity and rightful place in society.

Religiously, Islamic traditionalism is the very warp and woof of community. But there is a strong undercurrent of folk Islam which draws millions into its sphere of influence.

In the Arab world there is a great deal of emphasis on belief in innumerable demons, spirits, jinn, the evil eye, and ritual worship of saints who wield supernatural powers. Magic beliefs and practices are found among villagers in all Arab countries.

7. Phil Parshall, *New Paths in Muslim Evangelism: Evangelical Approaches to Contextualization* (Grand Rapids: Baker, 1980), pp. 65, 67.

Simple practices are known to everybody, but if more effective action is required, the service of magical specialists are available for a fee.[8]

I find such religious anomalies do not overly disturb the *ummah* of the Middle East. These folk practices are more or less absent, at least on a formalized basis, in Saudi Arabia. They are quietly tolerated by the *ulama* in other Arab countries. It will be interesting to see if the present fundamentalist resurgence will have any effect on folk Islam. I doubt that it will. The fundamentalists must deal with fighting the West, along with bitter political infighting among themselves.

Relations among Arabs

The conflict between the desire for pan-Arab *ummah* and the pragmatic need for a self-serving foreign policy has splintered the Middle East into many factions. Unity has never come easily for Arabs, but the present situation looks grim indeed. Desmond Stewart has criticized this tendency:

Except on two issues—colonialism and Israel—the Arabs do not speak with one voice. They have a gift for disunion and a gift for uniting against any leader who tries to unite them. Six centuries ago the great Arab historian Ibn Khaldun quoted the Quran, the scriptures of Islam, when speaking of Mohammed's miracle in uniting the Arabs: "If you had expended all the treasures on earth, you would have achieved no unity among them. But God achieved unity among them."

This divine miracle, however, took place seven centuries before Ibn Khaldun. Today, despite soothing assurances of brotherhood, it is often harder for the ordinary Arab to visit Arab countries than it is for the ordinary European to move about Europe. There is still no customs union. Currency regulations and the need for exit visas from many states are an additional obstacle. Nor are the Arab countries well informed about each other. It is rare for an Arab newspaper to maintain a full-time correspondent in another Arab capital.[9]

8. Tim Matheny, *Reaching the Arabs: A Felt Need Approach* (Pasadena, Calif.: William Carey Library, 1981), p. 25.
9. Stewart, *The Arab World*, p. 11.

If these words reflect an accurate assessment of pan-Arab disunity, then does it naturally follow that *ummah* based on Islam is an unobtainable goal? That depends somewhat on one's definition of Islamic community. If one considers it to be a comprehensive brotherhood which includes political alliances and military pacts, then achieving unity is almost certainly impossible. But if *ummah* is defined as a spiritual bond between individuals, then the Arabs will fare much better. "The tight emotional bond of heterogeneous believers locked together without formal organization in the Muslim *ummah*, has proved to be a more widely effective means of growth and endurance than any political structure whatsoever."[10]

Is it fair to fault Arabs for their internal state of confusion? The colonial powers had partitioned and repartitioned the Arab world under diverse Spanish, French, Italian, and British regimes into some twenty-five political entities. A sense of Arab cohesion was smothered under Western colonial rule. Leon Uris's novel, *The Haj*, although strongly biased toward Jews, gives an interesting historical and sociological insight into the life of the Arabs.

There are those who feel Arab unity is in a process of formulation and that brighter days lie ahead.

> Greater Arab unity is coming, anyway. The trend towards unity in the Arab world is beyond resistibility, whether from within or from without. Hindered and retarded it may be, but not indefinitely arrested.... In the free, unhindered advance towards Arab unity, as in dynamic Arab nationalism in general, lies the only hope for moderate, orderly, and peaceful progress towards the attainment of the human aspirations of the Arab peoples for the exercise of their God-given rights to liberty, solidarity, and a more abundant life.[11]

The world has been shocked to find Arabs suddenly at center stage in the ongoing drama of struggles between the superpowers. Western diplomats will be seriously remiss in their responsibilities if they dismiss Islam as an irrelevant, outmoded

10. G. E. Von Grunebaum, *Modern Islam: The Search for Cultural Identity* (New York: Vintage, 1962), p. 183.
11. Fayez A. Sayegh, *Arab Unity: Hope and Fulfillment* (New York: Devin-Adair, 1958), p. 212.

influence in Arab life. The shadow of the prophet Muhammad today looms large over every decision made in Arab palaces. Despite tensions within the camp, Arabs are full of optimism that the past glories of Islam are about to be restored. Just such a belief brings about a sociological dynamic that fosters a sense of internal community and solidarity.

Islam in Asia

Fifty-five percent of all Muslims in the world live east of Afghanistan. Muslim traders and Sufi missionaries had a major impact on Asia, for their religion imposed minimal demands on new converts. "All one had to do was utter the two words of the confession of faith, 'I bear witness that there is no God but Allah and that Mohammed is the Messenger of Allah,' and one was a convert and a member of the community of Mohammed."[12]

In many areas of Asia, Islam became a rather thin layer of ritualized religion overlaying a deeply imbedded folk religion. Pre-Islamic Asians were, to a large degree, people who lived in a world of fear and superstition. They gave themselves to prayers, sacrifices, and idol worship in the hope of appeasing the evil influences of fate and nature. Islam did not remove these sociological and religious realities. Rather, the early Muslim propagators allowed a natural syncretism between their foreign institutionalized tradition and the more animistic expressions of the Asian people. As we will see, Sufism was the most benign of propagating agents. Sufis were more interested in promoting a heartfelt quest for Allah than in demanding strict adherence to legalistic codes and observances.

Bangladesh, Indonesia, China, and the Philippines have been chosen to demonstrate Islamic influence in Asia. The reader will recall that Bangladesh and Pakistan were one country (East and West Pakistan) until the civil war of 1971. The three countries of India, Pakistan, and Bangladesh were all India prior to 1947.

Bangladesh

The name *Bangladesh* means "the country of Bengalis." Bengal is the geographical area and Bengalis are the people of

12. Kenneth Perry Landon, *Southeast Asia: Crossroad of Religions* (Chicago: University of Chicago Press, 1949), p. 135.

Bengal. Their language is Bengali, a vernacular which is spoken by all of the ninety million people of the country. Muslims comprise 85 percent of the population, Hindus 14 percent, and Christians plus other small religious groups the other 1 percent.

Sunnis are in the majority but there are small representations of Shiis and Ahmadiyyas. Sufi influence permeates the total Muslim community. Islam in Bangladesh is an interesting amalgam of the orthodox and the unorthodox. This is a direct result of Sufism.

In the thirteenth century, Muslim armies of Central Asian ancestry occupied Bangladesh. For more than five hundred years the land of Bengal remained under Muslim rule. Dom Moraes comments on the process of Bengali conversion to Islam:

The caste system introduced by the Aryans was by this time 3,000 years old, and the centuries had fossilized it. The untouchables and those of low caste, trapped on this unwieldy treadmill, now thought Islam, preaching the equality and brotherhood of its adherents, the only means of escape from an eternally inferior status in society. Mass conversions took place. These were often group conversions, where an entire village or professional community turned Muslim. Thus certain professions became largely the province of Muslims: weavers, tailors, and butchers, for example, all followed Islam. . . . The highly born Hindus, however, were in the main remarkably unaffected by the influence of Islam. As the historican R. C. Mazumdar wrote dolefully, "In particular it is strange that the wonderful social democracy of the Muslims, far from removing the barriers artificially planted between man and man, rather made them stronger and stronger": at least as far as the caste Hindus were concerned.[13]

Several interesting facts are documented in this historical note. One of the great attractions of Islam was a sociological release. Tailors and butchers were among those who converted in order to gain new status in society. It is important to note that today in Muslim Bangladesh, tailors and butchers are con-

13. Dom Moraes, *The Tempest Within: An Account of East Pakistan* (New York: Barnes and Noble, 1971), p. 3.

sidered socially inferior. One then can question the long-range sociological benefits of these people's becoming Muslims.

Conversion often took place communally. Family and friends accepted Islam in large groups. In this act they created community and thus minimized social opposition from other Hindus. Individual conversion from any tightly knit religious system invariably will lead to severe reaction from family and close friends and possibly from religious leaders as well.

The early influence of Sufis in Bengal was documented in a letter written by Mir Sayyid Ashraf Jahangir Simnani: "God be praised! what a good land is that of Bengal where numerous saints and ascetics came from many directions and made it their habitation. . . . In short, in the country of Bengal, there is no town and no village where holy saints did not come and settle down."[14]

It has been estimated that, at minimum, 75 percent of all Muslims in Bangladesh are deeply influenced by Sufism. One cannot travel more than a few miles in the countryside without observing the whitewashed tomb of some departed Sufi saint.

The sense of *ummah* is greatly enhanced throughout the rural areas of Bangladesh by participation in one of the many orders of Sufism. One of the common questions asked in Bengali between strangers is, "Bhai, apni kon tarikay achen?" which translates, "Brother, what order or path [of Sufism] do you belong to?" This is akin to a Mason observing the brotherhood ring being worn by a total stranger. There is an immediate acceptance and sense of camaraderie forged between fellow believers.

The annual meetings held in honor of a living or departed spiritual guide are numerous in Bangladesh. These gatherings build communal feeling. Devout pilgrims journey from long distances in order to participate in a sociological and religious experience that will sustain them in the hardships to be endured in the next year. This process is similar to Christians going annually to a Bible camp to hear their favorite expounder of God's truth. God, a man of God, fellow believers, and spiritual and physical refreshment are all foci in both activities.

Political allegiances also serve as a rallying point for people

14. Abdul Karim, *Social History of Muslims in Bengal* (Dacca: The Asiatic Society of Pakistan, 1959), p. 85.

of like mind. The desire for a particularistic expression of Muslim *ummah* was foundational in the establishment of Pakistan in 1947.

> It was this sense of the religious importance of the community along with the social and political importance of religion, that was the basis for the "two nation theory" and the founding of Pakistan. The source of mass support for the Pakistan movement lay less in a commitment to the abstract doctrine of the unity of church and state than in the strong emphasis placed on the social practice of Islam and on the solidarity of the community.[15]

Mohammed Ali Jinnah, the founding father of Pakistan, was not a Muslim in any traditional sense of the word. He was only nominal in following the religious dictates of Islam. But Jinnah was a master strategist who knew how to use Islam for political purposes. His plea was for Muslims to have a homeland of their own, a country where there would be a full realization of their desire for community. The consequence of this political division of the Indian subcontinent is written in the blood of literally millions of Muslims and Hindus slain in the 1947 partition and in the 1971 civil war. Community based on politics is at best an unstable expression of the religious *ummah*. In 1972, the Bengali people regarded Sheik Mujibur Rahman, the great statesman of Bangladesh, as almost a god incarnate. When he was assassinated by his own appointed military officers in 1975, there was a lack of grief or regret. Such are the fickle winds of political expediency.

Bangladesh has sought to relate to the worldwide *ummah* of Islam. The Palestine Liberation Organization has a large headquarters in the capital city. Arab diplomats are treated with great honor. Anti-Israeli rhetoric regularly appears in the media. Leaders of the country often reiterate the important role Bangladesh has as one of the three largest Muslim nations in the world.

But beneath this surface expression of unity with other Islamic states is a reservation that cannot be publicly stated. The "official line" of solidarity must be maintained. There is, how-

15. Donald N. Wilber, *Pakistan* (New Haven: Hraf, 1964), p. 88.

ever, a festering resentment against wealthy Arab countries
that spend their resources in fighting against each other, rather
than assisting Bangladesh, one of the poorest nations in the
world, in its developmental programs. Reaction to Ayatullah
Khomeini is generally negative. Bengalis regard him as a political and religious fanatic who has brought disrepute upon the
good name of Islam. A similar view is held concerning Muammar Gaddafi.

Stories concerning the worldly behavior of Saudis as they
visit the West have circulated among Bengalis, causing them to
question the rigid moral codes upheld within the borders of
Saudi Arabia. Most Bengalis who have gone to Saudi Arabia for
employment have returned with a host of negative impressions
concerning the people who are the keepers of the sacred homeland of the Prophet.

Then there is the whole issue of what happened in 1971 when
West Pakistan utilized brute military force to seek to keep East
Pakistan from obtaining greater political autonomy. Never will
the scenes of robbing, looting, raping, and killing be erased
from the minds of Bengalis. They were completely overwhelmed that such degradation could flow from the hearts of
fellow Muslims. Many Bengalis lost their faith in Islam, at least
temporarily, following the holocaust of 1971.

These are specific international encounters that have fractured the Islamic *ummah*. Balanced against this, however, is
the mystical quality of community which is perpetually renew-
ing itself internally. The heart of a Muslim still responds
warmly to the realization that he is part of a brotherhood of
people that circles the globe and encompasses one-sixth of the
world's population. What a joy and privilege to be a Muslim, a
follower of the Prophet, an adherent of the truth, and a true
devotee of Allah! This simple statement relegates political realities to the status of secondary concerns. It is my observation
that Muslims generally respond to emotion, experience, and
subjective reality rather than a cold objective statement of
linear argumentation. It is at this crucial point that Eastern
Muslims and Western Christians come into serious conflict.
Muslims can fairly easily minimize unpleasant facts and at the
same time emphasize a reality that causes them joy. A parallel
would be the satisfaction derived when a Christian states that
one billion people are followers of Christ and that Christianity

is the largest religion in the world. That is a factual statement with emotional impact. But any thinking person must go on and sadly refer to the innumerable divisions within Christendom. This truth mutes any sense of unjustified triumphalism. Muslims often do not follow truth to its broader conclusions.

It is seldom that a Muslim dares to break *ummah* and constructively criticize Islam in print. Mazheruddin Siddiqi has done just this in his comments on the need for reform within institutional Islam:

> Left to themselves the mosques will remain centers of fanaticism and obscurantism. The government has been afraid to touch this problem lest it be exposed to the criticism of the people who distrust official activity in this area, but some means must be found to organize the support of the mosques and to give proper education to the Imams who are responsible for their care. The strength and vitality of Islam springs from its social and institutional ideals. Islam started as a social order with a definite social and economic structure, but it has become a highly individualistic religion. At this time, when the people are moved by a strong urge for social equality and economic and political justice, there is a great need for a country-wide agency to look after their religious needs and to guide them to an understanding of the principles of Islam.[16]

The call, therefore, goes out to make official Islam more relevant to the needs of the masses. Recently, in Bangladesh, there have been government-sponsored seminars for Muslim religious leaders which are designed to broaden the *imam's* activities into areas beyond that which is technically religious. As far as I am aware, this program has met with broad acceptance on the part of the public. It would appear that such a movement will serve to strengthen the bonds of Islamic *ummah* at the grassroots level of society.

Bangladesh is considered by many Middle Eastern Muslims to be hopeless. Bengalis are also heavily criticized for allowing Sufi aberrations not only to be practiced, but also even to be endorsed by the country's political leadership. Yet, no one

16. Mazheruddin Siddiqi, "Muslim Culture in Pakistan and India," in *Islam: The Straight Path*, ed. Kenneth W. Morgan (New York: Ronald Press, 1958), pp. 342–43.

would propose excluding Bangladesh from the larger community of Islam. Tensions may exist on both sides, but it can be stated with a fair degree of certainty that Islamic brotherhood, at some level, will prevail.

Indonesia

It is somewhat ironic that the nation with the greatest population of Muslims lies on the extreme eastern end of the Islamic belt. Indonesia, a land of more than 150 million people, has a population of 130 million Muslims. It is a country still in the process of finding its own religious identity. The divergent forces of Communism, Christianity, Islam, and folk religion all vie for the ideological and religious allegiance of the masses. Only folk religion has solid Indonesian roots, and it has been denounced because of its conflict with the government's desire to promote monotheism.

Even though Islam is a foreign import benignly laid upon the Indonesian people, it has triumphed in much the same way it did in Bangladesh.

> From the Malay annals and some Arabic literature it appears that Arab missionaries assumed a leading role in the process of mass conversion, but it would be incorrect to say that there were no other influences. The faith was already established in north India and long before in China, and traces of Indian, Chinese, and even Persian influences can be found. Currents from all these directions appear to have converged about the same time, and to confine the credit to one source is to ignore the mass of evidence in favour of the others. If we speak of the earliest introduction of the faith in the area, however, it is most likely that this was done by the Arabs who appear to have established a colony on the west coast of Sumatra as early as A.D. 674.[17]

Indonesians were attracted to Islam because of its close parallel to their own mystical bent. Bridges to the Indonesian people included Sufi pantheism, veneration of saints, and belief in numbers of mystical importance. Animistic charms were discarded in favor of Islamic magic. Worship before idols was con-

17. Mohammed A. Rauf, *A Brief History of Islam* (Kuala Lumpur: Oxford University Press, 1964), p. 84.

tinued but with the addition of a confession of faith in Allah and Muhammad. The Indonesians made mystical use of numerology such as the first four caliphs, the four Arabic letters that spelled the name of the Prophet, and the twelve *imams* of the Shiis.

By the time mass conversions commenced in the latter part of the fourteenth century, the major Sufi orders had been established and their teaching widely disseminated. Most preachers of Islam in those early days belonged to some Sufi sect. Many of the Muslim missionaries had been commissioned and sent out by the disciples of some well-known saint such as Abd al-Qadir of Baghdad. Such propagators of Sufism were known for their patience, simplicity of life, and miraculous healing powers. These distinctive qualities considerably aided in the process of gaining converts.

Early Muslim teachers advocated cultural and religious syncretism. Islam was eager to adapt to folk religious culture and customs. This process went so far as to produce a Muslim practice described in the Indonesia constituent assembly in 1957: "On holy days our villages are full of the smell of incense and on such occasions our people do not fail to offer specially prepared rice and chicken to our Prophet Mohammed (may God's peace be on him)."[18]

The five pillars of Islam as practiced in Indonesia are, in varying degrees, distinct from the more orthodox beliefs and practices of the Middle East. The first pillar, the confession of faith, was simply a verbal accretion to the animistic beliefs already held by the Indonesians. Many regarded the statement as a new incantation that they hoped would influence the supernatural powers in their behalf.

The second pillar is the ritual performance of prayer five times a day. Many if not most Indonesian Muslims neglect the daily prayers as well as the purification before prayers that is incumbent on all Muslims. Indonesians are a clean people who bathe regularly, but this has nothing to do with religious rites.

Muslims in Indonesia had an unorthodox beginning which permitted them to feel that they were Muslims without paying much attention to the prayers. They had the idea that a man

18. G. H. Jansen, *Militant Islam* (New York: Harper and Row, 1979), p. 39.

could become united with his creator by mental exercises and that the bodily forms of worship were merely preliminary and could be dispensed with when one achieved the higher mystic level. This was an aspect of Indian yoga which had become attached to Islam in transit across India. For those persons who could not scale the mystic heights there were charms and other formulas which worked by magic. So we may conclude that the second pillar has never been sedulously observed among Muslims in Southeast Asia.[19]

The third pillar, fasting during the month of Ramadan, is unevenly observed. Devout Muslims regularly abstain from eating or drinking during the daylight hours of the fast. However, great multitudes ignore the strict regulations altogether or just fast in a token manner. Some abstain only on the first day and are mockingly referred to as "fasting like the *bedug*" (a drum covered on only one side). Others fast on the first and last day and are said to be fasting like a *kendang* (a drum with skins on both sides).[20]

Zakat, the fourth pillar, is the Islamic regulation of giving two and a half percent of one's income to assist the poor. In Indonesia this offering is often limited to rice and is given on festive occasions. "It is believed that what shortcomings were not equalized by the fast might be paid off by the offering of rice and thus God's books will be balanced for the year."[21] Tax which should be paid on other things such as cattle is seldom paid. There is enthusiasm shown just for the rice offering, the reason being its association with festivals.

All sources indicate the fifth pillar of Islam, the Hajj, is very popular with Indonesians. At present up to ten times as many Muslims apply for permission to go on the Hajj as are allowed to go under a tight quota system. The government charters ships and supervises the journey to Saudi Arabia.

Snouck Hurgronje summarized the importance of the Hajj for the Indonesians under three categories. The first is the opportunity to be initiated into the mystic societies represented at Mecca. The Indonesians' appreciation for religious mysticism

19. Landon, *Southeast Asia*, pp. 144–45.
20. P. A. Hoesein Djajadiningrat, "Islam in Indonesia," in *Islam: The Straight Path*, ed. Kenneth W. Morgan (New York: Ronald Press), 1958, p. 386.
21. Landon, *Southeast Asia*, p. 145.

was strengthened by social intercourse with Muslim mystics from other areas of the world. To some, this meant becoming a disciple of a particular saint and then propagating their new-found faith and allegiance upon their return to Indonesia. The second is that they were deeply impressed with the worldwide *ummah* of Islam as exhibited by the diverse group of Muslims who had made the Hajj. Islam became, for the pilgrims, much more than a localized expression of belief in Allah. They had come to experience firsthand the multiethnic dimensions of Islamic brotherhood. The third is that to other Indonesians the Hajj became a vehicle for their conversion to a more traditionalist belief and practice of Islam. They returned to their homes committed reformers, dedicated to purging all extraneous and non-Quranic practices from Islam.[22]

The Indonesian mosque is frequently found to be culturally unique.

> The traditional mosque in Indonesia has as its characteristic style what is known as a broken roof, consisting of two or three layers with an independent, curbed roof line. If there is a minaret it is a tower which stands apart from the mosque. In the new mosques a new architectural style is being introduced, influenced somewhat by the mosques of western Islamic countries. In Indonesian mosques the time for prayer is announced by powerful beating on a great drum made of a thick, hollow tree trunk covered with buffalo skin; then the call to prayer is usually chanted either from the mosque itself or from the roof of the mosque.[23]

It is interesting to note that many of the mosques of olden days look like pagodas with their layers of superimposed roofs. At first the mosques were oriented toward the west, but later the builders obtained better maps and built them with a west-northwest orientation. The director of the mosque is known as the *penghulu*. This is an office that is not common throughout the Muslim world. The *penghulu* is also the religious judge and as such has status with the government.

Among the Muslim Javanese there continues a belief that the

---

22. Snouk Hurgronje, *Mekka*, trans. J. H. Monahan (London: Luzac, 1931), pp. 249ff.

23. Djajadiningrat, "Islam in Indonesia," p. 385.

guardian spirit of the village dwells in a tree. Many Sundanese worship Lady Sri, the personification of the rice kernel, for whom many offerings are made in order to persuade her to ensure a good harvest. Other Indonesians believe in the good or evil power resident in an ancient sword.

Another expression of folk religion that has been accepted under the cloak of Islam has been the ritual feast. These festive occasions form one of the most important religious and social expressions of the Indonesians. Such feasts are common occurrences and are a serious financial burden to the poor. "One of the common arguments to attempt to persuade Indonesians to be converted to Christianity is that they would not need to continue the feasts and could thus save money. But this to an Indonesian is about as pointless as urging a Christian to give up Christianity in order to abolish Christmas."[24]

In family life, the feasts are held to commemorate pregnancies, births, marriages, and death. Often these celebrations are held in stages, resulting in three or four feasts for each commemoration. This is particularly true of the continuing feasts of remembrance held following the death of a loved one.

Festive days include January 31, the Muslim all souls' day. Before this day burial tombs are whitewashed and special worship performed; a feast follows. Muharram is the day set aside for remembering the martyrdom of Hussein. It, too, is an occasion for feasting. One of the great days of festivity is the celebration of the Prophet's birthday. It is equal to any two of the other major festivals of Islam. Pre-Islamic practices abound on this special day.

In Atjeh during the singing of the songs of praise, the singers tie knots in pieces of black thread which are then given to the children to wear around their necks as amulets. In West Java, the tying of knots in threads to be worn as amulets is done during prayer after the recital. There is also a practice in West Java associated with the final prayer which is associated with the passage, "and receive it (that is, our recital) from us . . . in good . . . acceptance." When the word "acceptance" is pronounced the participants take a handful of rice which has been served at the ceremony and this "acceptance rice" is then dried in the

24. Landon, *Southeast Asia*, p. 156.

sun and stored away to be used when a special blessing is
needed, such as when a long journey is to be undertaken. Because of the Prophet's blessing associated with the commemoration ceremonies, people in West Java used to start important
work during the recital, such as making the first knots in a fish-
ing net.[25]

It was natural for Indonesians to venerate Muslim saints.
From the most ancient time, they had honored their ancestors.
The revered men of Islam were simply added to their list.
Veneration of Hindu and Buddhist saints has continued. There
are many graves of early Islamic missionaries dating from the
fifteenth century. These tombs are frequently visited by people
in need who vow to do certain good deeds if their requests are
granted through the intercession of the departed saint. Offerings of incense, rice, and flowers are left at the tomb. The involved person has his head washed white at the gravesite as a
symbol of devotion and purification.

A word needs to be said concerning the immensely popular
wayang (puppet plays based on Hindu traditions) and *gamelan*
(native orchestra). These elements of national life were so popular with the masses that Islam basically left them alone. The
gamelan music is accompanied by the soft beating of drums.
Actors are usually engaged in some type of magical practice.
Islamic mysticism made the necessary adaptation to these local magical emphases.

Muslim Indonesian women are quite liberated when compared to their counterparts throughout the Islamic world. I
noted in a recent visit that most women do not wear the veil and
many work openly in the rice fields. They even dance in the
wayang-wong shows. Such dancing would be considered lewd
in a more traditional Islamic setting. They mingle freely and
easily with men in the business world. On occasion, they can be
the prayer leader for men as well as for women.

Are Indonesians Muslims? Is not Islam but a sanctimonious
verbal creed for a people given to traditional animistic practices?

The shape of their mosques is unorthodox. The position of the
penghulu in the mosque is unique in the Moslem world. They

25. Djajadiningrat, "Islam in Indonesia," p. 393.

depend on the magic of the charm and the mystic dhikr to ward
off evil. Their practice of circumcision is carried out according
to local custom. The position of their women is not Moslem in
character. They exceed all customary Moslem practice in the
veneration of saints. Their practice of feasts has forced Islam
to sanctify offerings to spirits and ancestors.[26]

Yes, Islam has settled for a syncretistic expression of faith
and practice in Indonesia. Yet, like Bangladesh with all of its
aberrations, Indonesia is still very much a part of the worldwide Muslim *ummah*. This process of assimilation prevails
throughout Asian Islam. Orthodoxy struggles against local
superstitions but almost always fails if the people involved regard such things as essential to their happiness. In fact, it must
be recognized that these so-called un-Islamic or pagan ideas
and practices become Islamized by adoption. Such is the case
in this the largest of all Muslim countries.

China

Islam spread to China from the Middle East very early in
Muslim history. For centuries there had been commercial contact between Arabia and China. When Arab merchants became
Muslims they began to propagate their religion in a number of
districts within China. In several histories of Islam, it is mentioned that the prophet Muhammad sent his maternal uncle,
Wahab bin Kabsha, with suitable presents, to the Emperor of
China to request him to accept the religion of Allah. A mosque
in Canton, according to an ancient inscribed monument, was
built by this uncle. His nearby tomb is visited annually by thousands of pilgrims.

The Muslims of China are Sunnis and followers of the Hanifi
school of Islamic law. Early in their history they came to be
known by the distinctive name *Hui-Hui*. The origin of this name
is difficult to ascertain.

The ideograph (doubled) is the common Chinese word for "return," but it is not clear whether *hui-hui* is an attempt to trans-
literate the Arabic Islam, or whether there is a real meaning. It
might allude to the custom of "turning" to Mecca in prayer
(possibly also returning in pilgrimage), or, as some Chinese

26. Landon, *Southeast Asia*, p. 164.

writers, possibly influenced by Taoism, suggest, the return of the body to its true place in death and the return of the mind to the path of truth. Quite another theory derives the name from the Hui-ho or Uigurs, who were powerful in Mongolia during the Tang period.[27]

All writers on Chinese Islam wrestle with the unreliability of population statistics. The *China Handbook* of 1943 estimates the community to number between ten and fifteen million. These figures are inflated to fifty million in the 1950 issue. The *Encyclopedia of Missions* estimates the Muslim population at thirty million. Some Islamic scholars have speculated on a figure as high as seventy million. Perhaps a realistic population estimate would be in the range of twenty to thirty million.

Muslims were converted in every province of China. The largest groups, however, are to be found in the provinces of Kansu, Szechwan, and Yunnan. There are significant groups in the northeastern provinces of Manchuria and Hopei. "Oxen Street" outside the city wall of Peking is a residential area of more than one thousand Muslim families. In Tsinan, Ch'angchow, and Tientsin, Muslims cluster in small communities outside the city gates. In Tungchow, they congregate in the southeastern corner of the city. Throughout China, this pattern of population concentration is clearly seen. Muslims feel most comfortable in clustered communities. The rationale for this is mostly pragmatic. Worship and dietary regulations are easiest to observe within cloistered groupings of like-minded people.

Few Chinese Muslims have become farmers. They also avoided government employment because there would be pressure on them to partake of pork and wine. Many Muslims have opened restaurants where they strictly follow taboos on pork but are found to serve liquor. There are also Muslim butchers, leather workers, and merchants who sell jewelry and curios. In certain localities there are occupations that are exclusively for Muslims—leather work in Ninghsia, bathhouses in Ch'angchow, and sedan transportation in Taishan. In a number of cities Muslims have their own trade guilds.

The majority of Chinese Muslims are descendants of Ara-

27. E. R. Hughes, *Religion in China* (London: Hutchinson's University Library, 1950), p. 104.

bian, Iranian, and Turkish parents. This led to an interesting ad-
mixture of cultures. "During the Ming dynasty Muslims began
to make cloisonne vases, plates and bowls covered with colorful
blues and with delicate Arabian and Persian designs or with the
writings from the Quran and the Prophet's Tradition."[28] Another art style was to form an outline of a Chinese character
and then fill it with the Muslim creed. At a distance it is a large
Chinese character meaning "tiger" or "long life" but on closer
examination it is found to be filled with Arabic phrases. Chinese Muslims paint flowers but not birds or animals. They have
a religious reservation about making artistic representations
of living beings.

There are certain practices that maintain Muslims as an
alien minority within China. Muslims greet one another in Arabic and Persian. Many wear white headdresses which resemble
turbans. As previously mentioned, they abstain from alcohol
and pork. Coffins are not used in burial rites. The community
takes care of its poor so that there are few beggars among the
Muslims. They shun usury, as it is religiously prohibited. Divi-
nation is not practiced.

In physical characteristics, Muslims are distinct because of
historical intermarriage with foreigners. They have a larger
build, longer face, deeper eyes, and a thicker beard than other
Chinese. There are some thirty family names such as Na, Ha,
Sa, and Tieh that are unique to Muslims.

There are areas of adaptation to Chinese culture. Few Mus-
lim women wear the veil. Circumcision, contrary to worldwide
Islamic practice, is not a requirement of Chinese Islam. Busi-
ness continues as usual on Friday, the Muslim holy day. The
Muslim attitude toward Muhammad as a sage is parallel to that
of Chinese belief concerning the respected teacher, Confucius.
The mosque in China gives evidence of a syncretism between
Islam and Chinese religions.

> The Muslims of China lost connections with other Muslim coun-
> tries for a long time and were influenced unconsciously by Con-
> fucianism in several ways—for instance, they call the worship
> place *shin*, the Buddhist word for temple, rather than mosque

---

28. Dawood C. M. Ting, "Islamic Culture in China," in *Islam: The Straight
Path*, ed. Kenneth W. Morgan (New York: Ronald Press, 1958), p. 374.

as in Islamic countries. The mosques constructed in China look exactly like Confucian and Buddhist temples from the outside. The responsible personnel in the mosques held ranks similar to those of the head priest, priest, and monk in Buddhist temples and lived in the mosque and received alms and performed all religious duties. At a wedding or a funeral and religious leaders of Islam were asked to say prayers and recite passages just as the Buddhist monks did in the temples. Just as the Buddhists emphasized silence and meditation, so also the Sufis among the Muslims stressed similar practices and shared the belief that meditation would finally give power to perform miracles. The men who gained such powers were called Shaikhs by the Muslims. The Shaikhs and Buddhist monks often had contests in magic, which Muslims frequently won.[29]

Mosques usually display three characters, *Tsing Chen Ssi*, which means "the temple of the pure and true religion." Only in Kansu and East Turkestan are mosques to be found with typical Middle Eastern architectural designs. The interiors of all mosques, however, are distinctive. Beautiful Arabic inscriptions adorn the walls. Ornate prayer rugs grace the floors. The interior is divided into the worship room, a lecture hall, conference rooms, offices, and the "dead man's room" for washing the deceased. Mosques are frequently endowed through earnings received from real estate which is held in the name of the mosque.

The leader of the mosque is called the *ahund*, which means "scholar" or "teacher of religion." He is assisted by an *imam* who leads the worshipers in the prayer ritual. In some mosques there is an "unclassified *ahund*" who knows Arabic but has had little formal training in Islamic doctrine. He is responsible for leading the chanting as well as arranging the practical details for funerals. There is a committee of three to seven members who are elected for a year, serve without pay, and have general oversight of the income and property related to the mosque.[30]

For centuries Chinese Muslims had little contact with the orthodoxy of the Middle East. Changes in thought and practice inevitably occurred. With an increase in travel and commerce, many Muslim scholars visited the heartland of Islam and be-

29. Ibid., p. 360.
30. Ibid., p. 361.

came aware of the variations which had become standard practice among millions of Muslims in China. As these insights were
brought back to the masses, there developed serious strains between the Chinese Muslims and the newly introduced traditional Muslim norms. This conflict continued for more than
five decades.

Jahriyah (which means "to pray aloud") is a Sufi sect whose
ritual includes the practice of communally praising God in
loud voices. The members, similar to the dervishes of Iran,
form a circle, clasp hands, and begin to pray as they walk first
to the left and then to the right. They close their eyes and commence to shake their heads as the prayer becomes an emotional
chant. The chanting is accelerated as the body movements become faster and faster. Finally the chanting is reduced to the
recitation of only one word, "Allah-Allah-Allah-Allah," until the
men begin to drop from mental and physical exhaustion. This is
why the Chinese call the *Jahriyah* the "shaking-head" religion.
The majority of Muslims reject this sect as deviant from the
norm of Islamic practice.

The five pillars of Islam are generally observed, although in
recent years the influences of Communism and materialism
have had a negative impact on the faith of a large number of
Muslims, particularly the young people. Most do not pray five
times a day. Many Muslims appear at the mosque only at the
time of the two major festivals of Islam. It is common for Chinese Muslims to fast only the last three nights of Ramadan.
Most Muslims are very poor and therefore do not participate in
zakat. Few make the pilgrimage to Saudi Arabia. This is because of poverty as well as the reluctance of the Communist
government to give visas for travel abroad. In the past, there
were fifteen thousand Chinese Muslims, all strongly anti-
Communist, who had gone on the Hajj and had taken political
refuge in Mecca.

A Chinese Muslim wedding avoids all superstitions such as
the reading of the horoscopes of the betrothed. If one of the parties is not a Muslim, the *ahund* receives that one into Islam a
few days before the wedding. It is customary to give clothing,
jewelry, or a small amount of money as a minimal dowry.

The ceremonies of engagement and marriage are quite similar
for Chinese Muslims and non-Muslims except that the Muslims

celebrate the event with a religious and a general ceremony, and they do not use old Chinese music or gongs or fire crackers since they consider them to be superstitious. . . . Muslims hold the marriage ceremony in the mosque. In modern times Western music has been adopted for marriages since it is not associated with the worship of other gods. Chinese Muslims obey the Civil Law of China by practicing monogamy almost everywhere except in the frontier provinces. There is no Muslim court to take care of divorce, adoption, and inheritance, as in other Muslim countries; all these matters are now handled in the general courts.[31]

Muslims of China follow Islamic rites in regard to funerals but are closer to Confucianism in the rituals for mourning and preparing a body for burial. As death approaches, the family is expected to be near and to encourage the dying person to repeatedly state, "All things are not God. Only Allah is God. Muhammad is his special Prophet."

For more than a thousand years after Islam came to China there was no translation of the Quran or Hadith. A Chinese Quran was published in Taiwan in 1955. There are very few books in the vernacular on Islamic philosophy, history, science, or literature.

Since the 1930s there has been a conflict of varying intensity between Muslims and Communists. In 1937 Muslim soldiers defeated the Communists and drove them out of Kansu province. This set the stage for mutual antagonism. Communists have given Muslims some measure of regional autonomy, but it is always closely supervised by officers of the central government.

A major thrust in the Communist effort to break down Muslim intellectual resistance was through education. Previously, most Muslims who had any education received it through mosque schools where they studied the Koran, Muslim teaching, and at least enough Arabic to understand the services in the mosque. Intensive efforts were made under the new regime to bring all Muslim children into government schools, where the Chinese language was taught and used as the medium of instruction and where courses in science were emphasized.[32]

31. Ibid., p. 369.
32. Richard C. Bush, Jr., *Religion in Communist China* (Nashville: Abingdon, 1970), p. 274.

It would appear that Islam has survived intact through all the violent upheavals in Chinese history, including the bloody purges of the Cultural Revolution. Communal feelings have deepened within Chinese Muslim society. Adversity has brought about a tenacious determination to survive.

Few Arab Islamic scholars have toured the Muslim areas of China and only a small number of Chinese have visited the heartland of Islam. This situation is undergoing change through the latest policy of openness on the part of the Chinese authorities. It is fair to assume the Muslims of China will respond enthusiastically to this new opportunity to enter into the mainstream of the international Islamic *ummah*.

The Philippines

Islam reached the shores of Sulu in the southernmost part of the Philippines at the end of the fifteenth century. The early Muslims were more interested in trade than in propagating Islam. Yet, they proved to be effective missionaries as they promoted their religion by marrying into local clans, adopting native customs, and generally entering into the societal structures of the area in which they settled. It is crucial to understand that Islam was introduced not as a dogmatic, exclusive religion but rather as an addition to the pagan beliefs of the natives. The end result of this syncretistic presentation was what Peter G. Gowing, the outstanding scholar on Filipino Islam until his sudden death in 1983, has called "Islamized paganism." As was true elsewhere in Southeast Asia, Islam was introduced into the Philippines in a most benign and gradual manner. Victor Hurley, an American writer, has commented favorably on the propagation style of early Muslim traders and missionaries:

> They had all of the fanaticism of the Spanish priests without the accompanying greed for gold. They were the most purely altruistic preachers in the world. Their utter sincerity inspired the confidence of their savage hosts. The priests of Mohammad were among the most potent spreaders of civilization in the history of man. Their religion did not tear down and destroy as did that of the early Christians. The priests of Mohammad brought culture and writing and the arts, and they added these things to

the culture they found in their new lands. They were not de-
stroyers but were satisfied to improve the old culture.[33]

By 1521, the sultanates of Mindanao and the Sulu archipelago were engaged in extending their rule all the way to the
northern island of Luzon. The Spaniards put a halt to the Muslim advance in 1570. If the Spaniards had not checked Islamic
expansion, it is possible the Philippines, plus perhaps Taiwan,
Korea, China, and Japan would be Muslim today. Because of
Spanish military influence, Islam was pushed south into an en-
clave centered in western Mindanao.

The force of anti-Islamic action is found in this 1578 communique written by Governor-General de Sande to Captain Fi-
gueroa, the commanding officer of an expedition against the
Muslims of Mindanao:

> You shall order that there be not among them any more preach-
> ing of the sect of Mohammed, since it is evil and that of the
> Christian alone is good. . . . And because, for a short time since
> the Lord of Mindanao has been deceived by preachers of Bor-
> neo, and the people have become Moros, you shall tell them
> that our object is that they shall be converted to Christianity,
> and that he must grant a safe place where the law of Christian-
> ity be preached and the natives may hear the preaching and be
> converted without risk or harm from the chiefs. . . . And you
> shall try to ascertain who are the preachers of the sect of Mo-
> hammed and to seize and bring them before me. . . . And you
> shall burn or tear down the house where the evil doctrine is
> preached. And you shall order that it be not rebuilt.[34]

The earliest propagation of the Christian message was of quite
a different nature than that of the Muslim!

Gowing listed three ways in which contemporary Muslim
Filipinos have been affected by history. First, they have inher-
ited a legacy of Christian-Muslim animosity. The Spaniards
utilized Christian Filipinos in the subjugation of the Muslims.
This made the Christian regard the followers of Islam as heathen savages who needed to be conquered and then civilized.

---

33. Peter G. Gowing, "Muslim Filipinos Today," *The Muslim World*, vol. 54
(January 1964), pp. 42–43.
    34. Ibid., p. 43.

This deep-seated communal hatred continues to the present day. Second, Muslim Filipinos have become a part of a secluded culture. For centuries they have battled hostile forces. The result is an ingrown and suspicious community that is close to being paranoid. Third, there has developed a tradition of alliance and kinship with the Muslims of Borneo and Indonesia. The Sultanate of Sulu once ruled over territories in North Borneo; Maguindanao Muslims have fostered close commercial ties with Java and Sumatra. The geographical proximity of Mindanao and Indonesia has created apprehension among Christian Filipino government officials. Their response to the problem has been to encourage Christian migration to Mindanao, thus diluting Muslim political strength.[35]

Muslims in the Philippines represent an ethnic mix of aboriginal, Polynesian, Indonesian, Malayan, Chinese, and Indian origins. Religiously their faith and practice have been influenced by animism, spiritism, Hinduism, and Buddhism. These influences are most evident in the Muslim rites associated with circumcision, marriage, and death.

Muslims of the Philippines number approximately two and a half million, which is 5 percent of the total population. Maguindanaons constitute 40 percent of all Muslims in the Philippines. Their superstitions and rites connected with pregnancy and childbirth reflect the syncretistic religious influences within society. During pregnancy, the couple must emphasize good qualities in other people. Failure to do so will reflect adversely on the unborn child. The food eaten by the expectant mother must not be unusually shaped. If it is, this will cause deformities in the child. If the husband has his hair cut during this period it will result in the stunted growth of the baby's hair. If the father wears headgear of coiled cloth, it will cause the umbilical cord to strangle the child. On the seventh day after the delivery the baby is baptized in a ceremony called the *pedtabungawan*. Special delicacies are served on the occasion. Religious rites are performed by the *imam*. The hair of the baby is dipped in a basin of water as an act of baptism. Both male and female Muslims are circumcised.[36]

35. Ibid., p. 45.
36. Sahid S. Glang and Manuel M. Convocar, *Maguindanaon, Field Report Series No. 6* (Quezon City: Philippines Center for Advanced Studies, 1978), p. 27.

Despite the dominant role of Islam in Maguindanaon belief system, local beliefs still retain substantial importance, affecting the ideas and deeds of the native populations. There is the widespread fear of evil spirits and conversely, there is the devotion of gentler supernatural beings. Magic is likewise believed. All these beliefs provide the Maguindanaon with security in the face of danger.[37]

Muslims have been reluctant to avail themselves of educational opportunities in government schools. Many are fearful that the school system is designed to convert their children to Christianity. This hesitation has resulted in a low literacy rate among Filipino Muslims.

Muslims of the southern Philippines have had in their midst a fanatical group dedicated to the religious and political autonomy of the Islamic people. These people have committed numerous acts of violence in order to publicize their plight. Libya has assisted in financing these groups. Recently, while talking to a Filipino Muslim, I asked what the *ummah* of Islam meant to him. He immediately identified Libya as the country to which Filipino Muslims can relate in a sense of religious brotherhood.

Both Christians and Muslims contribute to the problems. Political and religious components are mingled in a confusing quagmire of issues. The result is that Muslims feel little loyalty to their national government. Their concept of *ummah* is first of all internal within their own ethnic group. It then extends to other Muslims of Mindanao. Lastly, it embraces Islamic people of countries that have supported them in their quest for religious and political freedom.

Strengths of Muslim Community

Driss Ferdi, an intellectual Muslim who had spent sixteen years exposed to secular rationalism in Paris, returned to his Muslim village to attend the funeral of his father. He had wandered from his early convictions as a practicing Muslim. Ferdi had become a sophisticated man of letters far removed academically and emotionally from the simple rural life of his childhood. In this powerful autobiographical note, Ferdi traces

37. Ibid., p. 37.

the poignant reconversion he experienced as he encountered the force of Islam in the context of Muslim community:

> Then a man stood up and began to chant. What he chanted was of no importance. It was not the words, not the meaning, not even the symbolism which moved our hearts. We forgot we were there the moment he began to chant. It was the incantation, and the end of our woes and miserable little problems, the aching and yet serene longing for that other life which is ours and to which we are all destined to return. . . . There was all of that in the voice of the man who stood chanting in the sun, and we were in his voice. I was in his voice despite the vast legacy of incredulity that I had received from the West. When he reached the end of a verse, he paused, and so it came about—an outburst of fervour. And while he chanted it was like a man in the wilderness chanting his faith. And the voice rose and swelled, changed in tone, became tragic, soared and then floated down on our heads like a seagull gliding gently and softly, little more than a whisper. And so—never again will I go in search of intellectuals, of written truths, synthetic truths, of collections of hybrid ideas which are nothing but ideas. Never again will I travel the world in search of a shadow of justice, fairness, progress, or schemes calculated to change mankind. I was weary and I was returning to my clan. The man was not even aware of his voice or of his faith . . . a man who could not even have been a dustman in this world of founts of knowledge and of civilization. Peace and everlasting truth were in him and in his voice, while all was crumbling around him.[38]

Ferdi in these few words has captured the world view of literally millions of Muslims. They do not care for all of the brilliant pronouncements of Harvard and Oxford. Scientific achievement is irrelevant. What does matter is allegiance to the highest power in the universe. Allah is the supreme authority, and man's submission to him is the chief priority. To the Westerner this mindset is frustrating. We desire to drag the reluctant Muslim into a complex world described by Alvin Toffler as the "Third Wave," a wave of cosmic explorations, sophisticated "high tech," and drastically rearranged sociological structures. The Muslim pleads for the traditional, the stable, the satisfying

---

38. Kenneth Cragg and R. Marston Speight, comps., *Islam from Within: Anthology of a Religion* (Belmont, Calif.: Wadsworth, 1980), pp. 11, 12.

world of warm interpersonal relationships. *Ummah*, to a Muslim, cannot be expressed by a computer, an assembly line, a spaceship, or sitting in a physics class trying to figure out the latest problem of cosmic importance. *Ummah*, put very simply, means God's chosen community, a community which is engaged in worship of Allah and meaningful interaction with each of the members of the *ummah*.

Is all of this a strength or a weakness? I have categorized it as a strength, perhaps because of personal biases. As in most areas of life, a strength taken to an extreme becomes a weakness. Among some Muslims, I am sure this has occurred. There needs to be a balance between modernity and traditional social values. What some Muslims are protesting is what they perceive as a sellout by the West to the gods of money, knowledge, and power. The result has been the depersonalization of the human race. An illustration of what Muslims consider ultimate insanity was expressed in the television special, "The Day After," when in the midst of the rubble and desolation wrought by nuclear warfare, the American president's quivering voice comes over the radio and assures the few remaining survivors on planet Earth that the United States has preserved democracy! The ultimate technology of splitting the atom has been pronounced a victor . . . in the midst of crumbling buildings, decaying flesh, and total hopelessness. It is no wonder that in a day when the world can be destroyed in less than one hour, the Muslim protests and looks longingly back to the early days of Islamic stability and triumph.

Recognition of God

God permeates every area of the life of a dedicated Muslim. The name of Allah is constantly being spoken, not in a vain manner, but in a solemn recognition of his authority and power in the life of a believer.

Many of the routine events of daily life are occasions of ejaculatory petition—entering and leaving the house, entering and leaving a lavatory, retiring and rising, or visiting the sick, passing a graveyard, embarking and disembarking, before and after meals, in front of a mirror, after a bath, on first partaking of any item in the yearly harvest, in distress, and in trial. In many cases the words have come down from traditional practices or phrases of the Prophet himself. The purpose of such devotional recognition of God in the minutiae of the everyday is to make one's "Islam," or submission, comprehensive and alert and to evoke the spirit of gratitude and humility. Bodily functions which may so easily go awry and which in their wholeness are so wonderful should be the occasion of ejaculatory worship.[39]

For many years, I considered the Muslim phrase *Hai-Allah* to be equivalent to the English "O God." I faulted the Muslims for using these words in a vain, even cursing sort of manner. Only when I began to read the Hadith did I understand the correctness of Bishop Cragg's interpretation of the Muslim's constant references to God. In their holy books, Muslims are enjoined to make verbal reference to God in absolutely every act of life. A whole section in the Hadith refers to prayers to be said during the act of lovemaking. This strikes the Westerner as extreme, but I have no doubt that some very devout Muslims seek to follow such regulations to the letter.

Islamic community, then, is expressed in recognition of God. It is communicated every time a Muslim meets a fellow believer and greets him with *As-Salamu Alykum* (Peace be upon you). Upon departure, a Muslim warmly says *Khoda hafiz* (May God be with you). These short messages of spiritual greeting seem so much better than "Hi, how are you," or "Bye, see you later."

Family Solidarity

In reference to Arab women, I made mention of some of the tensions prevailing as new and old patterns clash. Modernity, with its so-called liberating influence, is calling upon Muslim women to discard the veil, take up the briefcase, and enter the university and the business world with a newfound boldness and assertiveness. Such moves have been denounced by many religious teachers as being contrary to Islam. The woman is to be a homebound, modest, submissive wife and mother. Historically, most Muslim women have fit into this category.

Iran and Egypt are case studies where many Muslim women have experienced social liberation and then, through the influence of the Islamic revolution, have turned back to the veil and to the home. This has not always been done under duress. Many

---

39. Kenneth Cragg, *The Call of the Minaret* (New York: Oxford University Press, 1956), pp. 110–11.

women have taken these steps voluntarily in order to better conform to the dictates of Islam.

Although it is necessary to take note of conflicting cross-currents, it is also important not to overestimate their impact on the solidarity of Muslim family life. Overall, Islam has preserved the integrity of the family. The West has a divorce rate of nearly 45 percent, while it is safe to estimate that the rate throughout the Muslim world is less than 10 percent. Separation and desertion are problems but probably less so than in the West.

The question then arises as to the quality of relationships within the family. The *Los Angeles Times* speculated that there are more than ten million battered wives in America. This is an overwhelming statistic in view of the freedom American women have to initiate divorce proceedings with the expectation of receiving a just financial settlement. It would be my considered opinion that wife beating within Muslim families is no more frequent than in America.

Westerners charge Islam with imposing extreme modesty, isolation, and deprivation upon women. Perhaps this is a legitimate charge if we value the miniskirt over the veil or the bikini over the sari. Most Muslim women regard the dress patterns of Western women as being simply a form of nudity which is utilized to cause men to lust after them. It is liberation which has become license. For most, it is labeled gross and blatant immorality.

The most common graffiti I have observed in one large Muslim country is centered in one word. It is a word found scribbled on bathroom walls, printed on notebooks, and artistically written on plaques. It is the word most frequently spoken or written, apart from Allah and Muhammad, within the rich language of that country. The word is "Mother," and it is written with deep respect and honor—never in derision or jest. The attitude toward motherhood is much like that recorded in the Old Testament.

The dialogue between Elizabeth W. Fernea and a group of Iraqi Muslim village women is illuminating:

> "And is it true," asked Basima, "that in America they put all the old women in houses by themselves, away from their families?" I admitted that this was sometimes true and tried to ex-

plain, but my words were drowned in the general murmur of disapproval.

"What a terrible place that must be!"

"How awful!"

"And their children let them go?"

"Thank God we live in El Nahra, where the men are not so cruel!"

It had never occurred to me before, but the idea of old people's homes must have been particularly reprehensible to these women whose world lay within the family unit and whose whole lives of toil and childbearing were rewarded in old age, when they enjoyed repose and respect as members of their children's households.[40]

Prostitution and pornography are minimal in Islamic countries. It is true that girls are often married at a young age as a safeguard against promiscuity, but is that not preferable to the problems of childbirth outside of wedlock as well as the alarmingly high rate of abortion found in the West? It should be mentioned that homosexuality is reputed to be a problem within Muslim society. Accurate statistics are impossible to obtain.

It has been a privilege to observe Dr. Ali's family at very close range over an extended period of time. I have seen love expressed consistently among the family members in a manner that I have seldom observed in Christian families. Perhaps the West has something to learn from Muslim social patterns where the home has basically retained its role as a haven from the harsh storms of life. I realize the critic will find exceptions and seek to discredit this section. I agree that there are weaknesses in the role of Muslim women in Islam. Some of these will be discussed in the next section. Seclusion of women, marriage without consent, wife beating, and other inadequacies are found among Muslims. No one can deny this. I merely protest against the critic who sees only the negative without a commensurate appreciation of the good. I am also annoyed by any writer who denounces Islam without a cross-reference to the

---

40. Elizabeth W. Fernea, *Guests of the Sheik* (Garden City, N.Y.: Anchor, 1965), p. 185.

terrible social ills of the West, which supposedly has been influenced by Christian ethics and morals for two thousand years.

Islamic Witness

Muslims believe in their responsibility to broaden the borders of Islamic community. Although this fact may not give me, as a Christian, much comfort, yet I acknowledge the positive effects such a witness has on solidifying Muslim *ummah*. Although Samuel M. Zwemer wrote these words in 1907, they are still applicable among most Muslims today:

> To the modern Christian world, missions imply organization, societies, paid agents, subscriptions, reports, etc. All this is practically absent from the present Moslem idea of propagation, and yet, the spread of Islam goes on. . . . It would be an exaggeration to say that every Moslem is a missionary, but it is true that, with the exception of the Derwish orders (who resemble monks), the missionaries of Islam are the laymen in every walk of life, rather than its priesthood.[41]

This is a subject in which Muslims take great pride. The sophistication and financial backing of the modern Christian missionary movement is totally absent in Islam. Our use of satellites linked to Christian radio and television stations is unthinkable, at this stage, for Muslims. An army of young people from Campus Crusade is crisscrossing the planet showing a film on the life of Jesus. Such a vision is absent within Islam. My personal library of two thousand Christian books probably exceeds the number of all books ever published on Islam in Bangladesh, the world's third largest Muslim country.

How can one account for the massive spread of Islam from the deserts and clans of Arabia to the prestigious position of being the second largest religion in the world? It is a "foreign" religion in most countries. Basic Arabic has had to be learned by converts. Few hospitals and social institutions have been built by high-powered missionaries. Missiologically, Islam would not earn very high marks. Yet, its propagation has been

41. Samuel M. Zwemer, *Islam: A Challenge to Faith* (New York: Student Volunteer Movement for Foreign Missions, 1907), p. 79.

eminently successful. Muslims would say, *Al-hamdu-Li-llah* (All praise to God). Many Christians would respond by attributing such a rapid expansion to the influence of Satan.

Pragmatically, the observer sees the warrior, the trader, and the missionary. These three symbolize Islamic propagation. But what of the receiving community? It is safe to generalize that the warrior, in the early days of Islamic expansion, met people so dissatisfied with the status quo that they were open to change. The trader became an integral part of the community in which he worked. His strong Islamic faith made a deep impact and led to multiple conversions. The missionary came as an earnest persuader. Each of the three was an enthusiastic advocate of the formation of social solidarity that can best be termed *ummah*.

> The preaching of Islam was earnest, and demanded as unconditional a surrender as did their weapons. The thunder of their cavalry was not more terrible to the enemy than the clamor of their short, sharp creed in the ears of an idolatrous and divided Christendom, or the ears of ignorant pagans: *"La-ilaha illa Allah! Allahu Akbar!"* These men of the desert carried everything before them because they had the backbone of conviction, knew no compromise, and were thirsting for world-conquest. Not Khalid alone, but every Moslem warrier felt himself to be the "Sword of God."[42]

Such a zeal outlived the early military campaigns of Islam. Muslims are totally convinced that they alone possess the authoritative Word of God and the message of truth for a godless world. Their *ummah* is superior to that offered by any philosophy, ideology, or religion.

Several books highlight the testimonies of converts to Islam. One of the most famous is the autobiography of Muhammad Asad as chronicled in *The Road to Mecca*. My impression, upon reading this 380-page book, was that Asad, a European journalist, had a sincere conversion to Islam, but a conversion more sociological than spiritual. One sees his appreciation of Islamic *ummah* on every page.

Another interesting book, *The Road to Holy Mecca*, is the conversion story of a Japanese journalist, Hussein Yoshio

42. Ibid., p. 78.

Hirashima. He portrays himself as an earnest seeker of truth, but in post-World-War-II Japan, he was disillusioned with what he saw as spiritual barrenness and a sense of despair. He had an opportunity to go to the Middle East, where he came into contact with many Muslims who deeply impressed him. He counted the cost of family alienation and officially converted to Islam.

Islam—Our Choice, compiled by Ebrahim Ahmed Bawany, is a book of documented testimonies published by the Muslim World League Printing Press in Geneva. It is clearly presented as a propagation effort by Islamic leaders. Most of the forty testimonies are given by Europeans who are well-educated and accomplished in their professions. The impact of Islamic brotherhood was instrumental in their conversions. This is also true of Muhtar Holland, an Oxford graduate who has been a professor at the University of London as well as the University of Toronto. Holland highlights two considerations that led him to become a Muslim in 1969 at the age of thirty-four.

> When I came to feel the need to espouse a religion (meaning to commit myself to one "for better or worse," as opposed to flirting with religiousness on the one hand, or the nominal membership from birth on the other), it was Islam that I chose to embrace. As for adopting a particular religion, I had come to the conclusion—after many misgivings—that this was an important part of the fulness of human experience. As for the choice of Islam, one consideration was the directness and blazing simplicity of its doctrine: I could see truth in other religions, but here the Truth was plainest to me. The second consideration was the Islamic emphasis on brotherhood.
>
> I had been stirred by the Quranic ideal of a brotherhood of believers "in the Way of God;" I had been moved literally to tears by accounts of the fraternal acts of the Prophet Muhammad and his companions (What openness in the feelings they must have known); I was also influenced by my personal encounters with Muslims of today. I had met Muslims from all walks of life, in my travels in Turkey and Syria, and during a five month study-leave in Egypt. I had lectured to students from all parts of the Muslim world; Nigeria, Egypt, Sudan, Syria, Iran, Pakistan, Malaysia, Bahrain, even Mecca itself. Now Muslims themselves would be the last to pretend that the Islamic world today embodies more than a fraction of the true religious ideal.

Nevertheless, I sensed that, among very many of the Muslims I came to know, the spirit of brotherhood was very much alive and expressed itself in their attitudes and behaviour.[43]

In this section I have sought briefly to allude to certain strengths found within Islamic *ummah*. I am sure my Muslim friends could add a great deal to these observations. Likewise, I am certain some fellow Christians would happily ignore or even severely criticize some of my thoughts.

I will attempt to be equally lucid in the next few pages as I highlight some serious weaknesses and defects in Islamic *ummah*.

Weaknesses of Muslim Community

It is human nature to point out the faults of a person or system with which we do not agree. Without exception, this is a relatively easy task, given man's individual and corporate propensity for evil. As Christians, we must remind ourselves of the ease with which Muslims could rightly criticize innumerable aspects of the community of one billion people who call themselves Christians. A non-Theist minister told me of her research in graduate school in which she compared, through the use of film clips, the "psychological manipulation and crowd-control techniques" of Adolf Hitler, Benito Mussolini, and Billy Graham. Her conclusion was that there was absolutely no difference in the three men in their efforts to influence the masses! The presuppositions with which my Universalist-Unitarian friend began her research are rather obvious.

There are serious defects within all large structures that include people from diverse backgrounds, be that Islam, Christianity, or any other religion. As will be pointed out, historically one problem with Islam has been its reluctance to engage in self-criticism. This process, albeit a painful one, is absolutely essential to attaining any acceptable level of credibility. I offer the following comments to my Muslim friends not in a spirit of destructiveness or false triumphalism. Rather, it is my prayer that Muslims will be stimulated to look afresh at areas which

43. Muhtar Holland, *The Duties of Brotherhood in Islam* (Leicester: The Islamic Foundation, 1980), p. 11.

have contributed to the massive amount of antagonism that has separated the *ummahs* of Christianity and Islam.

Fanaticism

My intimate and very positive experience with the devout Ali family led me to anticipate a similar relationship with the Abduls. My wife, daughter, and I were on furlough in Detroit. We lived in an apartment just beneath the Abduls'. Soon after we got settled, we went up to meet the family. Dr. Abdul is an Egyptian doctor who is highly trained and by any standards has become professionally successful. He took his specialized training in the States. During that time he met Karen, an American, whom he later married. Karen has become a practicing Muslim. Dr. Abdul is now a naturalized American citizen.

From the start, it was obvious that Dr. Abdul was very anti-Christian. I sought to respond carefully to his many misconceptions about the Christian faith. Over the ten-month period we were in the apartment we had a number of social occasions together. It was particularly easy for Julie, my wife, to relate to Karen.

One of the most memorable nights in my life took place the night before we were to move out of the apartment. Dr. Abdul and Karen came down, ostensibly to bid us farewell. Instead he launched the worst verbal attack on me personally that I have ever experienced. Dr. Abdul charged that I am a missionary only because of financial remuneration; that I am incapable of doing any other work, therefore I have become a minister; and that I seek to induce Muslims to convert to Christianity through unethical means. In a spirit of unbridled anger, he stalked out the door and proceeded to return the several potted plants that we had given to him and his wife.

In retrospect, I strongly suspect that Dr. Abdul is a member of the fanatical Islamic Brotherhood. In our conversations, it had been evident he was a Khomeini sympathizer. Even as I write these words, I feel the hurt of that encounter—a hurt that includes a sense of failure that I had been unable to communicate better with Dr. Abdul and cause him to move toward a more sympathetic understanding of Christians and Christianity.

John L. Lamonte has said that "no issue is more calculated to

stir up ordinary citizens than that of religion."[44] Christianity
has had more than its share of fanaticism. The Crusades
against Muslims in the Holy Land are one of the darkest blots
on church history. From the present historical perspective, we
can only shake our heads in disbelief that nine shiploads of devout children set out for the Holy Land in order to participate
in its emancipation from "infidel Muslims." This infamous Children's Crusade ended with the sinking of a number of the ships.
The rest of them were diverted to Alexandria where the children were sold into slavery. Unfortunately, religious bigotry is
still with us, both in Christian and in Muslim communities.

Islamic fanaticism is seen to have a Quranic basis:

> Lo! Those who disbelieve Our revelations, We shall expose
> them to the Fire. As often as their skins are consumed We shall
> exchange them for fresh skins that they may taste the torment.
> Lo! Allah is ever Mighty, Wise. [4:56]

> If they turn back [to enmity] then take them and kill them wher-
> ever ye find them. [4:89]

> Whoso fighteth in the way of Allah, be he slain or be he victori-
> ous, on him We shall bestow a vast reward. [4:74]

These few verses give the flavor of similar teachings reiter-
ated throughout the Quran. Confusion results from the statement *There is no compulsion in religion* that is found in the
Quran. I have never had this contradiction explained to my
satisfaction.

Historically, the early spread of Islam was fueled by a fanatical sense of destiny on the part of the Arabs as they moved off
the deserts of Arabia. Later the Turks attacked the Christian Ar-
menians with such force that hundreds of thousands died. In
India, Muslims were often ruthless in their behavior toward the
Hindus.

> This contempt for the lives of the rebellious or vanquished was
> exemplified over and over in the history of Islam and India. The
> slave emperor, Balban, once slew forty thousand Mongols,
> whom he suspected of disloyalty, notwithstanding that they

44. John L. Lamonte, "Crusade and Jihad," in *The Arab Heritage*, ed.
Nabih Amin Faris (Princeton: Princeton University Press, 1946), p. 159.

had professed the Moslem religion. Timur (Tamerlane) felt encumbered by one hundred thousand Hindu prisoners taken at the capture of Delhi. He ordered them to be slain in cold blood. The Bahmanid Mohammed I, son of Hassan Gangu, once avenged the death of his Moslem garrison at Mudkal by the slaughter of seventy thousand men, women and children. Such were the deeds of the proselyting sword, which was unsheathed against the unbelieving world by the mandate of the prophet.[45]

The situation in Iran, Iraq, and Lebanon points to the ongoing militancy of Islam. Several Muslim scholars have clearly enunciated current Islamic policy as world revolution and conquest. "The objective of the Islamic Jihad is to eliminate the rule of an un-Islamic system and establish in its stead an Islamic system of State rule. Islam does not intend to confine this revolution to a single State or a few countries; the aim of Islam is to bring about a universal revolution. . . . No portion of mankind should be deprived of the Truth."[46]

The force of this statement clearly indicates where more fanatical Islam is headed. In another passage, Abul A'la Maududi postulates changes that will occur when the Islamic *ummah* gains political power. All forms of interest will be banned. Gambling, prostitution, immodest dress, and cinema attendance will likewise be prohibited.[47]

Khomeini, while still in Paris, gave a verbal preview of actions that were to follow:

O Scholars of Islam! Today the youths of all the Muslim countries are being led astray and separated from us by means of false propaganda. There are many centres of Christians, Jews, and Bahaies in Tehran who are bent upon uprooting the principles of Islam. Is it not our duty to wipe out these centres which are causing tremendous harm to Islam?[48]

45. E. M. Wherry, *Islam and Christianity in India and the Far East* (New York: Revell, 1907), p. 49.

46. Abul A'la Maududi, *Jihad in Islam* (Lahore: Islamic Publications, 1976), p. 22.

47. Ibid., pp. 27–28.

48. Mohiudden Ayyubi, ed., *Khumeini Speaks Revolution*, trans. N. M. Shaikh (Karachi: International Islamic Publishers, 1981), p. 25.

There are a number of documented stories coming out of Tehran that indicate Khomeini has particularly targeted these three groups as a focus of Islamic wrath. Little can be done in mediation with a man who is totally convinced he is God's representative on earth and that his actions are fully sanctioned by Allah.

The convert from Islam to Christianity has often felt the full fury of the wrath of the *ummah*. The norm has been for the apostate to Christianity to be expelled from the community and, in many instances, to suffer physical harm. The result of all this has been that very few Muslims have been willing to pay such a high price to follow Christ. Later in this book, I will seek to explore the options that will allow the new believer to remain within Islamic society, continue to be a Muslim culturally, and yet be true to his faith in Christ. There are no easy solutions to this age-old problem but it is one to which we must address ourselves. Until we do, it is likely we will see no more than a trickle of Muslims willing to cross the sociological, economic, political, and religious barriers necessary to become a Christian in an Islamic context.

A Muslim cries out the Shahadah (the Islamic confession of faith) as he drives a truck full of explosives into the Marine compound at Beirut Airport. Such an act of martyrdom holds much of the free world in fear. Concrete barriers are placed around the White House. Security at the Pentagon is greatly increased. America braces itself for the one crazed Muslim who is prepared to inflict a great tragedy at some unknown place and undetermined time.

> The concept *jihad*, however, covers not only a collective aspect, the conducting of a war by the Islamic state, but also a personal one. The participation of a Moslem in such a war is also called *jihad* and is considered a pious act that stands on the same level as asceticism and other good works. Numerous are the Koran-verses and Traditions in which Paradise is promised to those who fall in battle. Therefore it is likely that many Moslems took part in a war on the ground of personal and religious motives. In this sense it might be called a "Holy War," but in the past as well as recently these religious sentiments have been exploited by rulers with a view to mobilize people for wars.[49]

49. Rudolph Peters, *Jihad in Mediaeval and Modern Islam* (Leiden: Brill, 1977), p. 4.

Fanaticism, wherever found, is always counterproductive. It begins as a reaction against an external force, but soon turns inward and starts to purge all within the system who are deemed inadequately committed to the cause. This element of inbuilt self-destruction is tearing apart Muslim *ummah* in various parts of the world. If Islamic leaders would issue a call for a balanced exegesis of Quranic passages, this could assist in resolving the issues that are resulting in acts which are antithetical to the true *ummah* of Islam.

Self-Centeredness

Community is expressed outwardly. It begins with the individual, but it cannot remain there. It should embrace family and friends, and then move into a social structure such as an ideology, cult, religion, or some such grouping of people of common interest. The more embracive *ummah* is, the greater is its influence and effectiveness.

Islam, as stated before, has done very well in regard to the family. Interaction with and care and concern for relatives is unusually high. But when the circle expands beyond the extended family, such involvement with the needs of others lessens considerably.

The following critique by James L. Barton is admittedly harsh, but contains enough truth to make Muslims re-evaluate a concept of *ummah* which inadequately responds to pressing needs:

A Moslem community is essentially selfish. In times of severe famine among them, distributors of relief have frequently remarked upon the impossibility of securing the services of any Moslem to aid in saving life except by paying large prices. Moslem nature seems to lack that to which appeal can be made for a service of pure philanthropy. Human suffering as such seems to make little or no impression. A community appeal falls upon deaf ears. It will be a long and difficult task to impress upon them the brotherhood of humanity and to engender in them a genuine desire to improve the social order and to eradicate its evils.[50]

50. James L. Barton, *The Christian Approach to Islam* (Boston: Pilgrim, 1918), p. 177.

While resident in a Muslim country, I used to travel by train several times a week to nearby villages. I was always gripped by the needs of the scores of men, women, and children who had no other home than the boisterous, smelly area on the platforms from which passengers embarked and disembarked. Naked children defecated, women dressed in rags sat for hours staring blankly into space, men vociferously argued with one another, teen-agers picked pockets, and the bystanders watched—but did not see.

I expressed my concern to Dr. Ali. Immediately, he went to leading citizens and local government officers in order to enlist their support in alleviating the situation. He met with a cold response of total indifference. Yet, he was shortly thereafter able to mobilize a group of concerned citizens who visited every store in the immediate vicinity of the mosque and asked each owner to close during the Friday hour of prayer. Perhaps this story illustrates a Muslim hierarchy of values. Respect for the mosque becomes more important than the suffering of scores of fellow Muslims.

Few hospitals or orphanages have been established by concerned Muslims. Some would maintain that the reason for this is not a lack of desire to assist the needy, but rather inadequate financial resources. There are two responses to this argument. The first is that even in extremely poor countries, there are always people of wealth to be found. Secondly, oil-rich Middle Eastern Muslim nations have not had an exemplary record in aiding underdeveloped Islamic nations in programs of social assistance.

If Muslims have such little concern for their brothers in the faith, then it is obvious they will ignore the needs of minorities within their countries. This brings us to the next area of weakness within Islam.

Treatment of Minorities

Are religious and ethnic minorities ever treated as equals? It is true that some nations do better in this area of basic human rights than others, but the tendency is for the majority to lord it over the minority and to engage in either overt or subtle discrimination.

Christians were horribly persecuted by the Romans in the early centuries of their existence. However, the situation re-

versed in 380 when Christianity was adopted as the state religion of the Eastern Roman Empire. Christians became
respected citizens with full rights and privileges. But what happened to the former majority? "Pagans became martyrs and
pagan philosophers and teachers suffered exile."[51]

Muslim apologists occasionally indulge in unrealistic rhetoric in order to cast Islam in the best possible light. This has
been done by Maududi in regard to Muslim treatment of
minorities:

> In truth, it can be categorically stated that, compared with
> other systems of government, Islam has definitely enjoined the
> most just, the most tolerant and the most generous treatment
> to the minorities who choose to stay within the borders of its
> State and lead a life directed and governed by those principles
> which are different from and even hostile to the ideology of the
> majority.[52]

Regrettably, I must take exception to these comments. Islam
is a total code of life. It is meant to regulate every area of man's
existence. Therefore it naturally follows that Islam functions
best where it is dominant. Laws can be passed which are in harmony with the Quran. Banking systems can be introduced that
bypass the use of interest so that the Quranic prohibition of
usery can be maintained. Closing of restaurants during daylight hours of the month of Ramadan is enforceable. Eating
pork and drinking alcohol are easily banned. Polygamy is allowed. But what of the Christian who is born a citizen of such
an Islamic country? My observations lead me to conclude that
most minorities, be they Hindu, Bahai, Jew, or Christian, live
under considerable tension in Muslim lands. "Islam could
recognize the rights of other religious communities that were
monotheistic, but politically it could tolerate them only as sub-
ordinate."[53]

Islamic community is a tight, cohesive force that only reluc-
tantly can countenance disagreement in the form of an oppos-

51. Edwin E. Calverley, *Islam: An Introduction* (Cairo: The American University at Cairo, 1958), p. 16.

52. Abul A'la Maududi, *First Principles of the Islamic State* (Lahore: Islamic Publications, 1960), pp. 66–67.

53. Calverley, *Islam*, p. 17.

ing ideological commitment. Muslims, it seems to me, are easily intimidated by anything non-Islamic. Therefore they feel most comfortable in an *ummah* which affirms, protects, and strengthens their belief system. They are uneasy with any group within their borders which is a threat to their homogeneous structure.

It is not my purpose to document this thesis with case studies from throughout the Muslim world. That would belabor the point needlessly. I would, however, urge Muslims themselves to examine charges of discrimination against minorities. At the same time, they should recognize that Muslims are themselves minorities in scores of countries. It behooves them to treat minorities in an exemplary manner so that non-Muslim nations will find it psychologically easier to guarantee the legitimate rights of the millions of Muslims who are presently resident in the West.

Moral Standards

How can a Westerner criticize Islam for moral defects, particularly in light of our own problems of immorality? Would this not be a process of seeking to remove a splinter from a brother's eye while having a beam in one's own?

I have always sought to be nondefensive when Muslims attack the sexual promiscuity that is prevalent in the West. It is with shame that I acknowledge the excesses and blatant sins which are the result of an overemphasis on freedom of speech and action. Still, it should be obvious that two wrongs do not make a right. All societies must be judged by God's standard of righteousness, not by a civil libertarian who is always ready to defend personal freedom—regardless of how that liberty may infringe on the rights of other individuals or society at large.

Bribery is rampant in most Muslim countries. It is pervasive from the lowest level to the highest corridors of government authority. Inadequate salaries contribute to the problem. One may rightly question why we find bribery also, if less openly, in the affluent West. Among Muslims the motivation is more basic existence and in the West it is based more on greed.

For the remainder of this section I would like to consider briefly the subject of the treatment of women in Islam. This is the most controversial area of ethical confrontation between Islam and Christianity. I have consulted a number of books written by Muslims on this subject, but I will particularly refer to *Wives of the Prophet*, written by Fida Hussain, a Pakistani woman with good academic credentials. Her viewpoint is traditional and fairly well articulated. Hussain addresses the issue of the Prophet's multiple wives:

> This attack on the sacred personality of the Holy Prophet is not because of any scandal attached to his name but for the unappreciated reason that he married helpless widows from motives of humanity and altruism, as well as political expediency. Thus it comes about that the charge of sensuality has been levelled against a person who married at the age of twenty-five an elderly lady of forty and stuck to her until her death at the age of sixty-five when he himself was nearly fifty. Up to this advanced age, the Prophet of God wedded no other wife, nor is there any insinuation even in the writings of the most hostile critics, in regard to his moral integrity throughout his life, including the lifetime of his first wife, Khadijah. The charge, accordingly boils down to this that after his fiftieth year, when he was weighed down by the cares of his holy mission and the onerous duties of a rapidly expanding State, he (God forbid!) waxed sensual.[54]

The Prophet, according to Hussain and other reputable sources, married twelve times. His most controversial marriage was to Zaynab. The Hadith indicate that while she was married to Muhammad's adopted son, Zeyd, the Prophet visited her home and was stricken by her beauty. Zaynab was divorced by Zeyd and shortly thereafter married Muhammad. Surah 33:37–38 of the Quran states:

> So when Zeyd had performed the necessary formality [of divorce] from her, We gave her unto Thee in marriage, so that [henceforth] there may be no sin for believers in respect of wives of their adopted sons, when the latter have performed the necessary formality [of release] from them. The commandment of Allah must be fulfilled. There is no reproach for the Prophet in that which Allah maketh his due.

Westerners find the idea of a father marrying his adopted son's wife to be repugnant.

---

54. Fida Hussain, *Wives of the Prophet* (Lahore: Shaikh Muhammad Ashraf, 1952), p. 4.

Aishah, the daughter of Abu Bakr and the favorite wife of the
Prophet, was wedded to him at the age of six or seven. It is said
she was taken from her home where she was playing dolls with
her friends to the place of the wedding ceremony. The marriage
was consummated some five years later. Critics fault the
Prophet, well into his fifties, for marrying a girl young enough
to be his granddaughter. Muslim apologists insist the union
was solemnized because of Muhammad's desire to integrate
Abu Bakr into his immediate family.

Muslims are limited, by Quranic command, to four wives.
Surah 33:50 makes an exception for Muhammad. This special
privilege accorded to the Prophet has been the focus of cynical
debate for centuries:

> O Prophet! Lo! We have made lawful unto thee thy wives unto
> whom thou hast paid their dowries, and those whom thy right
> hand possesseth of those whom Allah hath given thee as spoils
> of war, and the daughters of thine uncle on the father's side and
> the daughters of thine aunts on the father's side and the daugh-
> ters of thine uncles on the mother's side and the daughters of
> thine aunts on the mother's side who emigrated with thee, and
> a believing woman if she give herself unto the Prophet and the
> Prophet desire to ask her in marriage—a privilege for thee
> only, not for the [rest of] believers—We are aware of that which
> We enjoined upon them concerning their wives and those
> whom their right hands possess—that thou mayst be free from
> blame, for Allah is Forgiving, Merciful.

A Muslim Filipino recently broached the subject of Muhammad's multiple wives. Very defensively, he spoke of Solomon
having seven hundred wives and three hundred concubines. He
strongly felt that Muhammad had done a great service for mankind by putting certain strictures on the practice of polygamy.

The Quran states that one may have as many as four wives
only if each spouse is treated fairly and equally. But then Surah
4:129 declares, "Ye will not be able to deal equally between your
wives, however much ye wish" to do so. It therefore seems the
Quran allows and then disallows polygamy. This problem of
Quranic exegesis causes no little embarrassment to Muslim
theologians. It should be added, however, that monogamy is the
norm in the Muslim world. Polygamy is the exception, not the
rule.

Surah 4:34 greatly troubles the more socially and economically liberated Muslim who still desires to be a submissive follower of Allah:

> Men are in charge of women, because Allah hath made the one of them to excel the other, and because they spend of their property [for the support of women]. So good women are the obedient, guarding in secret that which Allah hath guarded. As for those from whom ye fear rebellion, admonish them and banish them to beds apart and scourge them.

It is true, as mentioned earlier, that wife beating is a social ill in the West. But there is no biblical support for such an act. The New Testament commands the husband to treat the wife with great honor, dignity, and with a love that is pervasive in the relationship. Hussain seeks to apply the best interpretation possible on this Quranic teaching by saying,

> As regards the right of man to chastise woman, modern opinion may take exception to it, but a careful examination of some of the extreme cases of perversion will show that it is more humane to correct rather than to divorce and throw her out on the street. The Quran is careful in using the word "admonish" first and then the word "beat". Now-a-days women being more intelligent and educated than in ancient days, admonishing may be enough.[55]

The following are examples of other Islamic teaching that have been criticized by Christians:

Adultery is punishable, after confirmation by four eyewitnesses, by flogging each of the guilty parties one hundred times.

The Hadith present the Prophet as having seen a vision of more women than men in hell. He cited the ungratefulness of women toward men as the reason.

Women are commanded to dress modestly, lower their gaze in public, and generally avoid meeting with the opposite sex. In many Muslim countries this has led to the seclusion of women.

If they go out of the home, they wear a veil which completely covers the body.

55. Ibid., p. 28.

Surah 2:282 indicates that the testimony of two women witnesses equals the testimony of one man.

Other illustrations could be cited, but these are generally
representative of the problems Muslims confront when seeking
to explain their position on the status of women in Islam. It is
important for the Westerner to realize these issues are more
blatant and have more impact because of contemporary Western views concerning women. Muslims, who accept a more traditional historical position of the woman as homemaker, do not
feel the force of the arguments against their behavior.

Lack of Internal Criticism

In recent years word has swept through the Muslim world
that Neil Armstrong heard an unusual sound on the moon.
When, years later, he visited Egypt, he heard the call to prayer
and immediately recognized the *azan* as that which he heard on
the moon. Upon further inquiry, he was led to a study of the Quran and subsequently became a convert to Islam. I have seen
this story in newspapers and magazines and heard it from the
lips of Muslims in the most remote villages of Islamic countries. It is always presented as an absolute, irrefutable fact, a
fact that causes great rejoicing in the heart of the one telling the
story. Official government publications have also joined in
spreading this rumor.

While we were in the States, my wife called Armstrong's office and talked to his private secretary. The secretary was
aware of the rumor and the impact it was having in the Muslim
world. Subsequently, she sent us an official denial of the story
on Armstrong's personal stationery. She also enclosed a copy of
a communique sent by the State Department to U.S. embassies
in all Muslim countries. This communique instructed consu-
late officials to refute the rumor of Armstrong's conversion to
Islam. Another enclosure told of Armstrong's phone conversation with Muslim leaders in India in which he again denied his
conversion.

Why did Muslims so quickly and uncritically accept this rumor? Are they insecure and desperately in need of affirmation?
This is to some extent probably true, but it is important to note
a lack of academic critical processes among Muslims as a

whole. Another example is Hussain's statement, "It is heartening to note that the largest selling book in America last year was the English translation of the Holy Quran."[56]

Blind faith is a cornerstone of Islam, although many Muslims will deny it. For example, Muslims have never seriously questioned the mode of mechanical dictation by which God is reputed to have given his word to the Prophet. "In contrast to the tradition, the Koran itself has remained almost untouched by any breath of evolutionary criticism. Only a few Indian liberals and still fewer Arab socialists have yet ventured to question that it is the literally-inspired Word of God and that its very statement is eternally true, right and valid."[57]

Most Muslims I have met have stated that the original Quran as compiled in Muhammad's day is in Mecca. It does little good to point out the error of such a statement.

There is a general hesitation to accept rational and historical investigation as valid methodologies to investigate religious claims. Faith is faith. How can faith be verified? Any such attempt, to most Muslims, is proof of disbelief. Such prejudice is hard to reason with. Needless to say, such a view is also found among some Christians.

Islam has been hesitant to open itself to serious academic dialogue with Christian scholars.

> The greatest task that has always faced Islam and that will continue to face it until it actually faces it is to study its own roots in Judaism and Christianity. There has never been a single Muslim who dedicated his whole life to the study of Christianity and who wrote or perhaps could write a single authoritative work on Christianity that would be accepted by the Church or by recognized Christian scholars, whereas there have been innumerable Jews and Christians who dedicated their whole life to the study of Islam, and who wrote works on Islam, accepted, always to be sure with reservations with respect to certain points, and respected and referred to by Muslims themselves. This is strange, especially as a good half of the Koran itself explicitly touches on Judaism and Christianity. We had competent Christian scholars who took part in this Islamic

56. Ibid., p. 184.
57. H. A. R. Gibb, *Modern Trends in Islam* (New York: Octagon, 1972), p. 50.

Symposium and who made notable contributions to it; we
could not have Muslim scholars who could take part in the
Christian Symposium and who could make notable contributions to it. The self-isolation of Islam from Christianity is one of
the most important acts of radical discontinuity that occurred
in history.[58]

Some Muslims will argue that Islamic *ummah* is strengthened by scholastic isolation. They would see exposure to the
critics of the West as counterproductive to Islamic unity. Thus,
in many circles, the fortress mentality prevails. This suspicion
applies as well to Islamic scholars like Fazlur Rahman, who
has dared to question from within the camp. He is definitely
not in the good graces of fundamentalist Muslims.

It is my conviction that Muslims would profit by allowing
themselves to respond to both internal and external criticism.
Faith is indeed faith. But faith without a basis of rationality and
historicity is open to ridicule. The objective in a religious system is as important as the subjective. Muslims would do well to
recognize this.

Future Direction Within Islam

One Muslim author has identified five schools of thought
which are operative today in Islam. The first is that of the tradi-
tionalists. These so-called no-changers are allergic to any
alteration of Islam as presently found in the world. The second
group desires to shift emphasis from the comprehensive to the
private. This dual-domain world view translates into something like the separation of church and state. Third, there are
the apologists. They are totally committed to the truthfulness
of Islam and seek to defend its veracity before a doubting
world. Usually this small group of defenders engages in superficial rhetoric rather than dealing in depth with substantial issues. The fourth school is that of the revivalists who want
Muslims to retrace history and recover the pristine purity of
first-century Islam. Last are the modernists who seek to express Islam in up-to-date terminology. They are convinced of

58. Charles Malik, "Introduction," in *God and Man in Contemporary Islamic Thought*, ed. Charles Malik (Beirut: American University of Beirut,
1972), p. 88.

the relevance of Islam for the twentieth century. But they see the need to adapt unchanging principles and truth to the sophisticated age of modernity in which man now finds himself.[59]

> The very fact that after independence most of the Muslim countries are trying to bring their laws into conformity with the Quran and the Sunnah and are anxious that no law is passed which is in any way repugnant to the teachings of the Quran and the Sunnah shows the trend of thought in the modern Muslim world. This pro-Islam trend is found not only in the field of jurisprudence but in other branches of life also, e.g., in various countries efforts are being made to Islamicise education; likewise efforts are being made for the revival of the socioeconomic moral ideals of Islam. The Muslims are trying slowly but steadily to rediscover themselves. They fully realize that they had deviated from the *Siratul Mustaqim*—and they are making sincere efforts to find the Path. Individual life and collective life according to the will of God was translated into the context of his times by the Holy Prophet; and with the ever-resounding words of Divine Revelation and the inspiring example of our Prophet, we Muslims are determined to transform our individual and collective lives as desired by God in the modern context.[60]

The pressing question for Muslims relates to the determination of what that transformation means in the modern age. Certainly the answer given to that question would be expressed in antithetical terms by such influential Muslims as Rahman and Khomeini. It is likely both are correct. Muslim *ummah* is not a simplistic homogeneous reality. Its heterogeneity demands many varying expressions of community.

It seems obvious that, in spite of such heterogeneity, the dominant trend today is toward a return to the fundamentals of Islam. Writing in 1971, J. Spencer Trimingham observed that "Islam is clung to because of its social and cultural implications, but its spiritual power has weakened."[61] It is doubtful if

59. Inamullah Khan, "Islam in the Contemporary World," in *God and Man in Contemporary Islamic Thought*, ed. Charles Malik (Beirut: American University of Beirut, 1972), p. 11.

60. Ibid., p. 12.

61. J. Spencer Trimingham, *The Sufi Orders in Islam* (London: Oxford University Press, 1971), p. 249.

Trimingham would declare Islamic spiritual power weak in the present context of Muslim resurgence. As more Muslims embrace fundamentalism the cause of Islamic *ummah* is strengthened. A Muslim of prophetic insight wrote words that were penned in the chaos of the Second World War. For many Muslims these words still capture the optimism and confidence they have in the ultimate triumph of their cause:

> Therefore, let us shake off despair; let us take a step forward; let us keep steady our ambitions. With constant discipline, with will and determination to march onward, and with correct understanding of the essentials of "Imam" (true faith) taught by the Quran, let us strive and continue to strive. Know that if we do so our hopes and aspirations will soon be realised.[62]

62. Amir Shakib Arsalan, *Our Decline and Its Causes*, trans. M. A. Shakoor (Lahore: Shaikh Muhammad Ashraf, 1944), p. 135.

4

The Structure
of Christian Community

In order to consider the possibility of Muslim converts remaining within the *ummah* of Islam, it is necessary to examine Christian community from the same perspectives that we have surveyed the brotherhood of Islam. What is the biblical position on the mystical, spiritual, and symbolic community of believers in Christ? How does the theory of brotherhood translate into practical institutional forms? The gospel is supracultural but its manifestation will emerge within each culture where it takes hold. Will there be similarities of expression? Should each Christian community look so similar that there evolves an international Christian *ummah* on the formal level? That is, do we encourage every cluster of believers, whether in Senegal or Brunei, to sing "Amazing Grace" and pray in comfortable postures?

Other questions arise. What of the cataclysmic divisions that have taken place among Christians? Separations of Roman Catholic, Eastern Orthodox, and innumerable Protestant denominations can only cause the observer to shake his head in bewilderment. Each group claims hermeneutical truth and tends to inflate its own "uniqueness" to a position nearing that of the third heaven. Political considerations regarding the separation of church and state add to the confusion. Muslims often point to Northern Ireland as an example of hatred and violence within the body of Christ.

Do we applaud diversity or repent in shame that Satan has weakened Christian brotherhood through fragmentation? Is it proper to extend our support to the ecumenical movement or should we see such efforts as a demonic tool that weakens the witness of biblical Christianity? Is the Lord pleased that nationals identify themselves by the foreign mission to which they are related rather than by the Savior to whom they belong? I have heard Asian evangelists introducing themselves to each other by saying, "I am New Zealand"; "I am English"; "I am American"; and "I am Swedish"! They were simply referring to the missionary societies which paid their salaries. How repulsive it would be for a Muslim to overhear such a conversation.

This chapter will seek to define and describe Christian *ummah*. The last chapter will explore legitimate perimeters wherein the brotherhood of believers can be expressed within the *ummah* of Islam.

The Biblical Basis of Christian Community

Perhaps the briefest definition of Christian community is found in Matthew 18:20: "For where two or three have gathered together in My name, there I am in their midst."

"One person is not enough. Church is a community of people gathered around Jesus, committed to him, worshipping him, and ready to serve his kingdom in the world. People gathered around Jesus is the irreducible minimum of the church."[1]

From the fifth century B.C. onward, the Greek word *ekklesia* referred to an assembly of citizens who gathered to discuss their welfare. An example of this usage is found in Acts 19. During Paul's third missionary journey, the silversmiths of Ephesus were fearful that their trade would be adversely affected by his preaching. They therefore provoked a demonstration against Paul and his companions. In response, the town clerk urged the crowd to quiet themselves and to allow their complaints to move through the courts in an orderly manner. In verse 39 the word *ekklesia* describes the group of men who settle disputes, that is, the "lawful assembly." In verse 41 the same word designates the riotous crowd. Both instances refer to an assembly of people. *Ekklesia* did not inherently connote a religious gathering.

1. Howard A. Snyder, "The Church as Community: Subculture or Counterculture?" *Christianity Today*, 8 April 1983, p. 29.

But Paul then chooses this same word and fills it with a powerful new spiritual content.

> In these early letters of Paul, the term *ekklesia* consistently re-
> fers to actual gatherings of Christians as such, or to Christians
> in a local area conceived or defined as a regularly-assembling
> community. This means that "church" has a distinctly dy-
> namic rather than static character. It is a regular occurrence
> rather than an ongoing reality. The word does not describe all
> the Christians who live in a particular locality if they do not in
> fact gather or when they are not in fact gathering. Nor does it
> refer to the sum total of Christians in a region or scattered
> throughout the world at any particular point of time. And never
> during this period is the term applied to the building in which
> Christians meet. Whether we are considering the smaller
> gatherings of only some Christians in a city or the larger meet-
> ings involving the whole Christian population, it is in the home
> of one of the members that *ekklesia* is held—for example in the
> "upper room". Not until the third century do we have evidence
> of special buildings being constructed for Christian gather-
> ings and, even then, they were modelled on the room into
> which guests were received in the typical Roman and Greek
> household.[2]

It is interesting to note that the word *church* is now used to designate the institution, the building, and the corporate body of believers. "Church" is a unifying and comprehensive term. In John 17, Christ prays to the Father for the church to

receive eternal life (vv. 2, 24)

know God and Jesus Christ (v. 3)

keep God's Word (v. 6)

be unified (vv. 11, 21–23)

receive Christ's joy (v. 13)

be not of the world while still being in it (vv. 14–16)

go into the world as a witness (v. 18)

be sanctified in truth (v. 19)

How sincerely interested Christ was in the lives of those who

2. Robert J. Banks, *Paul's Idea of Community: The Early House Churches in Their Historical Setting* (Grand Rapids: Eerdmans, 1980), p. 41.

had believed and those who would yet believe. He was committing his whole earthly program to a few novice believers. Such a radical step of faith was vindicated as these men, so inadequate in themselves, were forced to rely upon the resources of God and thus became the instruments of successful Christian witness. This expansion of Christian community is described in Acts 2:41–47.

> So then, those who had received his word were baptized; and there were added that day about three thousand souls. And they were continually devoting themselves to the apostles' teaching and to fellowship, to the breaking of bread and to prayer. And everyone kept feeling a sense of awe; and many wonders and signs were taking place through the apostles. And all those who had believed were together, and had all things in common; and they began selling their property and possessions, and were sharing them with all, as anyone might have need. And day by day continuing with one mind in the temple, and breaking bread from house to house, they were taking their meals together with gladness and sincerity of heart, praising God, and having favor with all the people. And the Lord was adding to their number day by day those who were being saved.

Three thousand new believers formed the first Christian *ummah*. Baptism was the initiatory rite that gave the community a sense of cohesion. Immediately, there was an emphasis on fellowship. How desperately the Christians needed one another. They were "continually" together and "day by day" they met to worship and observe the Lord's Supper. Meals were taken together; a sharing process helped weld the people together in a caring relationship. The result of all this was a natural expansion of the gospel that caused others to be drawn into the orbit of faith. Awe and excitement permeated that early *ummah* of Christians.

This does not mean that serious rifts and divisions did not soon cause fragmentation within the body. Consider the classic passage where Paul forcefully rebukes the early believers:

> Now I exhort you, brethren, by the name of our Lord Jesus Christ, that you all agree, and there be no divisions among you, but you be made complete in the same mind and in the same judgment. For I have been informed concerning you, my brethren, by Chloe's people, that there are quarrels among you. Now I mean this, that each one of you is saying, "I am of Paul," and "I

of Apollos," and "I of Cephas," and "I of Christ." Has Christ
been divided? Paul was not crucified for you, was he? Or were
you baptized in the name of Paul? [1 Cor. 1:10–13]

Paul's writings are laced with urgent pleas for unity among
those coming out of Judaism and into the light of the liberating
gospel of Christ. He had to contend with theological conflicts
and ethnic misunderstandings, as well as personal alienations
such as were found between Euodia and Syntyche (Phil. 4). How
sad it is that human nature moves naturally toward alienation
and fragmentation. It is the norm. Only a concerted effort leads
to unity of purpose and direction. Christians have a poor record
in regard to following biblical exhortations to express oneness
of faith. And yet, such oneness is always before us as the ideal.
We can never totally dismiss unity as unattainable. The Bible
emphasizes an *ummah* that is filled with loving care and service.

G. C. Berkouwer writes of the relationship of the individual
to the community:

> The individual does not disappear behind the vague contours
> of a "totality," but he is liberated from individualization and
> solitariness in order to have a place in this new fellowship. That
> the Lord cares for the sheep includes, not excludes, specific at-
> tention for one lost sheep (Luke 15:4ff). Every individual need
> receives His undivided attention; yet, at the same time, ways
> are opened by which the individual receives a place in a human
> fellowship, ending all individualism. A new, clear light breaks
> through into human relationships, in struggle and frustration,
> fragmentation and dispersion.[3]

The problem is to balance human propensity for individualism with the need to unite individuals in a community. Should
all individualism be ended, as Berkouwer suggests? I think not.
God has not created robots who look alike, think alike, and act
alike. It was the Lord's desire that there be individuality among
his creatures. After a masterly discussion on this subject in
1 Corinthians 12, Paul, in verse 27, sums up: "Now you are
Christ's body, and individually members of it." The analogy of

---

3. G. C. Berkouwer, *The Church*, trans. James E. Davison (Grand Rapids:
Eerdmans, 1976), p. 77.

the human body with individual parts all working together for the good of the body is superb. To me, this is much more expressive than Islam's "cable of God."

Love is the integrating force of community. Within 1 Corinthians 13 we find love defined in all its beauty and sensitivity. With this kind of love as its motivation, Christian community emerges as a strong alternative to all the world has to offer in terms of religions and ideologies. "By this all men will know that you are My disciples, if you have love for one another" (John 13:35). Without this love, the professed *ummah* of believers will be as "noisy gongs and clanging cymbals."

Donald A. Burquest stated, "It is a crucial principle of our existence that each of us needs support from others. Indeed, it could be argued that this is the major driving force behind the notion of the Christian community found in Scripture—we need each other and we belong to each other."[4] C. Rene Padilla, a Latin American evangelical of repute, reinforces Burquest's comment when he observes that "the Bible knows nothing of the human being as an individual in isolation; it knows only of a person as a related being, a person in relation to other people."[5]

Another biblical metaphor which highlights interrelatedness within the Christian *ummah* is that of the "household of God." Israel, in the Old Testament, is frequently referred to as God's house. In the New Testament, verses like Acts 2:36; 1 Timothy 3:15; Hebrews 3:2–6; and 1 Peter 4:17 all describe the church in the same manner. God is the Head of the household and all of the house relates to him in love and obedience. Although God is Head, yet he gives respect to the members of his household by calling them his children.

Acts 15 describes the transition in Christian witness. The initial propagation was directed toward the Jews. Paul, after successfully preaching among Gentiles, went to the Jerusalem council to seek the blessing of the church elders. At that historic moment the church recognized ethnic and cultural diversity in the emerging *ummah* of Christendom. Each culture and people was to be allowed the freedom to create brotherhood ac-

4. Donald A. Burquest, "A Celebration Feast of Forgiveness," *Christianity Today*, 9 April 1982, p. 24.

5. C. Rene Padilla, "The Unity of the Church and the Homogeneous Unit Principle," *International Bulletin of Missionary Research*, vol. 6 (January 1982), p. 23.

cording to local norms as long as these did not conflict with biblical teaching. This did not mean Paul had license to adulterate the gospel or to syncretize biblical truth with pagan belief. It simply meant Christian truth could be expressed in terms that each community could appreciate. There would be a free flow of understanding because of linguistic and cultural sensitivity on the part of the communicator. It was an exciting day in church history when the Jewish leadership at Jerusalem recognized and encouraged the true universality of Christian community!

Berkouwer gives a synopsis of what *ummah* was to have become in church history:

> Because of the nature of the church, as described in the gospel, one could take unity for granted, not in a simplistic or trivial sense, but because the being of the Church, as willed by God, implies unity. This is so clear from the entire New Testament that all disunity, rupture, and schism within Christ's Church, which is His body, appear to be ridiculous and impossible. The New Testament does speak in the plural of "churches" (*ekklesiai*), but that does not signify any rupture or disunity, since different groups of believers in different places are meant; they together form the Church of Christ (cf. Gal. 1:2; Acts 15:41; 16:5, etc.). It is a unity that cannot be affected by any "*diaspora*". The light of grace and of reconciliation falls on this one Church. She has not arisen from her own initiative, but has been called, gathered, and chosen as the people of God, obtained by the blood of the Cross (cf. Acts 20:28). Who can think here of multiplicity, or many churches, or of divided churches?[6]

Divided churches there are! The next section will briefly overview the sad state of Christian community, both historically and contemporarily. This is a necessary although painful process if we are to understand the dissonance found within Islamic *ummah*. It is so much easier to criticize others when we neglect to give proper weight to our own failures.

Denominational Fragmentation

Lesslie Newbigin, a missionary statesman with several decades of ministry in India, tells of being challenged by young Indians who have visited the West:

6. Berkouwer, *The Church*, p. 30.

What right do you think you have to come here with your foreign religion? Do you imagine that you have the full truth? Do
you Europeans suppose that you—with your frightful wars,
your hydrogen bombs, and your dirty films and magazines—
are in a position to offer spiritual leadership to the world? Can
you really think that you, of all people, are entitled to invite the
whole world into your fellowship?[7]

That angry outburst demands a thoughtful response. Is the
Indian guilty of giving a careless caricature of Christian influence and community or is there significant truth within his
statement? If it is basically true, then how did we ever end up in
such a sad state?

An intellectual Muslim professor, Badru D. Kateregga, adds
his critique:

While appreciating that the Church has accepted cultural diversity, we learn that at times this has led to misunderstanding
among Christians, even occasionally causing divisions in the
Church. In contrast, Islam has come up with a single universal
Islamic culture, generally common to the entire *umma*. Although there is some diversity in the *umma*, ideally, the *umma*
surpasses ethnic, national, linguistic, and racial boundaries. It
is for this reason that Muslims cannot talk of African, Turkish,
Chinese, or American Islam. Perhaps it is for similar reasons
that the *umma* has not experienced so many divisions as char-
acterize the Church today.[8]

Kateregga has made an interesting comment about "universal Islamic culture." His point deals basically with Islamic ritualistic uniformity. Prayers, for instance, are performed in the
same manner in Arabic in every part of the Muslim world. He
looks at Christianity and finds not only cultural and linguistic
variety, but most importantly, theological diversity and contradiction. How did it all come about?

Kenneth Scott Latourette, one of the great church historians
of the twentieth century, stated, "Never have all those who have
professed themselves to be followers of Christ been one. From

7. Lesslie Newbigin, *Is Christ Divided? A Plea for Christian Unity in a
Revolutionary Age* (Grand Rapids: Eerdmans, 1961), p. 21.
8. Badru D. Kateregga and David W. Shenk, *Islam and Christianity: A Muslim and a Christian in Dialogue* (Grand Rapids: Eerdmans, 1981), p. 148.

the first generation of Christians, divisions have existed."[9] Later, in the fourth century, important church councils were called to deal with heresies. The resulting statements of faith and denunciations of deviance assisted in giving some semblance of homogeneity to Christian *ummah*. But throughout the first fifteen hundred years of church history there was little to cheer the heart of the purist. Religion was often corrupted, with the priestly hierarchy favoring the rich and fleecing the poor.

As a Protestant, I am grateful for my heritage which is identified with Martin Luther and John Calvin. In the midst of spiritual darkness came these two men whose courage and forthrightness radically altered the church scene in Europe. They were emboldened of God to rebuke evil and proclaim righteousness. Thousands became their followers. Their accomplishments in leadership and writing are impressive.

Yet these men were the products of an age in which intolerance and coercion were standard. As we look backward from a twentieth-century perspective, it is hard to understand some of the things they condoned in the name of Jesus Christ—almost as hard to comprehend as the violence perpetrated by Iranian and Iraqi Muslims in the name of Allah!

For instance, word came to Luther that some believers were being induced to renounce Christ and become Jewish proselytes. In great anger, he wrote a tract which recommended that all Jews be deported to Palestine. If some should refuse to go, "they should be forbidden to practice usery, should be compelled to earn their living on the land, synagogues should be burned, and their books including the Bible should be taken away from them."[10] Such a lack of forbearance and Christian charity seems shocking.

The Anabaptists were a great problem to the Roman Catholics, Lutherans, and Zwinglians. This group of passivists rejected government oaths and marriages outside the faith. One of their most controversial acts was the discontinuance of infant baptism and acceptance of adult believers' baptism. Luther felt this was a direct threat to his teaching and would

9. Kenneth Scott Latourette, *A History of Christianity* (New York: Harper and Row, 1975), pp. 4–5.
10. Roland H. Bainton, *Here I Stand: A Life of Martin Luther* (New York: Mentor, 1950), p. 297.

produce a heathen society apart from the church. Philipp Melanchthon composed a memorandum which charged the Anabaptists with sedition and blasphemy. Luther lent his prestige to the persecution of these sincere God-seekers by signing the memorandum of 1536 and writing at the bottom, "I assent. Although it seems cruel to punish them with the sword, it is crueler that they condemn the ministry of the Word and have no well-grounded doctrine and suppress the truth and in this way seek to subvert the civil order."[11] They, along with hundreds of others, were executed, some by drowning, some by beheading, and others by burning.

Calvin was a theological genius. His *Institutes of the Christian Religion* remains obligatory reading for any scholar seriously pursuing the academic discipline of theology. Calvin's insights have influenced millions. Yet, he, too, was intolerant of those who disagreed with him. Michael Servetus was an intellectual who accomplished much in life. At one point, he made a personal study of the Bible which convinced him that Jesus was not God, but simply a good man; that children are born innocent; that babies ought not to be baptized; and that man determines his own eternal destiny. Calvin was overwhelmed by such heresy. He put forth thirty-nine accusations against Servetus. They debated against each other in the harshest manner. Anger and even hatred put distance between two of the great intellectuals of the age.

Calvin arranged for the council to arrest Servetus. He brought forth charges which sought to prove that the heresy of Servetus was threatening the church of Christ. Although Calvin had no part in the verdict to execute this condemned heretic, he did approve of it. His only act of mercy was to urge execution by beheading rather than burning at the stake—a recommendation the council did not follow.

Today there is a stone on the spot where Servetus died. It was put there long afterward by followers of Calvin. On the stone is this inscription in French: "As reverent and grateful sons of Calvin, our great Reformer, repudiating his mistake, which was the mistake of his age, and according to the true principles of the Reformation and the Gospel, holding fast to freedom of

11. Ibid., p. 295.

conscience, we erect this monument of reconciliation on this 27th of October, 1903."[12]

How do we evaluate a "mistake of [an] age"? Will Muslims look back from the year 2300 and declare their deeds in the late twentieth century to be acts of the age? Will this modify any harsh assessment of what many people today consider to be dastardly acts of ultrafanaticism? Do we excuse Calvin by glossing over what he must certainly have considered to be a spiritual position? Is sincerity adequate? These are hard questions.

Undoubtedly, Calvin and Luther were men of God. Just as certainly, these men had feet of clay. These specific illustrations of their fallibility were shared with the purpose of helping us all to moderate our harshness toward Muslim leaders who seem to be unspiritual and inconsistent. To some extent, we in Protestantism have to deal with similar historical realities.

The use of the word *denomination* to describe a religious group first came into popularity during the early years of the Evangelical Revival. John Wesley's use of this term has been frequently quoted: "I refuse to be distinguished from other men by any but the common principles of Christianity. I renounce and detest all other marks of distinction. But from real Christians, of whatever denomination, I earnestly desire not to be distinguished at all. Dost thou love and fear God? It is enough! I give thee the right hand of fellowship."[13]

As the early settlers came to America from Europe they brought with them a felt need for *ummah*. They were in a strange land, a new and frightening environment. Attack from hostile Indians was an ever-present possibility. The Pilgrims were drawn close one to another in the face of loneliness, adversity, and danger. A pious faith in God was central in the lives of the immigrants to the New World.

As new settlers arrived, diversity of belief and theological conviction multiplied within the community. Early in the eighteenth century, voluntary national associations of believers be-

12. Thea B. Van Halsema, *This Was John Calvin* (1959; Grand Rapids: Baker, 1981), p. 199.

13. Winthrop S. Hudson, "Denominationalism as a Basis for Ecumenicity: A Seventeenth Century Conception," in *Denominationalism*, ed. Russell E. Richey (Nashville: Abingdon, 1977), p. 21.

gan to be formed. These "denominations" spread quickly throughout the colonies, giving institutional form to those of similar belief and practice. These institutions sponsored colleges, hospitals, publishing societies, and mission outreaches. Denominationalism, then, was launched in a nation where it would proliferate as it had not done since Pentecost. In most countries, five or six major denominations have become prominent. But no country can match the hundreds of denominations that are found within the borders of the United States. Much of this tendency can be understood by pondering a statement by Elmer L. Towns:

> There is no other nation in history quite like the United States. We are a nation created by liberty, individualism, and revolt against European forms. Our nation is nurtured by pragmatism, industrialism, mass media, and mobility; creating conditions in which the church/denomination thrives or dies. Every church is a product of its times and culture. The American church is no different.[14]

Americans are individualists, admittedly, but such individualism is most comfortably expressed within community. An American may want to attend a church of a small denomination which has an outgoing, well-educated preacher; a pastor's wife who is unobtrusive; a church covenant which denounces use of alcoholic beverages, makes no mention of movie attendance, takes a proinerrancy view of biblical authority, is eschatologically pretribulational, and is anticharismatic; a congregation made up of people in the upper middle class; a building with a lighted cross on top, well-kept lawns, and padded pews. All of these preferences indicate individualism. But the American does not desire to attend such a church alone. He wants to choose an *ummah* in which he, along with others, is very much at home. Homogeneity is important to an American within his choice of community life. If he does not find a church that meets 75 percent of his desires, he will likely commute long distances so he can attend such a place of worship. If nothing is available, it is quite possible he will gather a like-minded group around him and start a new church!

14. Elmer L. Towns, *Is the Day of the Denomination Dead?* (Nashville: Nelson, 1973), p. 12.

Many are the Christian leaders who fervently denounce fragmentation within the *ummah* of the church. They deplore the individualism that has, in their view, led to separations within families, churches, and communities because people disagree over minor points of doctrine and practice. These thoughtful leaders postulate an all-inclusive denomination, with reasonable autonomy for member churches, as the corrective for fragmentation and divisiveness.

"Will a Christianity which has drawn all mankind to professed allegiance be able to achieve world-wide unity? Will all men through it become a single brotherhood? Will there be an all-embracing Church which will know no strife of parties or nations or theologies and no rivalries among strong leaders? Obviously that time is at best far distant."[15]

Latourette's assessment is accurate. Even two Presbyterian or two Lutheran bodies negotiate for years before they can merge. Our differences have gone deep into our individual and collective psyches. But what is at least understandable in our predominantly Christian culture is actually deplorable in a Hindu city like Madras. Suppose two Hindu brothers go to two different mission schools and are genuinely converted. Because of differences between the two churches, these new believers, who are members of the same physical and spiritual families, may be unable to take communion together!

In one square mile of Madras there are thirteen different churches. Which of them is the perplexed Hindu to join, if he desires to follow the Christ of the Bible? Each of the churches has some teaching that is at variance with that of the other twelve. Yet, each piously affirms the Bible as its basis of faith and practice.[16]

In some countries a partial answer to the confusion generated by multiple denominations has been the formation of councils of churches that express a unified *ummah* to the on-looking non-Christian community. The World Evangelical Fellowship is one such body which brings together both churches and missions on a national basis.

Howard A. Snyder has made a plea for a return to simplicity of church structure and worship:

15. Latourette, *A History of Christianity*, p. 67.
16. Stephen Neill, *Men of Unity* (London: SCM, 1960), p. 8.

Sacrifice, priesthood, tabernacle—all instituted through Moses in the Old Testament. Theologically all passed away with the coming of Christ and the birth of the church. Historically, all passed away with the destruction of Jerusalem in A.D. 70. They had become irrelevant, anachronistic.

And so the church was born without priesthood, sacrifice or tabernacle because the church and Christ together were all three. The church faithfully embodied this truth for more than a century, and overran the Roman Empire.

The great temptation of the organized church has been to re-instate these three elements among God's people: to turn community into an institution. Historically, the church has at times succumbed. Returning to the spirit of the Old Testament, she has set up a professional priesthood, turned the Eucharist into a new sacrificial system and built great cathedrals. When this happens, a return to faithfulness must mean a return—in both soteriology and ecclesiology—to the profound simplicity of the New Testament. Usually, however, reformation in doctrine has not been accomplished by sufficiently radical reform in church structure.[17]

What does "profound simplicity" mean to Snyder? All church buildings are to be sold. Offerings are given to the poor. Congregations of more than two hundred members are to be divided in two. Worship takes place in storefronts, garages, or small, cheap rented halls. Sunday-school promotion as well as other church publicity is dropped. Small Bible studies in homes take the place of the midweek prayer service. Pastors no longer receive salaries from the church. They engage in secular employment for their needed income. In effect, they become trained laymen instead of salaried professionals. Laymen, then, take the lead in all activities of the church, including the preaching. Church services are aimed toward believers, not non-Christians. The church meets on a day and at a time most convenient for the congregation.[18]

Would such a radical departure from the norm enhance *ummah* on a local level? Perhaps, but what about on a broader

17. Howard A. Snyder, *The Problem of Wine Skins: Church Structure in a Technological Age* (Downers Grove: Inter-Varsity, 1975), p. 58.
18. Ibid., pp. 23–24.

scale? It would seem to me each church would become a law unto itself, resulting in an even greater diversity of practice and doctrinal interpretation than we have today. At least denominations and informal church groupings offer guidelines that help to regulate deviation.

Are we driven to the despair of one author who assesses the church of Christ as "hopelessly divided" and then goes on to say, "We are forced to ask ourselves whether God's work has failed"?[19] Or what of the cynicism, perhaps justified, of the famous Plymouth Brethren theologian F. F. Bruce:

> If Peter and Paul could come back to earth for a week or two—say, to one of the cities, such as Rome, which they knew in their day—where would they find most congenial fellowship on a Sunday morning? If this question were asked in some mixed audiences, the questioner would have to beg his hearers to answer one at a time; otherwise there would be a deafening babel of conflicting replies. Many of the replies, however, could be reduced to a common formula: With us, of course![20]

But through it all, "listen carefully, and you will hear today the muffled cry and sigh for community."[21] That is, without doubt, a worldwide cry. It knows no cultural, ethnic, or religious boundary. Muslims and Christians alike desire a deep, meaningful bond between coreligionists. Both communities are grieved because of factions which divide and engender strife from within.

Political Issues

In a celebrated passage Jesus identified his view of the believer's relation to the state:

> Then the Pharisees went and counseled together how they might trap Him in what He said. And they sent their disciples to

19. F. R. Coad, "Christian Unity," in *In God's Community: Essays on the Church and Its Ministry*, ed. David J. Ellis and W. Ward Gasque (Wheaton: Shaw, 1978), pp. 115–16.

20. F. F. Bruce, "Lessons from the Early Church," in *In God's Community: Essays on the Church and Its Ministry*, ed. David J. Ellis and W. Ward Gasque (Wheaton: Shaw, 1978), pp. 153–54.

21. Snyder, "The Church as Community," p. 28.

> Him, along with the Herodians, saying, "Teacher, we know that
> You are truthful and teach the way of God in truth, and defer to
> no one; for You are not partial to any. Tell us, therefore, what do
> You think? Is it lawful to give a poll-tax to Caesar, or not?" But
> Jesus perceived their malice, and said, "Why are you testing
> Me, you hypocrites? Show Me the coin used for the poll-tax."
> And they brought Him a denarius. And He said to them,
> "Whose likeness and inscription is this?" They said to Him,
> "Caesar's." Then He said to them, "Then render to Caesar the
> things that are Caesar's; and to God the things that are God's."
> And hearing this, they marveled, and leaving Him, they went
> away. [Matt. 22:15–22; see also Mark 12:13–17; Luke 20:20–26]

Caesar and his empire would soon be engaging in a bloody
persecution of the followers of Christ. Surely Christ, through
his divine power of foreknowledge, was aware of the atrocities
that would be inflicted upon his small, nonviolent band of disciples. Also, the imperialistic designs of Rome were clearly
evident in first-century Palestine. Caesar was no friend of godliness or biblical truth.

Was Christ a revolutionary or a reactionary? This is a debate
I am happy to leave with the theologians. Suffice it to say, Jesus
did not advocate the violent overthrow of Roman rule. He was
more concerned with the hypocrisy of the Pharisees than the
colonialism of Rome.

This simple passage in Matthew has often been quoted as the
New Testament argument for separation of church and state.
Jesus made the distinction between the reign of God, which is
spiritual and eternal, and temporal rule. The power of government, apart from a token given to Jewish authorities, was in the
hands of Romans. It was necessary to have an authority to for-
mulate and enforce laws, or society would degenerate into
chaos. Christ made no significant point of the temporal authority of Palestine being that of a foreign power.

Paul also made use of Roman law.

> The apostle Paul is standing before Caesar's judgment seat and
> crying out, "I appeal unto Caesar!" (Acts 25:11). How can this
> be? During the period of Jewish persecution, Paul and other
> members of the early Church survived because of the protect-
> ing care of the Roman magistrates and rulers. In an important
> period of the primitive Church, the Roman Empire fulfilled its

God-given duty of protecting the innocent from ill-treatment or death for religious convictions.[22]

There is, however, some ambivalence in the early church leaders' regard for state law. Paul was happy to appeal to Caesar rather than be sent back to Jerusalem to face his accusers (Acts 25). Yet, Peter took part in a jailbreak which led to the execution of innocent guards by King Herod (Acts 12). One wonders whether we do not see a great deal of pragmatism in their actions.

Samuel P. Schlorff represents a rather extreme hermeneutical position in regard to the church/state controversy: "In the Bible, the Church is seen as an apolitical, supracultural, spiritual, eschatological fellowship, acting somewhat as a leaven upon society, but never being, or attempting to become identified with society."[23] Liberation theologians would take strong exception to such a view. A book which well articulates the evangelical appeal for involvement within society is Orlando Costas's well-documented work.[24] This brilliant Latin American theologian takes the lead in prodding fellow evangelicals to show a concern for the poor and oppressed of the Third World.

The Bible speaks frequently of the kingdom of God. Christians do not believe that political power can establish or maintain the kingdom of God. When his followers urged him to become a politician, Jesus never accepted such a worldly opportunity to achieve fame and fortune. Christ, by example, conveyed to mankind that the kingdom of God becomes present in the world through redemptive suffering rather than political caucuses.

This kingdom is not ostentatious, but rather quiet in its outworking. Through it, God's love and mercy are introduced into a hateful and vengeful world. Its appeal is spiritual reality, not self-serving gain. The *ummah* of Christ's disciples is the vehicle of the kingdom. From the community there issues forth a love which irresistibly draws many into its orbit of influence.

22. J. Marcellus Kik, *Church and State: The Story of Two Kingdoms* (New York: Nelson, 1963), p. 8.

23. Samuel P. Schlorff, ed., *Discipleship in Islamic Society* (Upper Darby, Penn.: North Africa Mission, 1981), pp. 34–35.

24. Orlando Costas, *Christ Outside the Gate: Mission Beyond Christendom* (Maryknoll, N.Y.: Orbis, 1982).

The church, then, in spite of its many weaknesses, is called to be a sign among nonbelievers of the kingdom of God. This kingdom transcends every cultural and ethnic boundary. It refuses to be owned by any religious or political system. It cannot be institutionally bound.[25]

Have Christians been able to adequately grasp such an exalted view of the kingdom of God? Regrettably, the natural tendency of the church has been toward institutionalization. All too frequently the institution reaches out to grasp temporal powers. This is piously done in the name of God, but, shamefully, more often is for the glory of ecclesiastical authorities. The history of the Roman Catholic Church in Europe is replete with examples of this church/state tension. Many of these actions have caused great embarrassment to true, devout believers in all denominations.

Until 300, Christian *ummah* was scattered and informal but with deep roots. Believers were prepared to lay down their lives for their faith in Christ. There was a natural and deep bond between those who were willing to sacrifice everything temporal for the sake of gaining Christ. It was a sobering experience to go down into the catacombs just outside of Rome and view this hiding place of Christians during this early period of history. Their altars and etchings on the walls have been preserved, thus providing a vivid reminder of the cost involved in being a follower of Christ in a time of persecution. Yet, the church flourished! It had no status, no large institutions, and no hierarchy. Christ was the dynamic in the hearts and lives of thousands of simple, devout believers. There was a compulsiveness about their witness. Lives had been freed from the slavery and bondage of idols and spiritual darkness. The state was the oppressor and the force of Antichrist. There was a clear dichotomy between the forces of evil and good. The state was no friend of the children of light.

But then a dramatic event occurred. In 312 the emperor Constantine faced the heathen Maxentius in a battle on the outskirts of Rome. Constantine was unsure of the outcome of such an important confrontation. The night before the engagement, Constantine dreamed that he saw a cross with the inscription:

25. Kateregga and Shenk, *Islam and Christianity,* p. 53.

"By this sign thou shalt conquer! The battle with Maxentius was won and the Edict of Milan was issued the following year. Through this edict Christian societies received, for the first time, the acknowledgment and sanction of law. At this point in history, Christianity and politics, along with the spiritual and the secular, all began to merge.

The Edict of Milan is a document of toleration, one that is quite remarkable for the age in which it was written. The following is a portion of the Edict:

> We believe that among the very first things to be settled are what related to the reverence due the Divinity,—an enactment which may give both to the Christians and to all others free power of following whatever religion each man may have preferred; that whatever of divine there is in the heavenly seat may be pacified and be propitious to us, and to all who sit under our authority. . . . We have given free and absolute power to these Christians of exercising their own religion. And as this indulgence has been granted to them, so you understand that a similarly free and unrestricted power is, with a view to the peace of our time, conceded to all others as to their own religion or observance, that each may have the free liberty of the worship which he prefers; for we desire that no religion may have its honour diminished by us.[26]

Paganism, by a stroke of the pen, ceased to be the state religion of the Roman Empire. All religions were tolerated. Christianity, however, was accorded a preferred position. It was later that Christianity became the official religion of the state. Constantine believed paganism would slowly decline and thus he refrained from passing laws or restrictions against pagan priests or their temples.

During Constantine's reign, Christian clergy were exempted from military and civil duties, Christian slaves were freed, gifts to churches were legalized, and Sunday began to be officially recognized as a holiday. Constantine became a bishop in the church and took part in ecclesiastical decisions as a member of the assembly. It was not long, however, before he was recognized as the bishop of bishops and the de facto head of the

26. Kik, *Church and State*, p. 40.

church. Constantine delayed baptism until just before his death. This was due to the common belief that baptism brought about the forgiveness of all sins. Constantine was anxious to have the maximum number expiated.

In subsequent years there was persecution of pagans as Christian temporal and ecclesiastical power became functionally one. As this process evolved, Christianity began to lose its spiritual focus. When bishops could influence decisions of state, they opened themselves to corruption. Recently, I saw a painting which depicted this period of church history. The setting was a room exquisitely decorated with deep carpets and full-length velvet curtains. Cushioned chairs trimmed in gold were placed around the room. Pictures of church authorities were hung on the wood-paneled walls. Several arrogant-looking churchmen dressed in purple robes and wearing skullcaps were standing in the center of the room. Some were smoking; others held wine glasses. To insert incongruity into the picture, the artist added two shabbily dressed peasants who were obsequiously bowing before the priests with petition papers in their outstretched hands. The church had come of age! It now had wealth and influence. How sad that for more than one thousand years this alliance between church and state was a powerful deterrent to spiritual reality.

A few specific illustrations from this period will assist our understanding. In 800, Charlemagne, the Roman Emperor, knelt in prayer before the altar of Saint Peter's as Pope Leo III placed a golden crown upon his head. The people shouted in unison, "To Charles Augustus, crowned by God, the great and pacific emperor of the Romans, life and victory!" The significance of the coronation has been debated, but to many, it meant the pope had the right to crown secular rulers as well as the authority to terminate their reign.

Gregory VII, better known as Hildebrand, was pope from 1073 to 1085. He wrote *Dictatus Papae*, which defines papal authority in twenty-seven affirmations. One excerpt from his writing powerfully highlights the church/state relationship: "The Roman Church was founded by God alone; the Roman pope alone can with right be called universal; he alone may use the imperial insignia; his feet only shall be kissed by all princes; he may dispose the emperors; he himself may be judged by no one; the Roman Church has never erred, nor will it err in all eternity."[27]

Such a dogmatic statement is overwhelming. But one must remember the context of the age and how such a power structure became almost impregnable over the centuries. If we are surprised at the acquiescence of the public, it would be good to recall how charismatic leaders of our own century have been able to sway the millions.

Boniface VIII (1294–1303) celebrated the jubilee in 1300. Sitting on the imperial throne, crowned with the triregnum, and girded with the secular sword, he cried out, "I am Caesar; I am Emperor." His famous bull, *Unam sanctam*, states,

> The spiritual and the material sword are both in the power of the Church, but the former is to be used by the Church, the latter only for it. The former is in the hand of the priest; the latter is no doubt in the hand of the monarch and the soldier, but it is to be used at the pontiff's beck and will: the one sword must be subject to the other, the temporal to the spiritual.[28]

The sense of *ummah* among Christians was not strengthened during this period of history. One might speculate that an alliance of church and state would contribute to unity. There would be no conflict of loyalty between divergent forces of society and religion. Unfortunately, such a merger serves only to corrupt rather than to edify. Spiritual emphasis is muted under the secularizing influence of the profane.

Calvin, in his day, was the most powerful person in Geneva. He has been charged with setting up a theocracy in which he and the clergy dominated the civil administration of the city. In fact, Calvin never occupied a political or civil office. He is on record as opposing church involvement in political affairs:

> For as no city or town can exist without a magistracy and civil polity; so the Church of God ... stands in need of a certain spiritual polity; which, however, is entirely distinct from civil polity, and is so far from obstructing or weakening it, that, on the

27. Ibid., p. 6.
28. Ibid., p. 66.

contrary, it highly conduces to its assistance and advancement. This power or jurisdiction, therefore, will, in short, be no other than an order instituted for the preservation of the spiritual polity.[29]

Yet Calvin, just by the force of his personality, was the person to whom civil authorities looked for advice and direction. They were reluctant to make legislation which would be in opposition to Calvin's views. He was regarded as being a spiritual leader who had an intimate relationship with God. What legislator would desire to be at odds with the will of the Almighty? "Calvin's interest and genius were such that there was scarcely a facet of Genevan life that he was not consulted about and his advice asked."[30]

Missionary work in the period of the Reformers was regarded as the work of the civil authorities. Melanchthon, Calvin, Ulrich Zwingli, and Martin Bucer held to this view. It is likely they had been influenced by their observation of Roman Catholic countries. Priests accompanied soldiers and seamen in their colonizing. Protestant mission work began with the political and economic expansion of such Protestant countries as Holland, England, and Denmark.[31]

America presents an interesting case study of the interrelatedness of religious and secular influences in civil government. The Constitution provides that "no religious test shall ever be required as a qualification to any office or public trust under the United States." The First Amendment to the Constitution further stipulates that "Congress shall make no law respecting an establishment of religion, or prohibiting the free exercise thereof."

What is the correct interpretation of these two brief statements? Would the average American agree with Erich W. Bethmann?

Separation of the State and church is one of the fundamental principles of American life; any mixing of the two is rejected almost with abhorrence. Americans are living in a completely secularized society. . . . Religion is a private concern. The indi-

29. Ibid., p. 81.
30. Ibid., p. 83.
31. Costas, *Christ Outside the Gate*, p. 59.

vidual enjoys complete freedom in choosing the manner and form of worship most suitable to his personal needs. This is the American way of handling the delicate subject of state-church relationship. It results in a clear separation. Church and state are considered to be of two different realms.[32]

We who are evangelicals react strongly to the proposition that we are destined to live in a "completely secularized society." Church and state are distinct realms, but it cannot be argued that overlap was never forseen by the authors of the Constitution. The founding fathers of the United States were for the most part Christian or at least favorably disposed toward Christian ethics and standards. They simply desired to be sure the fledging nation was not committed to any exclusive form of religious expression. Sectarianism was not to be advocated by the Constitution.

Christian expression is woven into the very fiber of government. An evangelical chaplain opens Senate meetings with prayer. Oaths of office are taken on the Bible. Our coins bear the phrase *In God We Trust*. The Pledge of Allegiance declares the nation to be under the authority of God. Thanksgiving, Christmas, and Easter are special occasions when the linkage of government and religion is apparent. Recent presidents have overtly professed their faith in Christ as their personal Savior.

The framers of the Constitution felt it necessary to erect a legal wall between church and state. This barrier, however, was not to be of a moral or spiritual character. Legislation has often been based on biblical ethical teaching.

All of this has not been accomplished without tension. One example would be the passage of the Eighteenth Amendment. National prohibition was regarded as a positive Christian position. Yet, soon after the passage of the amendment, many sincere Christians concluded that more harm than good would be done if prohibition were allowed to continue.

What is true of the liquor question is true in greater or less degree of all attempts to enforce upon the entire community by

32. Erich W. Bethmann, *Steps Toward Understanding Islam*, Kohinur series, no. 4 (Washington, D.C.: American Friends of the Middle East, 1966), p. 27.

legislation standards which can be maintained only in a truly Christian society. Accordingly we see a gradual relaxation of pressure by the churches in the interests of uniform legislation in the field of public morals (e.g., marriage and divorce, Sunday observance, etc.). This has been accompanied, it is to be feared, by a breaking down of standards in the churches themselves, which makes it increasingly difficult to draw any clear line between the morality appropriate to a Christian and that of the community at large.[33]

William Adams Brown has identified the conflict a Christian encounters when he ponders whether it is right to seek to impose his moral and ethical standards on others through legislative processes. For instance, it is a criminal offense to sell marijuana but not to sell liquor. Both drugs affect behavior and can result in causing harm to innocent people. Pornography contributes to the breakup of homes. Should it not be legislated out of existence? Abortion is felt by many to be nothing short of murder. Why is it allowed to continue? We live in a pluralistic society. Differences of opinion abound. Unfortunately, even true Christians hold varying views on many of the social issues of the day. These controversies will continue.

Even with these apparent tensions, few would opt for the Islamic practice of mosque/state unification. Most of us support Christian influence in government, but stop short of any type of integration which could lead to a situation described by educator Humphrey Lee: "There must be no coercion of the state by the church. The church with political power has been a church in danger. When the church enters the political field, the church is either inept or proficient. When inept, the church makes itself ridiculous: when proficient in political actions, the church becomes proficient in deviousness and compromise."[34]

Sociological Considerations

Man is a social creature. Many sociological studies have revealed the necessity of linkage between humans. Loneliness

33. William Adams Brown, *Church and State in Contemporary America* (New York: Scribner's, 1936), p. 125.
34. Joseph Martin Dawson, *America's Way in Church, State, and Society* (New York: Macmillan, 1953), p. 164.

leads to a life of meaninglessness and neurosis. It is of no small significance that God created the human race in such a way that two people involved in an act of the greatest intimacy are necessary for its perpetuation.

The East has traditionally placed the highest value on social interrelationships. In the farming communities of the pre-industrial age the same was true in the West. A new day dawned in the eighteenth century when factories replaced the plows. Man became anonymous on the assembly line. This process has continued at an accelerated pace in the latter years of the twentieth century.

But, can it be that in the midst of Alvin Toffler's "Third Wave," mankind is once again beginning to reconsider the value of relationships? A *Time* cover story (9 April 1984) was entitled "Sex in the 80's: The Revolution Is Over." Casual sex was depicted as empty and unsatisfying. Instead, people seek meaningful companionship based on mutual commitment between the sexes.

Megatrends was on the top of the best-seller list for months. One of John Naisbitt's interesting observations concerns the felt need for social intercourse. The shopping mall is the third most frequented place in the United States. This Naisbitt interprets as a result of the American desire to be in a place where it is possible to interact with others. He goes on to link high-tech achievement with a parallel growth in a movement which emphasizes personal relationships:

> But something else was growing alongside the technological invasion. Our response to the high tech all around us was the evolution of a highly personal value system to compensate for the impersonal value of technology. The result was the new self-help or personal growth movement, which eventually became the human potential movement. Much has been written about the human potential movement, but to my knowledge no one has connected it with technological change. In reality, each feeds the other—high tech/high touch. Now, at the dawn of the twenty-first century, high tech/high touch has truly come of age. Technology and our human potential are the two great challenges and adventures facing humankind today. The great lesson we must learn from the principle of high tech/high touch is a modern version of the ancient Greek ideal—balance.

We must learn to balance the material wonders of technology with the spiritual demands of our human nature.[35]

To proclaim the "wonders of technology [and] the spiritual demands of our human nature" in the same breath is a rather uncommon phenomenon!

Another bestseller, *Algeny*, sounds the warning against bio-engineering. Author Jeremy Rifkin protests that genetic manipulation will lead to a world without feeling: "In the end, it is companionship we give up, the companionship with other life that is at once both describable and essential, and without which existence becomes a meaningless exercise."[36]

Toffler, one of the world's most widely read authors, adds his comments on the dangers of a strictly technosociety: "Any decent society must generate a feeling of community. Community offsets loneliness. It gives people a vitally necessary sense of belonging. Yet today the institutions on which community depends are crumbling in all the techno-societies. The result is a spreading plague of loneliness."[37]

Can it be that the influential secular writers of the day are instruments of challenge to the contemporary Christian church? In light of a well-defined need for relationships, it becomes incumbent on the church to re-evaluate all of its programs and strategies to see if these are effectively reaching out to a society plagued by the pain of solitary existence.

In 1912, Émile Durkheim, after spending years studying the religion of the people of the South Sea Islands, published *The Elementary Forms of the Religious Life*. In it he suggested that the primary purpose of religion at its earliest stage is not to put people in touch with God, but rather to put them in touch with each other. Rituals of religion taught them how to share with their neighbors the cycles of birth, marriage, and death. Other sacred rituals related to planting and harvest. Through these ritualistic celebrations, the community was able to share joy

35. John Naisbitt, *Megatrends: Ten New Directions for Transforming Our Lives* (New York: Warner, 1982), p. 40.

36. Jeremy Rifkin and Nicanor Perlas, *Algeny* (New York: Viking, 1983), p. 252.

37. Alvin Toffler, *The Third Wave* (New York: Morrow, 1980), p. 383.

and sorrow. No one would be forced to stand alone in the climactic moments of life.[38]

Without denying Durkheim's basic thesis, I would add the vertical dimension. Man has a deep spiritual need that can be satisfied only through a relationship with his Creator. When one combines the vertical with the horizontal, there emerges a wholeness that is spiritually as well as psychologically fulfilling. At times, churches are known to overemphasize one aspect of relationship to the exclusion or near exclusion of the other. A friend of mine attends a great Bible-preaching church. Yet, she told me, "When I leave the church, I feel like crying. No one has spoken to me or shown any concern as to whether I am dead or alive." Situations like this highlight the need for a congregation to be more attuned to the hurts of lonely Christians within its midst.

Community is important for the individual believer. Mainline Protestantism, from its structures to its hymns and gospel songs, has emphasized the individual over the community. It has had a keen sense of the individual person's responsibility before God but little corresponding sense of the communal life of the Christian. Too often the Church has been seen more as a mere collection of saved souls than as a community of interacting personalities. Christian growth has been a matter of individual soul culture rather than the building of the community of the Spirit. Saints who lived isolated, solitary lives were often placed on a pedestal above those whose lives were spent in true community. These tendencies, of course, were part of Protestantism's pre-Reformation heritage.[39]

The church of Jesus Christ has too often incorporated the inadequacies of the culture in which it is found. The Westerner in contemporary society is a fast-moving individualist. Therefore, he all too often is content to fulfill his religious obligation by spending one hour in the Sunday morning worship service. This makes it impossible for him to enter into the community

38. Harold S. Kushner, *When Bad Things Happen to Good People* (New York: Schocken, 1981), p. 119.
39. Howard A. Snyder, *The Community of the King* (Downers Grove: Inter-Varsity, 1977), p. 74.

dynamics of biblical Christianity. Too few churches make a concerted effort to integrate their parishioners into a loving community. Rather, they meet only superficial needs.

Islam is proud of its brotherhood. It is, Muslims feel, a privilege to belong to a worldwide community. While visiting Muslims in various mosques in Asia, I have been often mistaken for a Muslim. Immediately, there is warm acceptance as I am brought into the circle of their fellowship. When they discover I am a follower of Christ, there develops a bit of remoteness between us. The *ummah* of Islam is very real. It behooves the church to equal if not excel the Muslim sense of brotherhood.

It is hoped this brief historical overview will help us as Christians understand the errors of the past, the inadequacies of the present, and a new hope for the future. Only then will we begin to offer Christian *ummah* that will be a viable alternative to Muslim community.

5

Christian Presence
Within Muslim
Community

The critic puts forth an emotive argument. How can light co-exist with darkness? Truth is an absolute that demands separation from all that is false. If Christianity is truth, then the convert from the erroneous system of Islam must of necessity come into direct conflict with his past religious heritage. Because religion and culture are so intertwined in Islam, this dictates that the former Muslim completely forsake his family, friends, and acquaintances.

Is there a valid counterargument to this set of propositions? Is there ever a converging set of circumstances that will allow converts to remain members in good standing within Islamic community? The answer is multifaceted and complex. It may be geographically and ethnically influenced as well as dictated by theological and sociological considerations. This chapter will seek to explore and identify some of the relevant areas which relate to this crucial issue.

Sociological Adaptations

As has been pointed out in earlier chapters, sociology and theology are inseparable components of Islam. Therefore, it is a serious mistake to approach the religion of 850 million Muslims from only a theological perspective. On the other hand, some Christian authors, in my view, have gone too far in proclaiming the obstacles encountered in Muslim evangelism to be primarily sociological. They seem to contend that, given an ideal set of societal circumstances, Muslims will convert to Christ in large numbers. This simply is not true. The offense of the cross and the divinity of Christ remain as major stumbling blocks to the Muslim. We should, however, be committed to reducing every unnecessary hindrance, both sociological and theological, to the Muslim becoming a follower of Christ. My postulate is that we can do a much better job of evangelism among the Sons of Ishmael than we have in the past.

Extraction Evangelism

Tim Matheny identifies extraction evangelism among Arabs as that which militates against church growth:

> It remains a fact that the process of extracting individuals from their setting in Arab communities does not build a church, but on the contrary, it builds barriers against the spreading of the Gospel. In spite of this, most Protestant missionaries and those of the Churches of Christ have emphasized the right of the individual to make his own religious choices. This is not a basic Arab conception, because Arab society and Islam do not recognize the right of the individual to make his own religious decisions.[1]

Among Muslims the extended family is paramount. The son or daughter is never really free from parental authority. Nor is there any desire to be. There is security within the fold of a loving, caring family. Few, other than the prodigal or the maladjusted, would desire to deliberately destroy this deep bond of unity.

It is sad that we as Westerners have sought to understand Muslim societies in terms of our own preference for individualism. We have even felt it incumbent upon us to demand immediate and solitary conversion. This we have done with biblical conviction and fervor. What we have often failed to compre-

---

1. Tim Matheny, *Reaching the Arabs: A Felt Need Approach* (Pasadena, Calif.: William Carey Library, 1981), p. 117.

hend is that the basic sociological realities of Bible times still prevail today in the world of Islam. The Bible repeatedly exalts family relationships. Mothers and fathers are to be obeyed and reverenced. One of the great disgraces is to bring disrepute on the family name. That is why, in the Old Testament, the rebellious son was to be stoned to death and the person who cursed his parents was to be executed.

"As long as the Christian missionary effort appears to be a frontal attack against this group solidarity it will effectively oppose the progress of the Gospel."[2] Islam responds to "attacks" by violent counterattacks. Social solidarity is actually enhanced when it is threatened. Warnings go out to the community. Parents become extremely watchful of their children. *Imams* begin to preach with greater force concerning religious and social *ummah*. The missionary outsider seldom understands the turmoil his evangelistic presence has created within the Muslim community. But the paucity of results for his labor confirms the cohesiveness of the community. "The community is the primary seat of social control. Here it is that deviation is penalized and conformity rewarded. It is noteworthy that ostracism from the community is widely regarded as the direst of punishments and that its threat serves as the ultimate inducement to cultural conformity."[3]

I have personally observed the overwhelming despair that a convert experiences when he is confronted with the choice, "Renounce Christ or immediately leave home." At times physical violence is threatened. Within a short time, the new believer appears at the door of the missionary or national pastor and begins to emotionally relate his tale of abandonment. In a demonstration of love, the Christian arranges for shelter, usually in a distant location, for the protection of the new believer. The bewildered convert gratefully accepts the offer. Linkage to community is forever severed. Family and friends feel deep revulsion for their loved one as well as the offending Christian party. Court cases, as well as retributive violence, may follow.

The missionary lauds the courage of the convert who is willing to pay such an extreme price for his faith in Christ. The nov-

2. Ibid., p. 74.
3. George Peter Murdock, *Social Structure* (New York: Macmillan, 1949), p. 82.

ice believer may then be held up as an example that the gospel works. But the price is fractured relationships and deep alienations. Is there not a better way?

The learned and gracious Kenneth Cragg has struggled with these issues:

> Is it possible to familiarize the Muslim with the truth that to become a Christian is not a mere shift of communities, that it does not rob Muslim society, as such, of a potential servant and the local community, as such, of a loving son? How can we demonstrate that to become a Christian is to remain responsible in some sense for "Muslim" citizenship? . . . If we believe in a Church within a culture, shall we make the door into that Church, a door right out of the culture? "Let not thy good be evil spoken of," said the Apostle. He meant that we have a responsibility toward the concepts others form of our institutions in so far as we can affect and shape those concepts. What, then, can be done to encourage in Islam the truth that becoming a Christian is not ceasing to belong with Muslim need, Muslim thought, and Muslim kin?[4]

This quote from one of Cragg's writings enunciates the problem we Christians have as we see Muslims come to the Lord. It is, however, frustrating to have a good perspective on the obstacles but to lack clear guidance on how to overcome them.

The Problem of the Mosque

An American friend who is a warm Christian with a deep desire to win Muslims to Christ has shared his experience of prayer in the mosque with me:

> Let me tell you about my first experience of worshiping in a mosque in Los Angeles. I went there with a lot of apprehension, but I felt God was saying, "Jim, it's time for you to enter the mosque." And I went planning that I probably would do the prayers with the Muslims. I went and sat on the back row with the Muslims—shoulder to shoulder. Then came the time that we had to stand up and I stood up with them. Nobody knew the difference until, all of a sudden, everybody went down and I was standing up. I just could not make myself bend over and

4. Kenneth Cragg, *The Call of the Minaret* (New York: Oxford University Press, 1956), p. 348.

worship. I think I had an uneasy feeling in my heart that maybe I was worshiping an idol. But anyway, they came up again and I was relieved, and then as they went down, I felt bad. I just couldn't make myself go down. The third time, I said to myself, "This is going to be it. I'm going to go down." And I did go down. I had a feeling like my guts were ripping up inside. I went all the way down and put my head on the ground. And I felt a relief. I was wondering if that feeling was my salvation going away or something. I wasn't very sure what it was, but I felt like I had incarnated into Islam; not completely, but in a new way for me. I went on and learned the entire Islamic prayer ritual. I found my love towards Muslims greatly increased. I possessed a new compassion, a new ability to be in their company.

I believe that 98 percent, maybe 99 percent, of Islamic worship can be used by us. When a Muslim comes to know Christ, he should be encouraged to go back to the mosque and be regular and say his prayers in the Spirit.

He goes on to state that he has prayed in mosques in Los Angeles and Washington, D.C. He recognizes that it may not be possible for a Christian to pray in the mosques of countries where Muslims are the majority of the population. But he feels strongly that converts should remain a viable part of Muslim community—and that includes participation in prayers at the mosque.

Another personal experience is related by Tom, a Westerner, resident in a Muslim nation. This young missionary felt a deep desire to identify with the Muslims in his adopted country. Tom cycled out to a remote small town where he was unknown. Soon, he was able to establish rapport with the local people, including the *imam* of the mosque. Tom requested the Muslims to teach him the prayer ritual, which they gladly did. As it was Friday at 1 p.m., Tom proposed that he join them in their prayer time. Permission was given and Tom lined up with the Muslims and did the prayer forms according to the prescribed ritual. Immediately following the prayers, Muslims who had come in late became angry when they heard a Christian had defiled the sanctity of the house of worship by actually praying in their mosque. The situation was extremely tense and could easily have turned violent. Finally, it was decided that Tom could leave safely but that he was never to return to that town.

My own experience is limited. I have visited mosques in

many parts of the Muslim world, but I have prayed in only two of them. In the Philippines, I entered a beautiful mosque which was completely empty of people. I knelt on the lush carpets, raised my hands in Muslim fashion, and proceeded to pray silently. Apparently no Muslim observed me.

The more relevant incident occurred in a crowded mosque in a suburb of Detroit. It was Friday noon when I arrived. Prayers were already in progress. Several hundred Muslims had lined up shoulder to shoulder and were in the process of prostrating and rising, all the time mumbling Arabic phrases from the Quran. As I slid in next to a Muslim near the door, no one even noticed my presence. I felt uncomfortable as I stood when others were kneeling. Likewise, I was conspicuous by kneeling when others were standing. Finally, I made the plunge and prostrated myself. In the next few moments I moved my body in harmony with the praying Muslims. I cannot say I felt any particular emotion except that I was glad to have finally done what my friends have done thousands of times. It seemed no one even noticed me. I was basically ignored following the prayer time. I have no plans ever again to participate in formal Muslim prayers in the mosque.

We have several issues before us. Is it a compromise of our faith to join in the Muslim prayer ritual? If not, how, when, where, and by whom should it be performed? In most Islamic countries the non-Muslim Westerner, conspicuous by his white face, will be prohibited from taking part in the prayer time in the mosque. The larger issue is whether the convert should be encouraged to continue to participate in the ritual. Or should he be warned that such a continuance is antithetical to a vibrant faith and loyalty to Jesus Christ?

I cannot agree with my friend when he states that 98 or 99 percent of Muslim worship can be utilized by us. There is a large area of commonality. The recognition of the glory and majesty of God is beautifully illustrated by the Muslim bowing humbly with his forehead to the floor. The attitude of supplication as seen in the uplifted hands portrays sublime dependence and dignity. At a certain time, one finger is extended, signifying the unity of God. The conclusion of the prayer time finds the Muslim worshiper pronouncing the benediction of peace on his neighbors who are kneeling to his right and left.

Most of the content of the ritual is acceptable to the Christian. God is exalted by a recitation of his attributes. Egalitarianism is practically demonstrated by the community as the wealthy line up beside the poor in the prayer rows. There is no difference in the sight of God. All are equal.

Yet, there are a few items of such weighty theological significance that I conclude any true believer who permanently continues to participate in the prayer ritual is indeed compromising his faith in Christ. I hasten to add that I recognize the value of and need for a proper transitional time for movement out of the mosque. This may take weeks and even months. This will depend on the degree of social pressure from the community as well as the rate of the maturing process in the life of the new believer. To demand an immediate cessation of all that has been practiced for years leads only to extractionism.

Sadly, the biblical Christ has no place in the mosque. One statement from the Quran that is frequently quoted is, "God cannot beget nor be begotten." This is an attack on the incarnation.

Another significant conflict relates to the exalted position of Muhammad as the final and greatest of all the prophets of God. I personally have never been able to affirm Muhammad as a prophet. He was the initiator of a message that has drawn millions away from the Christ of the Bible. Muslims are perhaps the hardest people in the world to reach with the gospel. This relates directly to the distortions of the Quran as revealed through Muhammad. Although I can commend this religious reformer in many areas, I can only condemn the effect his message has had on solidifying opposition to Jesus Christ. In the mosque there is a constant repetition of the Islamic creed, "There is no God but God and Muhammad is his Prophet." In good conscience, I cannot affirm this statement—nor do I personally understand any Christian doing so. I have listened carefully to all the arguments set forth in favor of Christians affirming this creed, but they seem to me to have no validity. A Christian's participation in the ritual is a confirmation of the message of Islam—regardless of what he is privately thinking or praying.

Muslims do not want Christians joining in the uniquely Islamic prayer ritual any more than we want Muslims partaking in the bread and juice of communion. We have an obligation to honor their religious convictions. After all, it is their mosque!

Furthermore, I do not approve of any type of Christian witnessing or gospel propagation within the premises of the mosque. How would we feel if Muslims came to our church and started handing out Islamic-oriented tracts to our parishioners on Sunday morning? There is, of course, a legitimate place for visiting the mosque to observe the prayer times as well as to ask sincere questions about Islam. In 1983, I took my Islamics class to a large inner-city mosque in Chicago. We had arranged the visit in advance. How graciously we were treated. We were seated in chairs which were set up alongside the worshipers. Following the prayer time, the *imam* greeted us over the microphone. We were then led into a large side room where we were served cold drinks and delicious cookies. The *imam* came and answered our questions for about thirty minutes. I wonder if any church would be as considerate and kind to a delegation of Muslims?

Although I advocate that Muslims remain an integral part of their community, I am forced to stop short of encouraging continued involvement in prayers at the mosque. The ritual is too closely connected to Islamic belief, theology, and religious practice. I conclude that participation involves either compromise or deceit. Neither is acceptable for a Christian. Therefore, we must move "beyond the mosque" and explore other areas wherein our objectives can be fulfilled.

The Missionary's Standard of Living

Muslims look upon the missionary in their midst with grave suspicion.

> The Muslim polemic interprets the attacks of missionaries upon Islam as a campaign that has aims and effects not only religious, but of many kinds. It is a campaign against the solidarity of the Easterners, against the unity of the Islamic nation, against the purity and classic perfection of the Arabic language, and against the character and person of the great hero of the East, Muhammad.[5]

How frustrating it is to be perceived in such a negative frame of reference. The missionary is regarded as a destroyer of all

---

5. Harry Gaylord Dorman, Jr., *Toward Understanding Islam* (New York: Teachers College, Columbia University, 1948), p. 117.

the rich heritage and lofty values of Islam. James L. Barton captured the essence of a significant problem as it relates to missionary presence within Muslim lands:

> We declare the necessity of the Christian missionary's orientalizing himself before he may expect to achieve success in reaching the other man. Hitherto the effort has too often been to occidentalize the Oriental when he accepts Christianity. This is by no means desirable. The Westerner should recognize that Christianity is capable of being grasped and applied by the Oriental, in his Oriental method of thinking, and made a vital part of his Oriental philosophy, and of becoming a power in his Oriental life and in the society in which that life has passed.[6]

There is a heavy price to pay when one sets about to "orientalize" himself. This is particularly true in this age of such an overwhelming gap in the living standard between the developed and developing nations. Few Western families can adapt downward to the standard of living in the remote villages of Bangladesh or Morocco. Yet, there should be a concerted effort toward identification with the people among whom one is working.

My wife and I, during 1980–82, lived in a rural setting (as we had done for five years in the early 1960s) in a predominantly Muslim country. We chose a lifestyle that we felt to be as close as possible to what we could endure physically and emotionally and yet be somewhat in harmony with our Muslim neighbors and friends. We rented a three-room cement house for thirty dollars per month. Each room was twelve feet by twelve feet. Furnishings were according to local norms. Our bathroom lacked a Western-style commode. We possessed no vehicle, but rather made use of cycle rickshas, buses, and trains. Our dress style was identical to that of a conservative Muslim family. We often served local dishes to friends, who graciously reciprocated. Our standard of living was fairly close to that of a college professor within the community. It proved to be an acceptable compromise as we found that villagers, as well as our higher-class Muslim friends, were comfortable in our home.

6. James L. Barton, *The Christian Approach to Islam* (Boston: Pilgrim, 1918), pp. 246–47.

During our years of ministry in a large Muslim city, we lived at a higher standard. This did not seem to pose a serious problem in light of the greater affluence in the urban setting. My plea is for a sensitivity that will reduce distance between the Western missionary and the Muslims among whom he has come to minister. If new converts see a disproportionate standard of living between them and their spiritual guides, they are likely to become envious. Requests for financial assistance will inevitably follow. If they are not granted, alienation is likely.

This problem is more acute for the missionary than for the national Christian worker. The national is usually on a minimal salary scale. This becomes problematic as comparisons are made between white-skinned and dark-skinned Christian ministers. One sincere and well-educated national stated, "I understand servants of Christ are to sacrifice and live on minimal salaries. But why does this apply only to the national and not to the foreigner?"

Decisions for Christ

Often, there is too little consideration given regarding sociological issues involved in the conversion process.

> The implications of these principles in Arab society is that the initial approach may be made to a younger person, but the challenge for a decision to change should be made to the head of the nuclear family or extended family. Allowing sufficient time for the making of decisions is indispensable in the group oriented Arab society. The evangelist's tendency to encourage some especially responsive person to step out and make an individual decision, may often cause the people as a whole to reject the message. Until a people are able to make what seems to them a valid decision, any pulling out of members of the group immediately raises the fear of the loss of solidarity.[7]

In our evangelistic outreach, we have consistently urged the solitary convert to go back among his friends and family and discreetly share his faith. This is not to be done in a way that will stimulate social opposition. If necessary, we counsel the new believer to say nothing about his conversion until others notice a qualitative change in his life and this then opens the

7. Matheny, *Reaching the Arabs*, p. 63.

door for a quiet word of witness. We are extremely honest from the start with the convert; he is told he must remain within the Islamic community.

Our goal is to see a small cluster of believers within a given geographical area. When the ideal of sociological strength plus maturity on the part of the believers is reached, it becomes possible to consider baptism. Premature baptism has often sparked off intense persecution from the Islamic community. This must be avoided.

We have suggested that a mature national believer do the actual baptizing of converts. No foreign missionary on our local team has ever baptized anyone. We have a strong policy in this regard. Usually the baptisms take place in an unobtrusive manner at a nearby river. No white people with their expensive cameras are present. It is an indigenous ceremony and celebration in response to a biblical command.

Another word needs to be said concerning Muslim women and children. Perhaps there will be some disagreement, but it is worth noting Matheny's comment on the subject: "From the anthropological point of view, it is probably better for the evangelist to look upon the status of women in the Arab world as being an aspect of a very complex cultural configuration rather than as a phenomenon which must be changed."[8] It is almost impossible for any foreign force to radically alter the Muslim cultural view of women. Therefore, I suggest we work within the system. Our initial evangelistic effort should not be directed toward women or children. They have little independent voice. Men are decision makers and leaders of society. In one Islamic country I know of only two Muslim women who have accepted Christ apart from their other family members. One had a nervous breakdown and the other died alone, rejected by her family. I am sure there are exceptions, such as Pakistani Bilquis Sheikh, as well as women in various countries of Africa, but overall, this is a fair representation of the situation.

What then must be done? Surely our Lord loves Muslim women and children as much as men. Undoubtedly! To deal with this problem, our approach has been to seek to reach them through the men of the family. If a husband and father is truly converted, he will have a spiritual concern for his nuclear as

8. Ibid., p. 50.

well as extended family. We have chosen to take the culturally
acceptable route and work through heads of families.

One further word needs to be said regarding evangelism of
Muslim students. A case could be made that these young people
are often open to new ideas and may be somewhat disillusioned
with Islam. Should they not be a target group for evangelistic
effort? This may be appropriate in some countries, but not in
all. Students are considered immature. They are not to make a
major decision in life without reference to their parents. If they
do boldly become Christians, it is likely there will be a violent
reaction from all family members. This can well lead to their
expulsion from society. Again, it is wiser to reach them through
the father.

Homogeneous Convert Churches

Once believers begin to discreetly declare themselves openly
as followers of Christ, there immediately follows the problem
of formation of community. It is at this crucial point that the
work can be destroyed. Reversion or flight are not at all uncommon; in fact, they are the norm.

In most contexts the agent of conversion has advised the convert to sever all religious ties with Islam and become integrated
into a local Christian church as quickly as possible. Muslims
regard this act as a denial of all highly esteemed social and religious values. The church is an agent of foreign imperialism on
their soil. They tolerate it with great difficulty. For one of their
sons to turn his back on culture and family is seen as an act of
high treason—punishable at times by death. Esther, a young
Pakistani girl, came to Christ and was forced to take shelter in a
missionary residence. Early one morning she was discovered
dead in her bed with a cracked skull. There is little doubt that
behind her death is to be found the indescribable anger of her
family and former friends within the Islamic community.

Within the scenario of extractionism is also to be found the
emotional and spiritual turmoil the believer suffers as he
moves into a new and unique *ummah*. So much is strange. Worship patterns, theological content, rituals, and festival observances are distinctive. The security of the Islamic legal system
has vanished. The perplexity of liberty and freedom of choice is
experienced. The convert has suddenly become a member of a
despised minority community. He is condemned for relating to

a foreign-influenced "import." His head swirls with conflict as on one hand his forsaking all is lauded and on the other hand he is condemned as a traitor who has sold his soul.

Finally, the attitude of the local church must be mentioned. Perhaps the missionary and national pastor graciously receive the convert, but what is to be said concerning the church members? All too frequently, the church has a mentality which leads members to express grave suspicion concerning the motives of any Muslim who professes Christ. "Only too often Muslim enquirers are discouraged by the aloof and suspicious attitude of church members."[9]

Into this complex and frustrating set of circumstances comes the proposal to establish convert churches of a homogeneous nature. "Incorporating converts into ethnic unit churches would minimize the societal and cultural dislocation that often occurs."[10] This homogeneous unit principle (HUP) has evoked positive as well as negative reaction. Few church leaders are neutral.

> It is quite evident that the use of the homogeneous unit principle for church growth has no biblical foundation. Its advocates have taken as their starting point a sociological observation and developed a missionary strategy; only then, a posteriori, have they made the attempt to find biblical support. As a result the Bible has not been allowed to speak. A friendly critic of the "Church Growth" movement has observed that "lack of integration with revelation is the greatest danger in Church Growth anthropology." The analysis above leads us to conclude that the "Church Growth" emphasis on homogeneous unit churches is in fact directly opposed to the apostolic teaching and practice in relation to the expansion of the church.[11]

Strong words indeed! Critics of this principle assert that there is no evidence in the Book of Acts that indicates different churches for the educated and the uneducated, for the rich and the poor, for the Palestinian Jews and the Jews of the Disper-

9. Michael Nazir-Ali, *Islam: A Christian Perspective* (Exeter: Paternoster, 1983), pp. 162–63.

10. Matheny, *Reaching the Arabs*, p. 74.

11. C. Rene Padilla, "The Unity of the Church and the Homogeneous Unit Principle," *International Bulletin of Missionary Research*, vol. 6 (January 1982), p. 29.

sion. Rather, Acts is said to point toward an early church which had all things in common and Christians who were of "one heart and soul" (4:32).

Michael Nazir-Ali is an Anglican bishop in Pakistan. His family background is Muslim. Nazir-Ali is a godly person with a sincere burden for the world of Islam. His recent book, *Islam: A Christian Perspective*, is a scholarly and courageous exploration of the distinctives as well as commonalities found between Islam and Christianity. As might be expected, he has reservations regarding the HUP.

> The existence of such [homogeneous] churches seems to me, however, wholly against the testimony of Scripture and catholic tradition. In very early Christianity there was only one celebration of the Eucharist every week in the whole city, at which the bishop presided and was assisted by all his presbyters and deacons. It was only the rapid spread of Christianity which made it necessary for the bishop to delegate to his presbyters the authority to preside at Eucharists. There is no mention whatever in early Christian writings of churches organized on homogeneous lines. Going back to the scriptures themselves, both Paul (in I Cor. 11) and James (chapter 2) quite clearly envisaged a socially-mixed congregation.[12]

Nazir-Ali does, however, allow for a church to emerge with homogeneous characteristics in pioneer situations. Yet such a church should not remain isolated from other believers. He also makes allowance for a convert church in areas where existing churches refuse to accept Muslim-background believers. He cites, as an example, the ancient churches of Iran that would not readily accept converts from Islam.[13]

For a theological defense of the principle, I recommend the writings of Donald A. McGavran and C. Peter Wagner. Others from the Fuller Seminary School of World Mission have also written prolifically on the subject. It is fair to say that one finds a rather extensive strain of pragmatism in the writings of Fuller faculty. This is because the professors in the missions department have all had field experience and thus lace their insights with the empirical and the experiential. For this reason,

12. Nazir-Ali, *Islam*, p. 161.
13. Ibid., pp. 160–62.

I find myself quite comfortable with their findings, which I also evaluate to be biblical. I have dealt with this issue in greater theological depth in earlier writings.

Malcolm X, following his visit to Mecca, made a most interesting observation:

> There was a colour pattern in the huge crowds. Once I happened to notice this, I closely observed it thereafter. Being from America made me intensely sensitive to matters of colour. I saw that people who looked alike drew together and most of the time stayed together. This was entirely voluntary; there being no other reason for it. But Africans were with Africans, Pakistanis were with Pakistanis. And so on. I tucked it into my mind that when I returned home I would tell Americans this observation; that where true brotherhood existed among all colours, where no one felt segregated, where there was no "superiority" complex, no "inferiority" complex—then voluntarily, naturally, people of the same kind felt drawn together by that which they had in common.[14]

This is the essence of what missiologists are advocating: Nothing more than an informal, voluntary grouping of believers based on that which they hold in common. No one is forced to attend. None are excluded. But there is a natural clustering of those from Muslim backgrounds who now desire to express their love for the Lord with those who are pilgrims on the same path.

Our Western churches frequently are examples of homogeneity. Robert Schuller draws one type of parishioner, Charles Swindoll another. The huge Moody Church attracts those who appreciate large gatherings whereas the small Plymouth Brethren assembly preaches the same basic gospel but in an entirely different setting. A working-class church in Gary, Indiana, will be distinctive from a wealthy suburban church in Boston. An independent Baptist church in Macon, Georgia, will present the same message as an evangelical Presbyterian church in Washington, D.C., but the method of presentation will be unique—so much so that it is unlikely that members would ever agree to attend the other church even if a job transfer made it expedient to do so.

14. Bernard Lewis, *Race and Color in Islam* (New York: Harper and Row, 1971), p. 3.

This is not an advocacy of elitism. It is simply a recognition of human nature. When I attend an emotional, shouting, foot-stomping service, I am basically alienated from the content of the message, no matter how evangelical it is. Likewise, I am not particularly enamored with sitting under the ministry of a pastor who has little theological education and thus simply reiterates the plan of salvation in each service. Both approaches contain the truth of the Word of God, but are directed toward a homogeneous audience into which I do not fit. I do not denounce either group. Rather, I am pleased that there are churches that specifically meet needs of people who are different from me.

In 1978, a significant consultation was held in Colorado Springs for the purpose of exploring new methodologies in outreach to Muslims. The conference report included these words:

> Where there is resistance or reluctance on the part of national Christians to involve themselves in this task, we shall seek to develop separate Muslim convert churches. These latter congregations shall be encouraged to develop culturally appropriate forms of worship that arise out of the natural expression of earlier worship patterns that will be true to biblical teaching and yet will neither deliberately flaunt our Christian liberty nor carelessly involve the believers in syncretistic belief or conduct.[15]

Such a convert church will aid new believers to maintain ties to their former *ummah* as well as begin to relate to a new community based on the Word of God. They have not gone to the established church which is regarded so negatively by Muslims. Rather, they will meet informally as a cluster of the redeemed who have come out of similar backgrounds and can now worship the Lord utilizing relevant forms that uniquely communicate spiritual realities to them. Most often the believers will meet in their own homes. This low profile will generate minimal opposition.

Christians of other than Muslim background would be most welcome, but they would be expected to fit into the style of wor-

---

15. Arthur F. Glasser, *The Glen Eyrie Report, No. 4, Muslim Evangelism* (Wheaton: Lausanne Committee for World Evangelism, 1978), p. 13.

ship that the converts have adopted. Informal fellowship links could be encouraged between all believers. Teaching would be given concerning the universal church so the converts would be aware of the larger *ummah* to which they belong. At a time when social conditions permit, there could be a careful move toward some degree of integration. I caution against premature merger. Such a move will only bring about persecution as well as cause inquirers to keep their distance from the believers.

Is this postulate ideal? No, it is not—nor are the hundreds of denominations of the West. Why should we judge the struggling group of converts in tight Muslim countries by criteria more severe than those we apply to our own homogeneous denominational proliferation? There is room here for a great deal of understanding.

In a few Muslim countries these proposals have been implemented. Initial reports have been encouraging. There needs to be constant review and evaluation. One unique experiment has been led by a teacher of mission theology in a large city in Pakistan. This professor felt the need to incarnate his teaching within the world of Islam. In a letter to me, he outlined his approach:

> I was convinced that our students must be exposed to the larger world in which they live, the world of Islam, the world of poverty and human distress. This led me to refuse all aid in the formation of our students. For the last five years we as a community of seven students and myself have lived by our own work and income. The house we live in is still middle class, but it is much poorer and simpler than the big institutions like our seminary. The house is always open. We have really endeared ourselves to the people around us . . . We have no servants and cook our own meals. All this generates a certain atmosphere. I have never experienced Providence as I experience it now.

It is evident why the community has endeared itself to the surrounding Muslims.

Christians as an Islamic Sect?

In chapter 2, I explored the sociological and theological deviations within Islam. Ahmadiyyas have been expelled from the Islamic community in Pakistan but few other sects have been so harshly treated. The racist American Black Muslims of the 1960s and 1970s were counted as part of the fold. Sufis who drink the menstrual blood of women have been lightly condemned, but never formally charged with heresy. Animistic practices are found within the Islam of Indonesia. Yet, Muslims proudly point to Indonesia as being the largest Islamic country in the world. Many Muslims strongly denounce the fanaticism of Libya and Iran, yet there has never been a move to formally censure these countries.

Are there perimeters of Islam within which believers in Christ may legitimately fit? Could "Followers of Isa" just be another sect of Islam? It would be a fine line between being a Muslim sect or a Christian sect. Syncretism of not only form, but also content, would be an ever-present danger.

I am open to seeing further experiments carried out in this area. But I feel it will not be possible for such a total integration (as an Islamic sect) to occur and still allow mutual integrity. There are four reasons for this:

1. The unacceptable exaltation of Prophet Muhammad.
2. The centrality of the mosque to religious expression within Islam.
3. The denial by Muslims of the Christian view of biblical authority as well as their rejection of our belief in the deity and atonement of Christ.
4. The desire of both Muslims and Christians to have an exclusive *ummah*.

What, then, is the way forward? As I see it, our responsibility is to lessen peripheral offense and distance between Muslims and Christians. This chapter is setting forth issues relating to the convert church and evangelistic approaches as well as worship forms. I hope that this combination of concerted moves on our part will make it just that much more realistic for Muslims to consider the Christ of the Bible without being offended by the Christ of Western culture. It is then possible that converts may be able to continue within the mainstream of life in a Muslim society, yet distance themselves from things compromisingly Islamic.

Evangelistic Approach

"We must become Moslems to the Moslem if we would gain them for Christ."[16] To a vocal minority of missionaries this statement is borderline heresy; that is, until they read that it was penned by the archconservative, Samuel M. Zwemer, apostle to Islam. Even seventy years ago it was recognized that we must do a better job in identification if we are to reach Muslims with the gospel. Methodology is an extremely important subject, one that should greatly exercise contemporary missionaries to Islam. In no way should this aspect of missiology diminish our emphasis on prayer and other imperative spiritual dynamics.

> Evangelism in crowded bazaars, handing out literature or preaching in churches may make contacts, stimulate interest and promote growth. On the other hand, it may offend, sometimes unnecessarily closing the minds that otherwise would have responded to the good news about Jesus Christ. World mission demands not only the indispensable fruit of the Spirit, it calls for the hard grind of study that opens the mind to an appreciative understanding of the cultural and religious background of those among whom one works.[17]

Does distribution of literature have a role in Muslim evangelism? Habel, to whom this book is dedicated, came to me fifteen years ago and simply stated, "I want to thank you for bringing me from darkness to light." This statement was perplexing to me. I knew Habel had recently come to Christ and had been baptized in the local Baptist church. Everyone was rejoicing in the conversion of this former Muslim. Yet, I had not talked to him personally until that moment. With heightened interest, I probed for further details. Habel then proceeded to tell me of the day he went for a walk in the crowded streets of a busy city. In the distance Habel saw a tall white man selling gospel

---

16. Samuel M. Zwemer, *The Moslem Christ* (New York: American Tract Society, 1912), p. 183.

17. Paul W. Marsh, "The Church and World Mission," in *In God's Community: Essays on the Church and Its Ministry*, ed. David J. Ellis and W. Ward Gasque (Wheaton: Shaw, 1978), p. 110.

packets to a group of Muslims. Out of curiosity, he walked over and bought the literature. That night, as he read God's Word in his home, the Spirit of the Lord began a work of illumination in his heart. Shortly thereafter, he went to the address given on the back page of the tracts. Habel was able to meet true believers and soon committed his life to Christ. Now he appeared before me identifying me as the white man who first put the message of salvation in his hand. Habel was beautifully discipled by Operation Mobilization and has emerged as one of the best evangelists to Muslims in the country in which he is resident. During my fourth term in the field, I had the privilege of ministering with Habel and forging a relationship with him that enriched me tremendously both as a Christian and as a missionary. It all began with the distribution of gospel packets.

So, the assumption is that I am an enthusiastic advocate of literature evangelism among Muslims. That I was director of a large correspondence school for more than ten years strengthens this view. Also, it could be assumed that I am aware of the role that literature has had in the conversion experiences of scores, if not hundreds, of Muslims worldwide. But, interestingly, I am ambivalent. C. George Fry and James R. King have penetratingly critiqued literature evangelism:

> Another questionable model, which certain Christians continue to find appropriate, however, is to fulfill the obligation to proclaim the gospel by handing out tracts and broadcasting radio messages. Such an approach, which avoids personal contact and involvement, appears to be indifferent as to who is listening or responding. It strikes us therefore, as a perversion of the Christian gospel and its message of caring for, loving, and nurturing individuals. Ultimately it is a denial of the incarnation. This kind of indifference is particularly serious in dealing with Muslims, who have such strong roots in the *"ummah"* or community.[18]

I can certainly understand such a strong sentiment. But, on the other hand, it can be said that literature was, for Habel, an introduction into Christian *ummah*. This is true for others as well. Can we not designate radio and literature as pre-

18. C. George Fry and James R. King, *Islam: A Survey of the Muslim Faith* (Grand Rapids: Baker, 1980), p. 131.

evangelism? These media are inadequate in themselves but can be used to stimulate interest and lead on to personal contacts with Christians. In our ministry, one of the converts picked up a tract from a gutter and read the account of Jesus dealing with the woman caught in the act of adultery. This story significantly helped prepare his heart for the moment we came on the scene to share the gospel with him.

Literature and radio programs which are disseminated in Muslim countries are all too frequently poorly produced. I protest against Western preachers and writers who export their "productions" with the stipulation that there can be no editing or revision of the material. Such copyrighted exports can be more of an ego trip than a humble ministry for Christ. It is time for radio programs, tracts, and books to be prepared by nationals in the countries in which the material will be utilized. The Western dollar which binds literature production to a specific author should be rejected. In our ministry we have sought to produce acculturated literature with Muslim art, Islamic linguistic forms, and illustrations that are relevant to the reader's daily life.

A further protest has been registered, this time against a polemical approach: "Therefore the approach is to confront the systems by hurling gospel grenades over the boundary walls in a process designed to raze the religious system to the ground. While this siege is in process, the attacking forces rescue what inmates they can, clean them up, baptize them and then use them as front line troops in the siege operations."[19]

Colorful writing indeed! Has not the history of Christian-Islamic confrontation been described in this paragraph? In past years there has been little allowance for the possibility that something good can be resident in Islam. Rather, the complete religious system has been denounced as demonic. All of the sincere, devout, humble God-seekers within Islam are overlooked.

Polemics lead nowhere. Both sides become entrenched and pay little heed to what the other party is saying. Logic is no longer the arbitrator of differing opinions. The loudest voice and hottest emotions prevail. The Muslim and Christian part,

19. Vinay Samuel and Chris Sugden, eds., *Sharing Jesus in the Two Thirds World* (Bangalore: Partnership in Mission—Asia, 1983), p. 192.

each convinced he has won the argument. In fact, Satan has triumphed as the two parties now feel a certain alienation.

I have never won an argument with a Muslim. To be effective, I have always had to stop short of confrontation. A respectful dialogue is the preferable path to pursue. It is difficult, if not impossible, to convey love to a Muslim in the midst of a heated debate.

One of the more controversial issues among Christians relates to the use of the Quran in witness to Muslims. There are those who see such usage as a bridge to the Muslim heart. Only verses of the Quran which do not conflict with biblical teaching are cited.

> The missionary to the Moslem will always be a preacher; but many of his ideas of a sermon and of preaching will undergo radical modification before the Mohammedan can be generally reached by the spoken address. It may even be necessary, in order to secure a sympathetic hearing from the very beginning, to take a text, not necessarily from the Bible, but from the Koran, or some traditional saying of Mohammed or from the Shariat, or some other Mohammedan source. There certainly can be no fundamental necessity for beginning a sermon to a Mohammedan, or to anybody else, for that matter, with a quotation from the New Testament or the Old. Missionaries to other peoples have often found it wise and rewarding to take a text from something outside of Christian writings. The missionaries in China and Japan frequently take their texts from some of the writings of Confucius. Is there any reason why some of the statements of Mohammed, while true, and capable of wide and large Christian development should not be made the basis of a Christian sermon to Moslems?[20]

The first chapter of the Quran is quoted literally millions of times each day throughout the Muslim world. Five times a day the devout believer recites this foundational chapter:

> Praise be to Allah, Lord of the Worlds,
> The Beneficent, the Merciful.
> Owner of the Day of Judgment,
> Thee [alone] we worship; Thee [alone] we ask for help.

20. Barton, *The Christian Approach to Islam*, pp. 193–94.

> Show us the straight path,
> The path of those whom Thou has favoured;
> Not [the path] of those who earn Thine anger
>   nor of those who go astray.

It seems to me this chapter contains no theological statement in opposition to biblical teaching. What a splendid bridge to the Muslim's mind. I have spoken on these verses, particularly emphasizing the words *show us the straight path*. This leads naturally to John 14:6 where Jesus identifies himself as the path to God.

Milton Coke, a friend of mine who has spent several years in a Muslim country, told me of an instance in which he had the opportunity to speak to a group of Muslims on Christmas. After much prayer, he decided to select several key passages from the Quran concerning the birth and life of Jesus and use them as a basis for his lecture. The audience swelled to more than one thousand Muslims. They were held in rapt attention and expressed great appreciation for Milton's message.

On the other hand, there are those who feel strongly that such use of the Quran gives our imprimatur to it. If we are to quote from it selectively, then it follows logically that Muslims will affirm that we believe in the whole Quran. Also, the point is made that our Lord is not the author of the Quran; Satan is. The Quran has led 850 million people away from God. How can we do anything which will lend credence or stature to it?

I can respect such personal convictions. My only plea is for Christians not to attack each others' positions on this issue. We should allow love and grace to prevail.

Theological Encounter

In the Christian section of a Pakistani village a hundred or so Muslims kindly came to listen to the news of Jesus Christ. Faced with the glorious challenge of such an opportunity the young missionary commenced, "I believe that Jesus Christ is the Son of God." These were true words, maybe brave words, but certainly foolish words, for to any Muslim it was blasphemy, implying that God had had sexual intercourse with a woman. And quite apart from anything else, they bluntly denied a basic tenet of Islam, that Allah neither begets nor is begotten. The missionary escaped with his life, but a hundred

Muslims' ears were closed to what might have been a life-
giving proclamation, because someone had failed to communicate truth in terms which could be understood correctly by
those who listened.[21]

Is the Muslim not logical in interpreting the words *Son of
God* literally? If this term does not imply a human being
brought forth from a God who had engaged in sexual relations,
then what does it mean? Further, the Quran indicates the Trinity is composed of God, Mary, and Jesus. "And when Allah
saith: O Jesus, son of Mary! Dist thou say unto mankind: Take
me and my mother for two gods beside Allah?" (5:116). Thus the
Muslim approaches a foundational Christian truth with a great
deal of bias as well as confusion.

Other Quranic verses speak against the Trinity:

> Lo! whoso ascribeth partners unto Allah, for him Allah hath
> forbidden Paradise. His abode is the Fire. For evil-doers there
> will be no helpers. They surely disbelieve who say: Lo! Allah is
> the third of three; when there is no God save the One God. If
> they desist not from so saying a painful doom will fall on those
> of them who disbelieve. . . . The Messiah, son of Mary, was no
> other than a messenger, messengers [the like of whom] had
> passed away before him. [Surah 5:72, 73, 75]

Throughout the Quran repeated emphasis is given to the
teaching that God can have no partner. Another common Muslim saying is, "God is not begotten nor can He beget" (Surah
112). Does the Christian agree with this in light of John 3:16
where we read that God gave his only "begotten" Son?

Muslims have stared me sternly in the face and made such
statements as, "Your God can be born in the womb of a woman;
my God could never so restrict himself"; or "Your God can die
on a cross and remain dead for three days, but my Allah will
never die"; or "You Christians believe God implanted the seed
of life into Mary. What about Mary's egg? If God used her egg,
then was not sin transmitted to Jesus? If God gave both sperm
and egg, then how ridiculous are the genealogies of Jesus as
found in the Bible. What does the Bible mean when it says that
Jesus is of the seed of David? If God did it all, what relationship
does David have with Jesus?"

21. Marsh, "The Church and World Mission," p. 110.

For the thoughtful reader, these are extremely difficult questions. Christians have been brought up accepting the trinity, incarnation, and deity of Christ as fact. We have given little thought to the Muslim who feels he has advanced an irrefutable argument by saying, "One plus one plus one must equal three. How can it possibly equal one?"

Within the New Testament we find assertions of Jesus that he and the Father are one. Also, the baptismal formula of the early church depicts the composition of the Trinity by stating, "In the name of the Father, Son, and Holy Spirit." Later, in the church councils of Nicea and Chalcedon, the divinity of Christ within a trinitarian theological schema was formulated.

Yet, this truth, broadly accepted throughout Christendom, has remained a fact clothed in mystery. Attempts have been made to explain the Trinity through analogy:

1. The sun, its rays, and its heat
2. Soul, body, and spirit
3. Water, steam, and ice
4. Root, branches, and fruit
5. The white, yolk, and shell of an egg

How totally inadequate are such human attempts to plumb the profound truths of our sovereign God. So where does this leave us? Where does it leave the sincere Muslim inquirer who feels he must have some degree of intellectual satisfaction before making a commitment to Christ?

It is wise to seek to divert the Muslim from this emotive subject until a firm relationship based upon mutual respect has been established. Never should one use the term *Son of God* without surrounding it with a great deal of sensitive explanation. Mark is not the best book of the Bible to use in initial evangelistic conversation with Muslims, as the first verse identifies Jesus as the Son of God.

I always vociferously deny the Islamic interpretation of God engaging in sexual union and declare such a thought to be utter blasphemy. Then I explain the biblical composition of the Trinity. This is followed by an attempt to highlight the spiritual nature of the term *Son of God* rather than the biological explanation Muslims have quite naturally accepted. There should be an effort to move the discussion away from form to content. Questions like the following should be explored: Why did God reveal himself in human form? What was the necessity for such a drastic action? Why have one billion people living today accepted this as fact? What can belief in Christ as God personally mean to me, both now and for eternity?

I have sought to counter the Muslim propensity toward literal interpretations by referring to their belief in the cable of God: "Tell me, do you believe that God has a special cable for all Muslims to grasp? Is Allah speaking of the tangible and material, or is he pointing to a spiritual truth which is to be understood and applied by the worldwide community of Islam? Similarly, the Quran speaks of Allah seeing and hearing (22:61), having hands (48:10), possessing a face (28:88), and ascending the throne after he completed creating the heavens and earth in six days (25:59). Does this mean God has a physical face, eyes, ears, and hands, as well as legs by which to mount a throne?"

More than a few times these words have given my Muslim friends a new insight into the teaching about the Christian Trinity. They can now interpret it within the general context of how their Quran presents a spiritual truth in human terms. I have stepped into their world view and engaged in a hermeneutic that fits their set of theological presuppositions. They acknowledge that Allah can make use of human analogy to communicate spiritual truth. My focus on explaining "Son of God" related to God revealing rather than so much on God becoming. Both are true, but Muslims can comprehend and accept the former more readily than the latter.

"The hour drew nigh and the moon was rent in twain" (Surah 54:1). I often request Muslims to logically explain how the moon can be severed and then come back together again. Logically, scientifically, and practically, such a happening is impossible. It is assumed this took place during Muhammad's lifetime, yet there is no historical or scientific verification of such an event. The earth's tides and weather would have been severely affected, so it is logical to assume some historian would have made note of such an unusual occurrence.

Almost all Muslims believe in the literal interpretation of Surah 54, which is entitled "The Moon." Verses 2 and 3 warn against those who will regard the splitting of the moon as mere illusion. "And if they behold a portent they turn away and say: Prolonged illusion. They denied [the truth] and followed their own lusts." When Muslims are pressed to explain this event, they simply respond that God is able to do anything he desires. The Quran has explicitly stated that the moon split and thus all believers are compelled to believe that it was an actual historical happening. Reason and logic are forced to submit to the higher authority of Allah.

At this point I refer to the miraculous events written about in our Scriptures. There are occurrences recorded which are shrouded in mystery. Our finite minds cannot begin to comprehend the infinite. Both Islam and Christianity are theologically pushed beyond the rational into the simple, yet ever so profound, arena of faith. The incarnation is one such faith encounter.

Another conflict relates to the authority of Christian Scripture. Muslims generally believe the Bible was accurate as initially revealed by God. However, it was altered and corrupted in the transmission process down through the ages. Therefore, the contradictions between certain passages in the Quran and the Bible are to be explained as being the errors of biblical scribes.

Muslims also believe in the abrogation of Christian Scripture by the Quran. God is reputed to have delivered a later revelation to Muhammad which is complete and final. As the New Testament supersedes the Old Covenant, so the Quran fulfills and finalizes God's revelation to man. Muslims tend to regard the Bible in much the same manner as some Christians view the Old Testament. Muslims believe that man had strayed far from God. There was a desperate need for a new word from heaven. Allah decided to reveal this universal message through a sincere God-quester who would faithfully follow the commands that would be given to him. Now the canon of Holy Writ is completed. Nevermore will there be another prophet or another God-given Scripture. All the revelations of Allah are complete. The Quran contains all the entire world needs to know in order to be saved from the eternal fires of hell. Man must flee to Allah in faith, submission, and good works. Thereby he will eventually attain the beautiful gardens of paradise which are populated by lovely virgins.

This basic view so undercuts scriptural authority that it is difficult to use the Bible in witness to Muslims. We must first ask the Muslim to prove his assertions. Where has the Bible been changed? Who changed it? When did this occur? I often ask Muslims to explain how Allah could ever allow his revelation to man to be altered and corrupted. If this is possible, then it also can happen to the Quran . . . and probably has!

If mankind needed a fresh scriptural revelation in the seventh century, is it not thinkable, in a day when the world can be destroyed within one hour, that once again there is a desperate need for a new prophet and a new word from God? Islam will not allow for such a possibility. In the same way, Christians believe in a closed revelation. The need was not for a new message from Muhammad in the seventh century, but rather an adherence to the Good News already shared with mankind in the first century.

The last verses of the Bible can be shared with Muslims to indicate how highly God regards his revelation.

> I testify to everyone who hears the words of the prophecy of this book: if anyone adds to them, God shall add to him the plagues which are written in the book; and if anyone takes away from the words of the book of this prophecy, God shall take away his part from the tree of life and from the holy city, which are written in this book. [Rev. 22:18–19]

In a day when the controversy about biblical inerrancy continues unabated, it behooves the Christian to have a good apologetic for his belief in scriptural authority. Certain Muslim scholars have published booklets attacking numerous biblical Scriptures, which are declared to be redundant, contradictory, and products of plagiarism. These critiques cannot be ignored. We must have an intelligent rationale and defense for our faith. It is not enough to brush aside such attacks and declare them unworthy of refutation. Alongside our faith must stand a credible explanation of what we have believed and why. The refusal to engage in this process is what sects have thrived on through the centuries. A significant number of books on biblical authority are available at any good Bible bookstore. I would particularly recommend the writings of Clark H. Pinnock.

There are other areas of theological conflict between Islam and Christianity. Muslims declare man to be basically good, but he has often chosen a path which takes him far from God. There is no such reality as transmitted sin through the line of

Adam and Eve. All stand or fall before God on the merit of their own faith and works. Attendant to this belief is the absence of any assurance of eternal life. Allah is the sovereign judge. He alone knows the innermost being of man. In the final day all will be made open before him and then a fair and equitable judgment will be made.

Muslims deny Christ died on the cross.

> And because of their saying: We slew the messiah Jesus son of Mary, Allah's messenger—They slew him not nor crucified, but it appeared so unto them; and lo! those who disagree concerning it are in doubt thereof; they have no knowledge thereof save pursuit of a conjecture; they slew him not for certain, but Allah took him up unto Himself. Allah was ever Mighty, Wise. [4:157, 158]

This Quranic scripture nullifies the crucial belief in the atoning work of Christ. There no longer remains a substitutionary offering for the sins of mankind. The Christian theological system is destroyed.

Quranic authority and the exalted position of Muhammad are unacceptable to the Christian, but one must be cautious in refuting these two crucial Muslim beliefs. In fact, it is best to just let them fade away as the new convert begins to focus spiritual attention on the Bible and the person of Christ. Any type of confrontation is usually counterproductive.

Theology became flesh in Jesus Christ. Is it not permissible to say that Christian theology must be incarnated in people within Muslim community? Cognitive and polemical approaches are cold and usually lifeless. Incarnated theology within the lives of believers can be the key to reaching Muslim hearts. Holiness of life must be an emphasis in any evangelistic strategy we pursue in reaching Muslims.

Material Assistance

A Pakistani Muslim bitterly reflects on the questionable ethics of missionaries:

> The missionary is an individual of peculiar mentality. He tries to benefit from the misfortune and difficulties of others. A person with any feelings of decency will shrink from taking advan-

tage of those in distress and dire need. Not so the missionary. He considers such unfortunates as his legitimate prey. He thrusts Christianity down the throat of poor sick humanity and ignorant young children. The patients are mostly illiterate and usually come from the poorest class.[22]

Adding to this searing critique, an evangelical missionary, Paul Marsh, raises penetrating questions relating to mission hospitals:

Shireen Mohammed joins the queue at the mission clinic, and two year old Maqsud, limply straddling her hip, needs pills for the fever which refuses to break. The clinic, however, does not open yet; first the "good news" is given—not that the pills have arrived, but that Christ the Savior has come. Is it good news to Shireen? Should she be forced, a captive audience, to swallow the gospel pill before she can get the other variety?[23]

One of the pressing controversies today within the Islamic world concerns what Muslims regard as the missionary strategy of using inducements in order to gain converts to Christianity. Muslims hold the following perceptions about hospitals and clinics:

Medical missions is simply a "front" for evangelistic persuasion.

Mission compounds are highly visible symbols of wealth, status, and power. They function in much the same manner as a prostitute does when she lures her weak prey into an immoral relationship.

Poor village Muslims are easily induced to become Christians through such a compelling strategy that subverts the mind by meeting felt needs of a physical nature.

How sad is such a perception. Medical missionaries over the decades have gone forth with the highest level of dedication to seek to express Christ's love through the art of rescuing lost souls and healing sick bodies. They have deliberately walked away from wealth, fame, and professional advancement. It is

22. Muhammad Akram, *A Look at the West* (Lahore: Islamic Publications, 1971), pp. 25–26.
23. Marsh, "The Church and World Mission," p. 103.

not uncommon for a surgeon to leave a potential or actual income in excess of one hundred thousand dollars per year in order to incarnate his faith among a community of desperately needy non-Christians. Long hours, inadequate facilities, and frustrating governmental regulations combine to stretch his faith and calling.

One would therefore assume that Muslim villagers would approach a mission-operated clinic or hospital with utmost gratitude. In most instances there is no other comparable medical care available within a hundred miles. What a privilege to have excellent humanitarian care extended to them by foreign doctors and nurses along with a competent national staff.

Mission hospitals traditionally have stressed a Christian witness within their overall program. There may be a nearby bookroom in which tracts and books are available. Evangelists share the gospel with patients who are awaiting treatment. In the wards, there is further opportunity on a long-term basis to present the Christian message to Muslims. There is no coercion; rather, one finds a sensitive, loving exhbition of Christian concern for the soul as well as for the body.

Yet, no matter how pure our motives are, we must deal with the reality of Muslim perception. Erich W. Bethmann has stated, "Most of our philanthropic work is not understood. Often it is considered to be a bait for catching converts and is resented."[24] A group of forty-six Muslim and Christian leaders meeting in Lebanon jointly stated, "It is especially unworthy to exploit the vulnerability of the uneducated, the sick, and the young."[25]

These criticisms by Muslims apply to many types of development, relief, and social assistance. What, then, is the missionary to do? We have often heard of the necessity to demonstrate the gospel rather than just make a cognitive presentation. Christ, we are told, must be shared as One who meets present as well as eternal needs. Christians such as Martin Goldsmith feel that Muslims are being unfair in their critiques of missionary social concern: "Christian missions have pioneered medical and education work in many countries throughout the world.

---

24. Erich W. Bethmann, *Bridge to Islam* (Nashville: Southern Publishing Association, 1950), p. 242.

25. "In Search of Understanding and Cooperation," *Al-Basheer*, vol. 2 (January-March 1973), p. 64.

Such institutions have not only aimed at the preaching of the Gospel, but have also been true expressions of Christian love. In recent years they have come under considerable attack for being mere underhand subterfuges for evangelism, but these attacks are not generally fair."[26]

L. Bevan Jones, who lived in prepartition India, was a prolific writer on Islam. In the milieu of desperate poverty which surrounded him, he struggled with the issues of "rice Christians" and then concluded:

> While scrupulously refraining from making promises of material assistance to the "inquirer," we should recognize that we have a very definite duty to the "convert" as soon as he has made his stand for Christ. We should now be as concerned for his body as we have all along been for his soul, since just because of his conversion, he will be, in most cases, desperately in need of the very means to live.
>
> Indeed, we have now a legitimate opportunity to furnish this kind of assistance as an object lesson bearing out our previous teaching. And the convert is certainly right in expecting such material help, until able to look after himself. He can quote our own Scriptures against us if we fail (Jas. 2:15; I John 3:17–18). We are often so afraid lest our charity do harm that it is well to remember that the real danger is not that we shall abuse the opportunity but neglect it altogether.[27]

This is a good presentation of the traditional view. Two comments are necessary. It is axiomatic that what the convert receives will be well known to the inquirer and thus fully qualifies for the category of inducements. Also, Jones assumes persecution and expulsion of the convert from the Islamic *ummah*. This is the very thing we are seeking to avoid. If this can be done, there will be no compelling financial need on the part of the convert. He will be engaged in the same job as before conversion. Of course, this assumes that people coming to Christ are not the unemployed or the rejects of society.

In *New Paths in Muslim Evangelism*, I have dealt in some de-

---

26. Martin Goldsmith, *Islam and Christian Witness* (Downers Grove: Inter-Varsity, 1982), pp. 109–10.

27. L. Bevan Jones, *The People of the Mosque* (Calcutta: Baptist Mission Press, 1932), p. 326.

tail with the postulate of parallel but not integrated models of social development and gospel propagation. I refer the reader to that source for a fuller explanation of that alternative. Here, I would like to present a brief proposal for a culturally appropriate medical ministry in an Islamic country. It can be enlarged and altered according to the particular needs of the people where it is implemented.

Staff: Two foreign doctors, two foreign nurses, two foreign men trained in public health and preventative medicine, along with a small national staff of dedicated Christians. All would be proficient in the local language and would have had considerable training in cross-cultural living. Each person would have studied Islam prior to involvement with Muslims.

Lifestyle: The staff would not cluster in one area. They would live in simple, rented accommodations among the people. If at all possible, motorcycles rather than expensive vehicles would be used. Public transportation would be utilized whenever possible. Efforts should be expended in having the Muslim community donate the use of a building for the medical facility. If this is not possible, then a small building should be rented. It is recognized that foreigners have recreational needs different from those of nationals. It is suggested they take regular breaks in a nearby large city, rather than construct a recreational facility where they live. The financial profile of the ministry should be commensurate with the immediate surroundings.

Ministry: Ten beds would be the maximum size. An outpatient facility would be open in the mornings only. Complicated surgical cases would be referred to the nearest alternative hospital. Patients would pay at least a portion of their medical fees.

Field workers would stress the preventative aspect of medical care. Evening classes would be held in villages.

There would be no formal gospel propagation. Only personal witness and friendship evangelism would be practiced. Carefully prepared, contextual literature could be discreetly shared with Muslims who express a more specific interest in the things of Christ. The name of the facility could be something like "Haven of Hope" or "Refuge of Peace."

The staff would strictly conform to the social expectations of the Muslim community by refraining from eating pork or doing

anything that would cause offense. Maximum social and professional interaction with Muslims would be encouraged. This
would lead to a natural and unstructured sharing of the Christian faith.

Would this proposal overcome the charge of missionaries *in-
ducing* the poor and diseased to become Christians? Possibly
not, but I feel it would move us significantly in that direction.
The important thing is for us to explore and experiment with
models that cause us to have ethical and moral credibility in the
eyes of both the Islamic government as well as the general Muslim populace. Much more can be done in this than has been
done in the past.

Felt Needs

Does all concern for the poor and needy have to be expressed
within institutional settings? What of the great fear that grips
millions of non-Christians: fear of failure, loneliness, financial
loss, evil spirits, and, finally, the fear of hell itself? These legitimate, pressing needs of the mind and heart are so often overlooked. It is easier to apply a bandage than to rebuke a demonic
presence. We have institutionalized our assistance with little
reference to the surging felt needs of the multitudes.

I, like other evangelicals, have hidden behind the statement,
"Yes, I should exercise believing prayer in a ministry of healing
sick bodies and consoling wounded minds. But I do not have
the supernaturally bestowed gift to be effective in this area of
spirituality. Therefore, I will continue dispensing medicine
along with a prayer for recovery of the ill."

In recent months, I have been challenged by a careful reading of Francis MacNutt's *Healing: An Act of Community*. This
balanced presentation urges involvement on the part of the
Christian community in a ministry of healing. The following is
a statement which I drew up after reading MacNutt's book as
well as going through the entire New Testament and doing a
study of each passage that relates to healing:

> The anointing of and prayer for the sick is a biblical teaching
> that has been largely ignored by the evangelical church. It
> should be reinstated as an expression of God's miraculous
> power and deep abiding concern for his suffering, hurting,
> alienated creation. Believers in Christ who are earnest seekers

of holiness are encouraged to anoint the sick with oil accompanied by laying on of hands and prayers of faith. This act should be performed in the context of a community of loving, concerned Christians. Administration of the rite must avoid mechanical or magical overtones. All concerned must acknowledge the sovereignty of God in the results of such a ceremony. No person may receive glory from acts of healing. To God alone be the exaltation and honor.

I have spent a significant amount of time watching "faith healers" on television. I admit to a rather high level of disgust when I observe how emotion is programed in order to get the setting right for the "slaying in the Spirit." Emotion seems to be a tool of the trade rather than a natural outflow from the Spirit of God. I have briefly attended a session in which a well-known evangelist was holding a workshop in which he taught his disciples how to speak in tongues and how to broaden their glossolalia vocabulary. He also gave demonstrations on how to dance in the Spirit. This man picked up his Ph.D in theology from a degree mill in Tennessee.

So I, like others, have seen enough to make me a skeptic, if not an outright unbeliever. Yet, I have been privileged to know intimately several Pentecostal missionaries who are very special men and women of God. I have no doubt whatsoever of their walk with the Lord and their commitment to the highest possible ethic in Christian service.

Added to this is my attendance at a healing meeting in which I documented to my satisfaction that a young girl, in response to believing prayer, was able to see for the first time in her life. It was a deeply touching moment to stand a few feet from the girl and see her blinking her eyes and excitedly saying to her father, "Daddy, I can see, Daddy, I can see!" That type of experience makes a believer out of a skeptic.

Perhaps I have less patience with a "gifts-not-for-this-age" theology than I do with faith healing. My study of the Bible simply does not allow me to conclude that the New Testament has closed shop on miracles. Some assert that we now have the completed canon and there is no further need of a miraculous authentication of the gospel. It seems to me that if Paul needed signs and wonders in his ministry, we who are in Muslim ministry need them every bit as much, if not more so. Eight hundred fifty million people are opposed to God's Word. It may well be that meeting their felt needs in some miraculous manner will be the only key to unlocking the hearts which have been so influenced against the message of Christ.

My concern is for an identification of felt needs among each people of the Muslim world. These areas of need will vary. May we be wary of a strategy based on the felt needs of the Bedouins of Morocco being transferred in total to the Punjabis of Pakistan.

We must also be careful to make our response community oriented. Heresies usually commence with one strong-willed, charismatic personality. So-called power gifts can be extremely dangerous. The checks and balances of the community will be an invaluable asset in guiding the utilization of gifts. This is why 1 Corinthians 14:29 speaks of collective judgment being passed on the person who prophesies in the name of the Lord. Is the prophecy of God or of the flesh? The body of believers assists in making that determination.

So, let us not forbid healings which pass the test of spiritual credibility. Our Lord is alive and active today. We must not confine a miracle-working God to the first century. As we cry out to the Lord for a new movement in the Muslim world, let us be prepared to follow where he leads us!

Church Forms

> The Christian missionary in approaching the Mohammedan, must be ready to make concessions respecting Christian customs and traditions. This in no way implies that there must be a concession in Christian truth, but a concession in practices and methods. We have been altogether too fixed in our forms of preaching and of conducting church worship, when approaching the Mohammedan of the East. He is also fixed in his methods and is often repelled at the outset by what he sees and hears, when the things that repel him have no particular significance to Christian worship, doctrine or life.[28]

A great fixed gulf separates Islam and Christianity. Both sides deeply appreciate their own worship forms and practices.

28. Barton, *The Christian Approach to Islam*, p. 257.

Christians, in light of accepted twentieth-century social norms, cannot comprehend squatting on the floor as they worship God. Muslims, on the other hand, consider sitting in pews as an objectionable style of worship. As Barton points out, it is the Christian who must be ready to make concessions in this area.

Indigeneity

The process of change is most interesting to observe. A few decades ago, the use of drums in African churches was prohibited by missionary overseers. Drums were considered to be an integral part of demon worship and thus totally unsuitable for Christian use. Today, drums are commonly found in churches throughout Africa. Barriers of resistance have slowly been lowered. Drums are now considered by most to be a neutral art form. Their appropriateness or otherwise is determined by context. In church, they are good; in animistic worship, they are unacceptable. An indigenous expression has come into its own among believers.

Only in recent years has Barton's call for Christian concession in areas of "practices and methods" been heeded. It has provoked no small controversy in certain evangelical circles. However, several missions have willingly experimented with the use of Muslim worship forms. It is my considered opinion that within ten to fifteen years there will be viable convert churches that will be utilizing indigenous forms in a good number of countries.

Francis A. Schaeffer has commented on the church's freedom of choice in regard to forms:

> Anything the New Testament does not command in regard to church form is a freedom to be exercised under the leadership of the Holy Spirit for that particular time and place. . . . It seems clear to me that the opposite cannot be held, namely only that which is commanded is allowed. If this were the case, then, for example, to have a church building would be wrong and so would having church bells or a pulpit, using books for singing, following any specific order of service, standing to sing, and many other like things. If consistently held in practice, I doubt if any church could function or worship.[29]

29. Francis A. Schaeffer, *The Church at the End of the Twentieth Century* (Downers Grove: Inter-Varsity, 1970), p. 67.

We as evangelicals are prone to declare the Bible to be a complete guide for all areas of life. But we must acknowledge the validity of Schaeffer's words. We in the West are living in the twentieth century, not the first. The fast-moving sophistication of the high-tech age demands a commensurate expression of appropriate church forms. The secular man who has responded to an invitation to visit a church will need to encounter the timeless message of Christ in a culturally relevant form. If he does not, it is likely the message will make little impact.

Likewise, we must give room to Muslim converts to construct an indigenous worship form which will be "contemporary" according to their preferences. If that means continuity with an age-old tradition, who are we as Westerners to declare it unacceptable?

Goldsmith has written concerning the influence of first-century cultural and religious norms on the formation of the early church:

> The weight of scholarship today would seem to lean away from any idea of a biblical blueprint towards the indisputable fact that the early Church based its forms on the religious background from which it sprang. Jewish synagogue worship and structures form the foundation on which the Christian Church was built. It may therefore be claimed that it is biblical for a church to relate closely to the religious and cultural context in which it is placed, although this must never be an excuse for doctrinal or spiritual compromise. This principle has profound implications for the Church in every land, for it means that the traditionalism must constantly yield to the pressures of our fast changing cultures. In Islamic societies too the Church will want to adjust to its milieu.[30]

It is encouraging to read comments such as these. When taken seriously, these words will change the face of missions in many lands of the world. The Western design of church buildings will give way to structures of indigenous relevance in countries like India and Algeria. Commonly accepted Western worship forms will be replaced by cultural and religious equivalents within each society in which a church is to be planted. Samuel P. Schlorff defines such an indigeneity as "a general

---

30. Goldsmith, *Islam and Christian Witness*, pp. 137–38.

continuity of customs and social practices between the new church and its society of origin."[31] Such a continuity can take place, I am convinced, without entering into a denial of theological integrity. This should be the goal of every missionary.

Another writer of early vintage has highlighted the tensions experienced by Muslim converts in the Indian subcontinent: "The Mohammedan wishes, and rightly so, to carry over into Christianity his national dress, language, and social customs in so far as they are not definitely anti-Christian; he finds himself conspicuous in a semi-Anglicized society, a "foreigner" in a religious community which seems to have lost all resemblance to those of the country of its birth."[32]

I totally concur with these sentiments and at the same time take issue with missionaries who declare that Muslims, upon conversion, desire to distance themselves from everything which could be even remotely considered Islamic. It would be my view that if converts do hold such a position, it probably can be traced back to the strong anti-Islamic bias of the missionary. The new believer has picked up his cues from his spiritual guide. Left to his own, I am confident the convert will happily express his newfound faith in Christ within his own society. In a country where most people are Muslims, this society is naturally impregnated with Islamic influence. This need not be evil or demonic. There should be an intelligent and rational evaluation process that defines areas of life which are in direct conflict with Scripture and those which are not. Some practices will be appreciatively retained while others will be quietly dropped. Is it not possible that the convert, with the aid of the Holy Spirit, can be a better judge of these issues than can the Western missionary?

Nazir-Ali has written of a large group of Christians who have sought to express indigeneity within an Indian Hindu context:

The Christians of St. Thomas of India (present membership approximately 3 million out of a total population of 18 million Indian Christians) have lived, for centuries, in an environment

31. Samuel P. Schlorff, ed., *Discipleship in Islamic Society* (Upper Darby, Penn.: North Africa Mission, 1981), p. 12.
32. T. H. P. Sailer, *The Muslim Faces the Future* (New York: Missionary Education Movement in the U.S. and Canada, 1926), pp. 196–97.

that is predominantly Hindu even to the extent that they are often treated as a caste within Hinduism. No one attending the
liturgy of (say) the Mar Thoma Church can fail to be impressed
by the degree of contextualization (I use a fashionable term)
that church has attained. The liturgy I attended was in Malaya-
lam with vestigial Syriac parts, the "Peace" and the "*Dominus
vobiscum*" were given in the form of the traditional Indian *na-
maste* greetings, the chanting and singing were typically Indian and the love-feast at the end of the Eucharist consisted of a
banana and a glass of tea! The whole thing seemed thoroughly
indigenous.[33]

Organizational Informality

Mission organizations, in the past, have tended to reproduce
Western-style denominations among their converts. This has
included the purchase of property and financing of church
buildings along with the construction of schools, orphanages,
and hospitals. Linkage between churches has necessitated a
central hierarchy of leadership. This has not been accomplished without a great deal of tension between nationals and
missionaries as well as among church members themselves.
Money and power have been sought in carnal and spiritually
destructive ways. Divisions in the body have ended up in dis-
graceful court cases. Jealousy has precipitated feuds that have
permanently alienated friends and families.

Muslims have successfully avoided many of these expressions of carnality within their religious life. The mosque is the
center of Islamic *ummah* but it is not a place where power seeking and financial considerations are prominent. There is little
linkage between mosques; therefore, the priests are not
tempted to seek positions of recognition and power. The function of the mosque is overwhelmingly spiritual; thus the cash
flow is minimal. Few institutions, other than religious schools,
are attached to the mosque. A small committee has oversight of
the mosque. This group of devout Muslims is responsible for its
care as well as for raising funds for the salary of the *imam*.

Can there not be continuity between what the convert has ap-
preciated in mosque organization and what he now experiences

33. Nazir-Ali, *Islam*, p. 146.

as he moves into the *ummah* of Christianity? Must he be exposed to structures, supposedly spiritual, which in reality will accomplish several very negative things:

1. He will be automatically distanced from his community by affiliation with a foreign "organization."
2. Most likely, he will feel very uncomfortable in such a new surrounding.
3. The convert may be repelled by the carnal actions of so-called Christians who are power mongers within the church structure. This could lead to reversion to Islam.
4. It has been historically documented that the new believer has, on occasion, been so overwhelmingly tempted that he has succumbed to the same sins that he has observed in the lives of older, yet extremely ungodly believers.

The critic can simply dismiss these comments as a caricature of the church and not a reality. Or, it could be stated, "So, what is new? This has all been happening since Paul's day." I have observed these phenomena throughout the church in many countries—not, of course, in every church, but in enough places to make me concerned. There were those who were carnal in Paul's day but that is never an excuse for desiring less than excellence within the Kingdom. What then can be done to construct an appropriate and relevant vehicle through which a dynamic Christian *ummah* can be realized? Perhaps house churches would be a good place to start. Watchman Nee wrote from the context of an emerging church in China in which many of the issues are parallel to those found in Muslim lands:

> The grand edifices of today with their lofty spires speak of the world and the flesh rather than of the Spirit, and in many ways they are not nearly as well suited to the purpose of Christian assembly as the private homes of God's people. In the first place, people feel much freer to speak of spiritual things in the unconventional atmosphere of a home than in a spacious church building where everything is conducted in a formal manner; besides, there is not the same possibility for mutual intercourse there. . . . Further, if the churches are in the private homes of the brethren, they naturally feel that all the interests

of the church are their interests. Still further, the meetings in
believers' homes can be a fruitful testimony to the neighbors.[34]

Westerners react against such thinking. We regard the home
as a family-oriented haven of privacy somewhat remote from
the demands and pressures of the outside world. The church is
to be a special building set apart for the express purpose of religious function. This preference is indicated by its export to the
non-Western world through the ministry of missionaries. Roman Catholics particularly were fond of planting huge cathedrals wherever their propagation took hold.

A number of Scriptures point to the earliest church being
formed and nurtured in the homes of believers:

Acts 2:46—The believers break bread.

Romans 16:5—Paul greets a house church.

1 Corinthians 16:19—The church which meets in Aquila and
Prisca's house is noted.

Colossians 4:15—Paul refers to the church that is in the
home of Nympha.

Philemon 2—Paul is writing to a house church.

As Jesus had met with the first disciples in small groups, and as
they had met together outdoors and in homes, so did the first
Christians. The life of the early church was nourished in
homes. First, it was built through normal family life. Second it
was fed through *koinonia* groups, cells of people who met together for prayer, worship, and the Eucharist, and who passed
on Jesus' teaching by word of mouth.[35]

Obviously there is a great deal of utilitarian value in church
buildings. But the negatives have often been overlooked. Consider the issue of cost. How many Muslim converts in poor Islamic countries can afford the high cost of property and
buildings? The only alternative is for Western money to come
to the rescue. This initiates the dependency that then becomes

34. Watchman Nee, *The Normal Christian Church Life* (Washington, D.C.:
International Students Press, 1962), pp. 116–17.
35. Howard A. Snyder, "The Church as Community: Subculture or
Counterculture?" *Christianity Today*, 8 April 1983, p. 30.

a permanent feature of the Christian *ummah* and which also creates deep tensions between nationals and missionaries. Is it not better for the church to meet in homes until such a time as believers themselves can afford the relative luxury of their own building? With proper guidance, believers can be motivated to donate a portion of land for the church. Others can then contribute building materials. In most villages of the Muslim world, the actual building of a simple house of worship can be done by the believers. They can then "own" the building communally. In this way true indigeneity has triumphed over financial dependence on the West.

Whether a building materializes or not, the emphasis should always be on the people of God, not on a manmade structure.

> The church is never a place, but always a people; never a fold but always a flock; never a sacred building but always a believing assembly. The church is you who pray, not where you pray. A structure of brick or marble can no more be a church than your clothes of serge or satin can be you. There is in this world nothing sacred but man, no sanctuary of man but the soul.[36]

Does this then prohibit relationships between bodies of believers? Are the dangers of hierarchical structuring such that each assembly must be an island unto itself? No, not at all. My plea is for informal fellowships to be be brought about by like-minded churches. The purpose of such groupings would be stimulation, encouragement, and *koinonia*. The financial liability of churches would be kept to a minimum. No slate of officers or paid coordinators would be required. A few men serving in a voluntary capacity would be the liaison between churches. When the fellowship becomes sufficiently large, it can then divide into two separate groups. Spiritual formation would be the major focus of the fellowships.

This church would rely heavily on lay leadership. It would be best to have either volunteer or part-time clergy. Once full-time ministers are appointed, there is a natural veering away from the prominence of lay leadership in the church.

> The New Testament doctrine of ministry rests therefore not on the clergy-laity distinction but on the twin and complementary

---

36. John F. Havlik, *People-Centered Evangelism* (Nashville: Broadman, 1971), p. 47.

pillars of the priesthood of all believers and the gifts of the
Spirit. Today, four centuries after the Reformation, the full implications of this Protestant affirmation have yet to be worked
out. The clergy-laity dichotomy is a direct carry-over from pre-
Reformation Roman Catholicism and a throwback to the Old
Testament priesthood. It is one of the principal obstacles to the
Church effectively being God's agent of the Kingdom today because it creates the false idea that only "holy men" namely, or-
dained ministers, are really qualified and responsible for
leadership and significant ministry. In the New Testament there
are functional distinctions between various kinds of minis-
tries but no hierarchical division between clergy and laity.[37]

These words are particularly appropriate for the norm of
very small Muslim convert churches. In our work we have actively sought to keep natural leaders within the boundaries of
lay leadership. We have not taken specially gifted men and sent
them to a distant area to attend a Bible school. This, in our
thinking, would impair a sense of group unity and continuity.
Training should take place on the local level as close as physically possible to where the believers live. We have found it expedient, because of possible persecution, to have our training
center some fifteen miles distant from where the converts are
resident. Yet, it is easily accessible to all. Sessions are held from
6 p.m. to midnight a few times each month.

More prayer, research, and creative thinking are called for
as, for the first time in many areas of the Muslim world, we begin to move from an exclusive emphasis on propagation to a balanced mix of evangelism and church formation.

Worship

For Muslims, worship is a broad term which is applied beyond
prayer (*salat*). Worship (*ibadah*) is the submission that Allah is
your Master and you are His servant, and so all that the servant
does in obedience to Him is *ibadah*. Every good deed performed to seek the pleasure of Allah is worship. This can be an
individual act, or a collective one. There are some rituals of
ibadah which have been made compulsory and, if left out, one
commits a sin or ceases to be a Muslim.[38]

37. Howard A. Snyder, *The Community of the King* (Downers Grove:
Inter-Varsity, 1977), p. 95.
38. Badru D. Kateregga and David W. Shenk, *Islam and Christianity: A
Muslim and a Christian in Dialogue* (Grand Rapids: Eerdmans, 1981), p. 154.

Worship is an all-embracive concept and practice for Muslims. A Muslim's eternal destiny is tied up in this word. You cannot be a true Muslim unless worship is an intellectual assent as well as a ritual. It must be cognitive as well as emotional. Worship is liturgical and repetitive, but it also must be dynamic if it is to be regarded as genuine.

The etymologies of the Hebrew and Greek words for "worship" in the Bible highlight the concepts of service and prostration. The English word *worship* is derived from the Anglo-Saxon *weorthscipe*, which means to ascribe worth, value, or honor to something or someone. The worship of God, then, points to an appreciation which is expressed by prostration. This worship is authenticated by going forth in service to God. Worship is an encounter between creator God and created servant.[39]

Apart from the prophetic passages of Revelation, my favorite Scripture regarding worship and service in the New Testament is found in Acts 2:46–47.

And day by day continuing with one mind in the temple, and breaking bread from house to house, they were taking their meals together with gladness and sincerity of heart, praising God, and having favor with all the people. And the Lord was adding to their number day by day those who were being saved.

In this passage is seen regularity, unity, sharing, fellowship, joy, sincerity, praise, service, and fruit. That is real Christian worship!

Are Muslims and Christians so far removed from each other in their respective understandings of worship? In one sense, the answer is negative. Both devout worshipers sincerely are questing for God. They long to adore and to serve. Yet, in a theological sense, the chasm is wide. For within worship is salvation. Once redemption is discussed, the distinctives of each religion become painfully clear. Yet, common ground should and must be explored.

As I mentioned earlier, I have serious reservations concern-

39. Alan G. Nute, "Worship," in *In God's Community: Essays on the Church and Its Ministry*, ed. David J. Ellis and W. Ward Gasque (Wheaton: Shaw, 1978), p. 40.

ing Christians praying in the mosque. This concern does not extend to praying with individual Muslims in a manner carefully calculated to avoid embarrassment to both parties. Dr. Ali and I thoroughly enjoyed praying with each other on numerous occasions. This was usually done in the privacy of my home. I would kneel in silent prayer while Dr. Ali would perform the prescribed ritual in Arabic. At the end we would both pray extemporaneously in the vernacular. Our prayer time would conclude with us embracing each other in the usual Muslim fashion.

In 1982, my wife, following an operation, was told she had cancer and that we should return immediately to the States. Our tranquil world was suddenly thrown into disarray. For the next six days we were stretched to our full capacity in making travel arrangements, packing, and serving cups of tea to our friends who had come to express their sympathy. At this crucial point in our lives, Dr. Ali became a real source of comfort. Each evening we would go into my small office, kneel on simple straw mats, and pray earnestly for grace, wisdom, and strength. Forever etched in my mind are the choked words and misty eyes of Dr. Ali as he cried out to Allah for Julie's healing. His expression of empathetic pain for what we were going through was deeply touching and reinforcing. God used a Muslim (as well as close Christian friends) to reach out to us in our night of stygian darkness.

Upon return to the States, we were told there had been a mix-up in laboratory tests and that actually my wife was as well as I am! When word went out to Dr. Ali's family, his aged mother first received the news on the phone. She shouted *Al-hamdu-Li-llah* (All praise to God) ten times. Such is the lifestyle of a dedicated Muslim family which takes worship seriously.

Cragg ponders the meaning of the Muslim call to prayer:

Here, then, is the Christian summons toward that fellowship which links the centuries in allegiance to Mahammad and proclaims itself from dawn to sunset each returning day. What does this Christian vocation mean in the light of the manifold moods and aspirations around the minaret today? Ascending with the remembrancer of prayer, how do we survey the life that spreads below him? Descending again into the bustle of multitudinous humanity, which through the waking hours the muezzin punctuates with prayer, what shall we be constrained to say? How shall we explain to the worship the minaret enjoins, the worship we owe to God in Christ? How shall we take the meanings of Christ into the summons from the mosque?[40]

If we as Christians are to go "beyond the mosque" physically as well as spiritually, then we are to equal or excel the Muslim desire for and practice of prayer. It is at this crucial point that I feel we as a community are found wanting. Our evangelical prayer lives are often cold, listless, and irregular. Perhaps following a five-times-daily regimen of prayer would be beneficial for the convert to retain as well as for the Western Christian to commence.

Fasting to the Muslim is an expression of worship. Ramadan is that special month of the year when Muslims worldwide abstain from food and drink during daylight hours. A sense of close fellowship prevails as a voluntary discipline is undertaken that has as its goal the spiritual cleansing of the believer. Goldsmith comments on the possible continuation of the fast after a person had converted to Christ:

> And then comes the question of the fast month. In connection with prayer, fasting is encouraged in the New Testament. Jesus gives teaching on the snare of pride in fasting and the dangers of sanctimonious piety, but true fasting has a significant place in Christian devotion. Is it permissible to introduce a fast month along Muslim lines into a Christian Church? Of course, it must be voluntary and practiced in conjunction with prayer. Good teaching from the New Testament would then instruct believers in the basic principles of Christian fasting.[41]

In 1982, in the Muslim country of our residence, I kept the entire month of the Muslim fast.

> The incessant ringing of the alarm clock at 3 a.m. slowly brought me to consciousness. A siren wailing in the background assured my groggy mind that another day of universal fasting was about to get under way. I made my way to our fifty-five-gallon drum of well water where a few splashes of cool water brought me to a functional state.

40. Cragg, *The Call of the Minaret*, pp. 184–85.
41. Goldsmith, *Islam and Christian Witness*, p. 140.

We (my wife and I) sat down to a light breakfast (which was not break-fast, but in reality the initiation of the fast) of toast and homemade cereal. Coffee and several glasses of water were forced down as an inadequate prophylactic to the deprivation of liquids which was to follow.

At 3:45 we read from the Bible and had a season of prayer together. Soon thereafter, the *azan* (call to prayer) was heard. It signaled the commencement of the fast. After returning to bed, we began the battle to subdue a fully alert mind and return to sleep once again. By 7 a.m., we were awakened by the more benign act of the sun shining through our bedroom window.

The Muslim fast in which I participated commenced on the longest day of the year, June 23, and ended at sunset on July 22. The actual time of the fast was from 4 a.m. to 7 p.m. During these fifteen hours, for thirty extremely hot days, I ate no food and drank no liquid. I sought to follow each prohibition as prescribed by the Quran and Hadith.

The first three days were the most difficult. I had recurring headaches, some dizziness, and moderate weakness. If one takes medicine, then the fast is automatically broken. The body seemed to adjust quite well to the new rhythm, but by the end of the month I was extremely weak.

During the fast, I sought to continue my ministry which included several trips out to our regional centers. I made two longer trips which involved nine hours of travel each day. Most afternoons I would take a two-hour rest and then indulge in a protracted period of pouring cool, refreshing water over my body. One concession to those engaged in the fast is being allowed to rinse out one's mouth with water. On one very hot afternoon I was forced to engage in this practice every twenty minutes.

My research indicates that, in the country where I lived, approximately 40 percent of the adult Muslims keep the fast. More villagers than city dwellers participate in the abstinence. There was almost no eating, drinking, or smoking in public. Even though forbidden, there was a notable increase in quarrels as the days of the fast slowly ground on.

It was a special delight to share the light refreshment (*iftar*) at the daily breaking of the fast with Muslim friends. There was an expressed appreciation that I, a Christian missionary, would participate in such a rigorous discipline of fasting with them. This led on to a time of joyous celebration together at the time of *Id-ul-Fitr*, the festival of feasting and gaiety which marks the end of the fast.

It is obvious that fasting cannot be legislated for Christians. There is, however, a place for a voluntary participation in the fast within Muslim contexts. I have often protested the tendency for converts to feel liberated from Islamic legalisms and thus end up as Christians with much less spiritual discipline than they had as Muslims. There is also the issue of inquirers. Many seekers would feel more comfortable in pursuing truth in a community where spiritual forms are not that distinct from those which they have followed throughout their lives.

Worship must be a primary emphasis in the emerging convert church. Devout Christians and Muslims have a common desire to reach out to God in adoration. This area of common experience can become a bridge over which the gospel can reverently be carried into the Muslim heart.

The New Community

We are still confronted with the specific issue of the convert remaining within Islamic *ummah* and yet simultaneously becoming a member of a new community. Matheny comments, "Would it not be acceptable for a convert to remain a part of his old community culturally, socially, and politically and still become a Christian? If the sect can be defined as basically social and cultural as opposed to religious then could not an Arab change his religious beliefs without necessarily having to change his sectarian affiliations?"[42]

The specific answer to this query will vary not only from country to country, but also from village to village. There is a fairly broad range of tolerance and intolerance among Muslims. The Sufis of northern India may well be graciously accepting of a convert who seeks to carefully continue within the *ummah* of his birth. In other more radical areas of the Muslim world, it may be extremely difficult to maintain continuity with Islamic society once a commitment to Christ is made. Difficult, but I trust not impossible.

It is definite that there will have to be a viable and dynamic

42. Matheny, *Reaching the Arabs*, p. 79.

community within the community. Christian *ummah* must be alive if it is to attract anyone into its midst. In the New Testament, the word that is translated "saints" is, with one exception, plural.

"The church exists in time and space and so must come together in time and space. Real community means shared time, shared meals, shared priorities, and some level of economic sharing. Specific patterns may vary, but New Testament *koinonia* does not exist without this shared life."[43]

There is a price to be paid for real community. Sharing costs. But within this principle of the shared life comes liberation and fruitfulness. Elizabeth O'Connor writes of how we in the West have positioned our church pews in such a way as to distance ourselves from our fellow Christians. She goes on to say, "We have not wanted to suffer in any serious way the encountering of one another, all unaware that avoidance deprives us of community that would evoke in our lives the experience of the unity of Psalm 133:1, 'Behold, how good and how pleasant it is for brethren to dwell together in unity.'"[44]

In whatever circumstances the believers find themselves, there is one assurance. The community in which they now find themselves will be a new community. "Therefore if any man is in Christ, he is a *new* creature" (2 Cor. 5:17).

Two of the most sacred mosques of the Islamic world look down from their sanctuaries eastward toward the trees of Old Gethsemane. From its olive-covered slopes the Garden of the Agony looks westward to the domes and minarets of the ancient skyline. In the still dawn the muezzin can be heard calling to prayer across the valley where Jesus communed with His spirit until midnight and went forth, the Christ of the Cross, the Saviour of the world. Through all their history, since the minarets were raised, the two faiths have been that near, that far. It is out of the meaning of the Garden that Christ's men have crossed into the world of the domes and the muezzin. We who, in our generation, listen to the call of the minaret may hear it most compellingly from the muezzin over Gethsemane. There

43. Snyder, "The Church as Community," p. 32.
44. Elizabeth O'Connor, *The New Community* (New York: Harper and Row, 1976), p. 3.

we shall best understand wherewith we must answer—and how—and why.[45]

So close, and yet so far. How true—and how sad. The world's two largest religions embrace almost two billion people, approximately half of the earth's population. Both promote monotheism, both maintain allegiance to biblical prophets, both are committed to high ethics and morals, both believe in a final day of judgment—yet how great is the distance between the crescent and the dove, the minaret and the cross, the Prophet and the Son of God. As Cragg points out, between Jerusalem's church and mosque is situated the quiet Garden of Gethsemane, a garden so symbolic of misunderstanding, loneliness, pain, hurt, and even betrayal. But there in the Garden we can visualize Christ bowed in deep agony of intercession. Not a time-bound supplication, but rather a prayer that embraces the world, for all ages, for all peoples—and for all eternity. Christ the catalyst between mosque and church. In Gethsemane, and in relationship to Jesus, we find the response to Cragg's question of "why." We now go forward—armed with love, humility, and the power of the Spirit.

The world of Islam waits before us . . . .

45. Cragg, *The Call of the Minaret*, p. 356.

The author invites correspondence at the following address:

Dr. Phil Parshall
5930 S.W. 112th Avenue
Miami, Florida 33173

Glossary

Ahmadiyya—a small but vocal sect within Islam
Azan—the Muslim call to prayer
Caliph—formerly, the spiritual leader of Islam
Dar-ul-Harb—territory outside of Islamic influence
Dar-ul-Islam—the territory of Islam
Dervish—a wandering religious mendicant
Dhikr—"remembrance"; a ceremony that centers around the recitation of the names and attributes of God
Druzes—a group in Lebanon that is an offshoot of the Ismailis
Faqir—a religious person who solicits alms in the name of Islam
Folk Islam—Islam as it is practiced by adherents on the grassroots level of society
Hadith—the Islamic Traditions
Hajj—the pilgrimage to Mecca
Id-ul-Fitr—the festival at the conclusion of Ramadan, the month of fasting
Iftar—the light refreshment eaten at the time of breaking the fast during Ramadan
Imam—the prayer leader in a mosque; in Shiite terminology, the title given to the spiritual leader of Islam
Ismailis—a sect among the Shiis
Jihad—Islamic religious war
Mazar—the shrine of a departed Muslim mystic
Mujaddid—the messiah, as defined in Islamic doctrine and belief

229

Murid—a follower of a pir
Murshid—a spiritual guide
Muta—temporary marriage
Naqshbandi—one of the four major orders of Sufism
Pir—a mystically-oriented Muslim spiritual guide
Qadiri—one of the four major orders of Sufism
Ramadan—the Islamic month of fasting
Shahadah—the Islamic confession in faith (There is no deity
     but God and Muhammad is his Prophet)
Shaikh—a spiritual leader within the Dervish order of Sufism
Shariat—the code of Islamic law
Shiis—a theological division of Islam; most Shiites live in Iran
Sufism—a mystically-oriented school of thought within Islam
Suhrawardi—one of the four major orders of Sufism
Sunnah—a record of sayings and activities of Muhammad
Sunni—a theological division of Islam; 90 percent of all Mus-
     lims are Sunnis
Surah—a chapter of the Quran
Tarika—a path or order within Sufism
Ulama—a body of learned Muslim theologians
Ummah—the community of Muslims
Urs—"marriage"; a union between a *pir* and God at the time of
     his death. This event is celebrated by disciples each year on
     the anniversary of the *pir's* death. The word also denotes the
     annual religious meeting of a living *pir*.
Wahhabis—the most fundamentalist sect of Islam
Zakat—a pillar of Islam; it mandates that Muslims give 2.5 per-
     cent of their income to Islamic causes

Bibliography

Abd-al Ati, Hammudah. *Establishment of Islamic Communities.* Plainfield, Ind.: Muslim Students' Association of the U.S. and Canada, 1974.

———. *The Family Structure in Islam.* Indianapolis: American Trust Publications, 1977.

———. *Islam in Focus.* Indianapolis: American Trust Publications, 1975.

Abduh, Muhammad. *The Theology of Unity.* Translated by Ishaq Musa'ad and Kenneth Cragg. New York: Arno, 1980.

Ahmad, Khurshid. *Fanaticism, Intolerance and Islam.* Lahore: Islamic Publications, 1957.

Ajijola, A. D. *Why I Believe in Islam?* Lahore: Islamic Publications, 1975.

Akhavi, Shahrough. *Religion and Politics in Contemporary Iran: Clergy-State Relations in the Pahlavi Period.* Albany: State University of New York Press, 1980.

Akram, Muhammad. *A Look at the West.* Lahore: Islamic Publications, 1971.

Al-Faruqi, Ismail. "Statement of Faith." In the catalog of American Islamic College. Chicago, 1983.

Al-Hujwiri, Ali Bin Uthman. *The Kashf Al-Mahjub.* Translated by R. A. Nicholson. New Delhi: Taj Company, 1982.

Ali, Syed Ameer. *The Spirit of Islam.* London: Christophers, 1922.

Ali, Zeyd A. "Deserving of Zukat." *The Voice of Islam*, June-July 1983, pp. 2–3.

Al-Khayyat, Sheikh Abd-allah. *The Muslim's Guide to Faith and Purification*. Translated by Abdul Kadir Al-Hubaiti. Muslim World League, 1975.

Al-Sawwaf, Shaikh Muhammad Mahmud. *The Muslim Book of Prayer*. Translated by Mujahid Muhammad Al-Sawwaf. Doha: Dar Ul Uloom Est, n.d.

Andrew, G. Findlay. *The Crescent in North-west China*. London: China Inland Mission, 1912.

Ansari, F. R. *Islam and Western Civilisation*. Karachi: World Federation of Islamic Missions, 1975.

Ansari, Zafar Ishaq. "Truth, Revelation and Obedience." *Al Basheer*, vol. 2 (January-March 1973), pp. 26–29.

Arberry, A. J. *The Doctrine of the Sufis*. Lahore: Shaikh Muhammad Ashraf, 1966.

Arensberg, Conrad M., and Solon T. Kimball. *Culture and Community*. New York: Harcourt, Brace and World, 1965.

Arnold, T. W. *The Preaching of Islam*. 1896. Lahore: Shaikh Muhammad Ashraf, 1976.

Arsalan, Amir Shakib. *Our Decline and Its Causes*. Translated by M. A. Shakoor. Lahore: Shaikh Muhammad Ashraf, 1944.

Asad, Muhammad. *The Road to Mecca*. 1954. Gibralter: Dar Al-Andalus, 1980.

Attar, Farid Al-Din. *Muslim Saints and Mystics*. Translated by A. J. Arberry. Boston: Routledge and Kegan Paul, 1966.

Ayyubi, Mohiuddin, ed. *Khumeini Speaks Revolution*. Translated by N. M. Shaikh. Karachi: International Islamic Publishers, 1981.

Azad, Abul Kalam. *Basic Concepts of the Quran*. Hyderabad, India: Academy of Islamic Studies, 1958.

Badawi, Zaki. *Islam in Britain*. London: Ta Ha Publishers, 1981.

Bainton, Roland H. *Here I Stand: A Life of Martin Luther*. New York: Mentor, 1950.

Bakker, D. "Islam in Indonesia." *The Muslim World*, vol. 62, no. 1 (January 1972), pp. 126–36.

Bammate, Haider. *Muslim Contribution to Civilization*. Brentwood: American Trust Publications, 1962.

Banks, Robert J. *Paul's Idea of Community: The Early House Churches in Their Historical Setting*. Grand Rapids: Eerdmans, 1980.

Barton, James L. *The Christian Approach to Islam*. Boston: Pilgrim, 1918.

"Battle of Two Islams." *Time*, 7 March 1983, p. 58.

Bawany, Ebrahim Ahmed, ed. *Islam—Our Choice*. Geneva: Muslim World League Printing Press, 1982.

Bell, Richard. *The Origin of Islam in Its Christian Environment*. London: Frank Cass and Co., 1968.

Bennigsen, Alexandre K. "Islam in the Soviet Union." In *Change and the Muslim World*, edited by Philip H. Stoddard, David C. Cuthell, and Margaret W. Sullivan, pp. 115-25. Syracuse, N.Y.: Syracuse University Press, 1981.

Berkouwer, G. C. *The Church*. Translated by James E. Davison. Grand Rapids: Eerdmans, 1976.

Bernard, Jessie. "Community Disorganization." In *International Encyclopedia of the Social Sciences*, pp. 163-69.

Berque, Jacques. *The Arabs: Their History and Future*. Translated by Jean Steward. New York: Praeger, 1964.

Bertocci, Peter J. "Bangladesh Composite Cultural Identity and Modernization in a Muslim-Majority State." In *Change and the Muslim World*, edited by Philip H. Stoddard, David C. Cuthell, and Margaret W. Sullivan, pp. 75-85. Syracuse, N.Y.: Syracuse University Press, 1981.

Bethmann, Erich W. *Bridge to Islam*. Nashville: Southern Publishing Association, 1950.

———. *Steps Toward Understanding Islam*. Kohinur series, no. 4. Washington, D.C.: American Friends of the Middle East, 1966.

Bonhoeffer, Dietrich. *The Communion of Saints: A Dogmatic Inquiry into the Sociology of the Church*. New York: Harper and Row, 1963.

Brockelmann, Carl. *History of the Islamic Peoples*. Translated by Joel Carmichael and Moshe Perlmann. New York: Capricorn, 1939.

Brohi, A. K. *Islam in the Modern World*. Lahore: Publishers United, 1975.

Brown, David. *The Way of the Prophet*. London: Highway, 1962.

Brown, William Adams. *Church and State in Contemporary America*. New York: Scribner's, 1936.

Bruce, F. F. "Lessons from the Early Church." In *In God's Community: Essays on the Church and Its Ministry*, edited by David J. Ellis and W. Ward Gasque, pp. 153-71. Wheaton: Shaw, 1978.

Burckhardt, Titus. *An Introduction to Sufi Doctrine.* Translated by D. M. Matheson. Lahore: Shaikh Muhammad Ashraf, 1959.

Burquest, Donald A. "A Celebration Feast of Forgiveness." *Christianity Today,* 9 April 1982, pp. 24–25.

Bush, Richard C., Jr. *Religion in Communist China.* Nashville: Abingdon, 1970.

Calverley, Edwin E. *Islam: An Introduction.* Cairo: The American University at Cairo, 1958.

Caskel, Werner. "Western Impact and Islamic Civilization." In *Unity and Variety in Muslim Civilization,* edited by G. E. Von Grunebaum. Chicago: University of Chicago Press, 1955.

Casserley, J. V. Langmead. *Christian Community.* London: Longmans, Green and Co., 1960.

Chan, Wing-tsit. *Religious Trends in Modern China.* New York: Octagon, 1969.

Chraibi, Driss. *Heirs to the Past.* Translated by Len Ortzen. London: Heinemann Educational Books, 1971.

Christian Witness among Muslims. Accra, Ghana: Africa Christian Press, 1971.

Coad, F. R. "Christian Unity." In *In God's Community: Essays on the Church and Its Ministry,* edited by David J. Ellis and W. Ward Gasque, pp. 113–21. Wheaton, Shaw, 1978.

Costas, Orlando. *Christ Outside the Gate: Mission Beyond Christendom.* Maryknoll, N.Y.: Orbis, 1982.

Cragg, Kenneth. *The Call of the Minaret.* New York: Oxford University Press, 1956.

————. *The Dome and the Rock: Jerusalem Studies in Islam.* London: S.P.C.K., 1964.

————. *Islamic Surveys 3: Counsels in Contemporary Islam.* Edinburgh: University Press, 1965.

————. *Muhammad and the Christian.* New York: Maryknoll, 1984.

————. *Sandals at the Mosque: Christian Presence amid Islam.* New York: Oxford University Press, 1959.

Cragg, Kenneth, and R. Marston Speight, comps. *Islam from Within: Anthology of a Religion.* Belmont, Calif.: Wadsworth, 1980.

Cutshall, Alden. *The Philippines: Nation of Islands.* Princeton, N.J.: VanNostrand, 1964.

Dawson, Joseph Martin. *America's Way in Church, State, and Society.* New York: Macmillan, 1953.

Dermenghem, Emile. *Muhammad and the Islamic Tradition.* Translated by Jean M. Watt. New York, Harper and Brothers, 1958.

DeVries, Bert. "Islamic Renewal in the Twentieth Century." *Reformed Journal,* vol. 30 (July 1980), pp. 9–11.

Diamond, Michael J., and Peter G. Gowing. *Islam and Muslims, Some Basic Information.* Quezon City: New Day Publishers, 1981.

Djajadiningrat, P. A. Hoesein. "Islam in Indonesia," In *Islam: The Straight Path,* edited by Kenneth W. Morgan, pp. 375–402. New York: Ronald Press, 1958.

Dodd, Peter, and Halim Barakat. "Palestinian Refugees of 1967: A Sociological Study." *The Muslim World,* vol. 60 (April 1970), pp. 123–42.

Donohue, John J., and John L. Esposito, eds. *Islam in Transition: Muslim Perspectives.* New York: Oxford University Press, 1982.

Dorman, Harry Gaylord, Jr. *Toward Understanding Islam.* New York: Teachers College, Columbia University, 1948.

Drewes, G. W. J. "Indonesia: Mysticism and Activism." In *Unity and Variety in Muslim Civilization,* edited by G. E. Von Grunebaum. Chicago: University of Chicago Press, 1955.

Elder, J. *The Biblical Approach to the Muslim.* Houston: Leadership Instruction and Training International, n.d.

Ellis, David J., and W. Ward Gasque, eds. *In God's Community: Essays on the Church and Its Ministry.* Wheaton: Shaw, 1978.

Emmerson, Donald K. "Islam in Modern Indonesia." In *Change and the Muslim World,* edited by Philip H. Stoddard, David C. Cuthell, and Margaret W. Sullivan, pp. 158–68. Syracuse, N.Y.: Syracuse University Press, 1981.

"Extremist gets death sentence in Jakarta." *Bangladesh Observer,* 27 September 1982, p. 12.

Farah, Caesar E. *Islam: Beliefs and Observances.* Woodbury, N.Y.: Barron's Education Series, 1968.

Faris, Nabih Amin, ed. *The Arab Heritage.* Princeton: Princeton University Press, 1946.

Faruqi, Ismail Al. "Islam as Culture and Civilization." In *Islam and Contemporary Society,* pp. 140–76. New York: Longman, 1982.

Fernea, Elizabeth W. *Guests of the Sheik.* Garden City, N.Y.: Anchor, 1965.

Ferré, Nels F. S. *Christianity and Society.* New York: Harper and Brothers, 1950.

Fry, C. George, and James R. King. *Islam: A Survey of the Muslim Faith*. Grand Rapids: Baker, 1980.

Gardet, Louis. *Mohammedanism*. Edited by Henri Daniel-Rops. Translated by William Burridge. New York: Hawthorn, 1961.

Gasque, W. Ward. "The Church in the New Testament." In *In God's Community: Essays on the Church and Its Ministry*, edited by David J. Ellis and W. Ward Gasque, pp. 1–13. Wheaton: Shaw, 1978.

Gaudefroy-Demombynes, Maurice. *Muslim Institutions*. Translated by John P. Macgregor. London: George Allen and Unwin, 1950.

Geertz, Clifford. *Islam Observed: Religious Development in Morocco and Indonesia*. New Haven: Yale University Press, 1968.

———. *The Religion of Java*. Chicago: University of Chicago Press, 1960.

Gibb, H. A. R. *Modern Trends in Islam*. New York: Octagon, 1972.

———. *Mohammedanism: An Historical Survey*. 2d ed. London: Oxford University Press, 1982.

Gibb, H. A. R., and J. H. Kramers, eds. *Shorter Encyclopedia of Islam*. Leiden: Brill, 1953.

Glang, Sahid S., and Manuel M. Convocar. *Maguindanaon, Field Report Series No. 6*. Quezon City: Center for Advanced Studies, 1978.

Glasser, Arthur F. *The Glen Eyrie Report, No. 4, Muslim Evangelism*. Wheaton: Lausanne Committee for World Evangelization, 1978.

Goitein, S. C. "The Origin and Nature of the Muslim Friday Worship." *The Muslim World*, vol. 49, no. 3 (July 1959), pp. 183–95.

Goldsmith, Martin. *Islam and Christian Witness*. Downers Grove: Inter-Varsity, 1983.

Gowing, Peter G. "Muslim Filipinos Today." *The Muslim World*, vol. 54 (January 1964), pp. 39–48.

Granet, Marcel. *The Religion of the Chinese People*. Translated and edited by Maurice Freedman. Harper and Row, 1975.

Grant, Robert M. *Early Christianity and Society: Seven Studies*. New York: Harper and Row, 1977.

Greeley, Andrew M. *The Denominational Society: A Sociological Approach to Religion in America*. Glenview, Ill.: Scott, Foresman and Company, 1972.

Guillaume, Alfred. *Islam*. Baltimore: Penguin, 1954.

Habib, Madelain. "Some Notes on the Naqshbandi Order." *The Muslim World*, vol. 59 (January 1969), pp. 40–45.

Haines, Charles Reginald. *Islam as a Missionary Religion*. London: S.P.C.K., 1889.

Haleblian, Krikor. "World View and Evangelization: A Case Study on Arab People." Th.M. thesis. Pasadena, Calif.: Fuller Theological Seminary, 1979.

Havlik, John F. *People-Centered Evangelism*. Nashville: Broadman, 1971.

Hirashima, Hussein Yoshio. *The Road to Holy Mecca*. Tokyo: Japan Publications Trading Co., 1972.

Hitti, Philip K. *The Arabs: A Short History*. Chicago: Henry Regnery, 1943.

Hodgson, Marshall. *The Venture of Islam: A Short History of Islamic Civilization*. Vol. 1, *The Classical Age of Islam;* vol. 2, *The Expansion of Islam in the Middle Periods;* vol. 3, *The Gunpowder Empires and Modern Times*. Chicago: University of Chicago Press, 1974.

Hoffman, Valerie J. "Researching the Religious Life of Muslim Women in Modern Egypt." Paper submitted to the American Research Center, Egypt, 1981.

Holland, Muhtar. *The Duties of Brotherhood in Islam*. Leicester: The Islamic Foundation, 1980.

Hottinger, Arnold. *The Arabs*. Berkeley: University of California Press, 1963.

Houtsma, M., A. J. Wensinck, T. W. Arnold, W. Heffening, and E. Levi-Provencal. *The Encyclopedia of Islam*. Vol. 2. London: Luzac, 1927.

Houtsma, M., A. J. Wensinck, H. A. R. Gibb, W. Heffening, and E. Levi-Provencal. *The Encyclopedia of Islam*. London: Luzac, 1934.

Hudson, Winthrop S. "Denominationalism as a Basis for Ecumenicity: A Seventeenth Century Conception." In *Denominationalism*, edited by Russell E. Richey, pp. 21–42. Nashville: Abingdon, 1977.

Hughes, E. R. *Religion in China*. London: Hutchinson's University Library, 1950.

Hurgronje, Snouck. *Mekka*. Translated by J. H. Monahan. London: Luzac, 1931.

Husaini, Ishak M. "Islamic Culture in Arab and African Countries." In *Islam: The Straight Path*, edited by Kenneth W. Morgan, pp. 224–52. New York: Ronald Press, 1958.

Hussain, Fida. *Wives of the Prophet*. Lahore: Shaikh Muhammad Ashraf, 1952.

Idris, Gaafar Sheikh. *The Process of Islamization.* Indianapolis: Muslim Students' Association of the U.S. and Canada, 1977.

Ikram, S. M. *Muslim Civilization in India.* Edited by A. T. Embree. New York: Columbia University Press, 1964.

Inrig, Gary. *Life in His Body: Discovering Purpose, Form, and Freedom in His Church.* Wheaton: Shaw, 1975.

"In Search of Understanding and Cooperation." *Al-Basheer,* vol. 2 (January-March 1973), pp. 61–69.

Iqbal, Muhammad. *Islam and Ahmadism.* Lucknow: Academy of Islamic Research and Publications, 1974.

―――. *The Mission of Islam.* New Delhi: Vikas Publishing House, 1977.

Ishaat-e-Diniyat. *A Call to Muslims.* New Delhi: Idara-e-Diniyat, 1944.

Islam, A. K. M. Aminul. *A Bangladesh Village: Conflict and Cohesion.* Cambridge, Mass.: Schenkman, 1973.

Jafri, Husain M. *Origins and Early Development of Shi'a Islam.* London: Longman, 1979.

Jansen, G. H. *Militant Islam.* New York: Harper and Row, 1979.

Jeffery, Arthur, ed. *Islam: Muhammad and His Religion.* New York: Bobbs-Merrill, 1958.

Johnstone, P. De Lacy. *Muhammad and His Power.* Edinburgh: T. and T. Clark, 1901.

Jomier, Jacques. *The Bible and the Koran.* Translated by Edward P. Arbez. New York: Desclee, 1964.

Jones, L. Bevan. *Christianity Explained to Muslims.* 1937. Calcutta: Baptist Mission Press, 1964.

―――. *The People of the Mosque.* Calcutta: Baptist Mission Press, 1932.

Joseph, John. *The Nestorians and Their Muslim Neighbors: A Study of Western Influence on Their Relations.* Princeton: Princeton University Press, 1961.

Karim, Abdul. *Social History of Muslims in Bengal.* Dacca: Asiatic Society of Pakistan, 1959.

Karim, M. N. "Hajj and Muslim Fraternity." *Bangladesh Observer,* 27 September 1982, p. 8.

Kateregga, Badru D., and David W. Shenk. *Islam and Christianity: A Muslim and a Christian in Dialogue.* Grand Rapids: Eerdmans, 1981.

Kee, Howard Clarke. *Community in the New Age.* London: SCM, 1977.

Khan, Inamullah. "Islam in the Contemporary World." In *God and Man in Contemporary Islamic Thought,* edited by Charles Malik, pp. 1–15. Beirut: American University of Beirut, 1972.

Khan, Muhammad Zafrulla. *Islam: Its Meaning for Modern Man.* New York: Harper and Row, 1962.

Khomeini, Imam. *Islam and Revolution: Writings and Declarations of Imam Khomeini.* Translated by Hamid Algar. Berkeley: Mizan, 1980.

Kik, J. Marcellus. *Church and State: The Story of Two Kingdoms.* New York: Nelson, 1963.

Kitagawa, Joseph M. *Religions of the East.* Philadelphia: Westminster, 1960.

Klein, F. A. *The Religion of Islam.* New York: Humanities, 1906.

Kushner, Harold S. *When Bad Things Happen to Good People.* New York: Schocken, 1981.

Lamonte, John L. "Crusade and Jihad." In *The Arab Heritage,* edited by Nabih Amin Faris. Princeton: Princeton University Press, 1946.

Landon, Kenneth Perry. *Southeast Asia: Crossroad of Religions.* Chicago: University of Chicago Press, 1949.

Lane-Poole, Stanley. *Studies in a Mosque.* London: Eden, Remington and Co., 1893.

LaPiere, Richard. *Collective Behavior.* New York: McGraw-Hill, 1938.

Latif, Syed Abdul. *Islamic Cultural Studies.* Lahore: Shaikh Muhammad Ashraf, 1947.

Latourette, Kenneth Scott. *A History of Christianity.* Vol. 2, *A.D. 1500–A.D. 1975.* New York: Harper and Row, 1975.

LeTourneau, Roger. "North Africa: Rigorism and Bewilderment." In *Unity and Variety in Muslim Civilization,* edited by G. E. Von Grunebaum. Chicago: University of Chicago Press, 1955.

Levy, Reuben. *The Social Structure of Islam.* Cambridge: At the University Press, 1969.

Lewis, Bernard. "Politics and War." In *The Legacy of Islam,* edited by Joseph Schacht, pp. 156–209. 2d ed. Oxford: Clarendon, 1974.

———. *Race and Color in Islam.* New York: Harper and Row, 1971.

Lings, Martin. *What Is Sufism?* Berkeley: University of California Press, 1975.

Loffler, Paul. "Religion, Nations and a Search for a World Community—Reflections from a Christian Theological Perspective." *Al Basheer*, vol. 2 (January-March 1973), pp. 17–21.

Malik, Charles, ed. "Introduction." In *God and Man in Contemporary Islamic Thought*, edited by Charles Malik. Beirut: American University of Beirut, pp. (1)–(100).

Marsh, Paul W. "The Church and World Mission." In *In God's Community: Essays on the Church and Its Ministry*, edited by David J. Ellis and W. Ward Gasque, pp. 102–12. Wheaton: Shaw, 1978.

Matheny, Tim. *Reaching the Arabs: A Felt Need Approach*. Pasadena, Calif.: William Carey Library, 1981.

Maududi, Abul A'la. *Ethical View Point of Islam*. Lahore: Islamic Publications, 1966.

———. *First Principles of the Islamic State*. Lahore: Islamic Publications, 1960.

———. *Jihad in Islam*. Lahore: Islamic Publications, 1976.

———. *Political Theory of Islam*. Lahore: Islamic Publications, 1960.

———. *The Process of Islamic Revolution*. Lahore: Islamic Publications, 1947.

———. *Unity of the Muslim World*. Lahore: Islamic Publications, 1967.

Mellis, Charles J. *Committed Communities: Fresh Streams for World Missions*. Pasadena, Calif.: William Carey Library, 1976.

Miller, Haskell M. *Compassion and Community: An Appraisal of the Church's Changing Role in Social Welfare*. New York: Association, 1961.

Milson, Menahem, trans. *A Sufi Rule for Novices*, being a translation of *Kitab Adab al-Muridin* by Abu al-Najib al-Suhrawardi. Cambridge: Harvard University Press, 1975.

Mitchell, Richard. *The Society of the Muslim Brothers*. London: Oxford University Press, 1969.

Mohs, Mayo. "Muslims Against Muslims." *Time*, 6 September 1982, p. 14.

Moraes, Dom. *The Tempest Within: An Account of East Pakistan*. New York: Barnes and Noble, 1971.

Morgan, Kenneth W., ed. *Islam: The Straight Path*. New York: Ronald Press, 1958.

Morton, Thomas Ralph. *Community of Faith: The Changing Pattern of the Church's Life*. New York: Association, 1954.

Murdock, George Peter. *Social Structure*. New York: Macmillan, 1949.

Mushir-ul-Haq. "Inter-Religious Understanding, A Step for Realization of the Ideal of the World Community." *Al-Basheer*, vol. 2 (January-March 1983), pp. 13-17.

Muslehuddin, Mohammad. *Sociology and Islam.* Lahore: Islamic Publications, 1977.

MacKeen, A. M. M. "The Sufi-Qawm Movement." *The Muslim World*, vol. 53, no. 3.

McAllister, Robert J. *Conflict in Community.* Collegeville, Minn.: Saint John's University Press, 1969.

McCurry, Don M., ed. *The Gospel and Islam.* Monrovia, Calif.: MARCC, 1978.

McDonald, Philip M. "Islamic Social Stratification in Rural Bangladesh: A Sociological Approach to Muslim Evangelism." Research project, Grand Rapids, 1978.

McDougall, William. *The Group Mind.* New York: Knickerbocker, 1920.

Nadwi, Abul Hasan Ali. *Islam in a Changing World.* Lucknow: Academy of Islamic Research and Publications, 1977.

————. *The New Menace and Its Answer.* Lucknow: Academy of Islamic Research and Publications, n.d.

————. *Qadianism: A Critical Study.* Translated by Zafar Ishaq Anseri. Lahore: Shaikh Muhammad Ashraf, 1965.

————. *Western Civilisation Islam and Muslims.* Translated by Mohammad Asif Kidwai. Lucknow: Academy of Islamic Research and Publications, 1978.

Naisbitt, John. *Megatrends: Ten New Directions for Transforming Our Lives.* New York: Warner, 1982.

Nasr, Seyyed Hossein. *Ideals and Realities of Islam.* New York: Praeger, 1967.

Nazir-Ali, Michael. "Christology in an Islamic Context." In *Sharing Jesus in the Two Thirds World*, edited by Vinay Samuel and Chris Sugden, pp. 205-28. Bangalore: Partnership in Mission—Asia, 1983.

————. *Islam: A Christian Perspective.* Exeter: Paternoster, 1983.

Nee, Watchman. *The Normal Christian Church Life.* Washington, D.C.: International Students Press, 1962.

Neill, Stephen. *Men of Unity.* London: SCM, 1960.

Newbigin, Lesslie. *Is Christ Divided? A Plea for Christian Unity in a Revolutionary Age.* Grand Rapids: Eerdmans, 1961.

Niazi, Kausar. *Role of the Mosque.* Lahore: Shaikh Muhammad Ashraf, 1979.

Nicholson, R. A. "Mysticism." In *The Legacy of Islam*, edited by T. W. Arnold and Alfred Guillaume, pp. 210–38. London: Oxford University Press, 1931.

Niebuhr, H. Richard. *Christ and Culture*. New York: Harper and Row, 1951.

Niebuhr, Reinhold. *Christian Realism and Political Problems*. New York: Scribner's, 1953.

———. *Man's Nature and His Communities*. New York: Scribner's, 1965.

Nute, Alan G. "Worship." In *In God's Community: Essays on the Church and Its Ministry*, edited by David J. Ellis and W. Ward Gasque, pp. 40–51. Wheaton: Shaw, 1978.

O'Connor, Elizabeth. *The New Community*. New York: Harper and Row, 1976.

Oster, Kenneth. *Islam Reconsidered: A Brief Historical Background to the Religion and Thought of the Moslem World*. Hicksville, N.Y.: Exposition, 1979.

Padilla, C. Rene. "The Unity of the Church and the Homogeneous Unit Principle." *International Bulletin of Missionary Research*, vol. 6 (January 1982), pp. 23–30.

Padwick, Constance E. *Muslim Devotions*. London: S.P.C.K., 1961.

Parker, Edward Harper. *China and Religion*. New York: Dutton, 1905.

Parshall, Phil. *Bridges to Islam: A Christian Perspective on Folk Islam*. Grand Rapids: Baker, 1983.

———. "Evangelizing Muslims: Are There Ways?" *Christianity Today*, January 1979, pp. 28–31.

———. *The Fortress and the Fire*. Bombay: Gospel Literature Service, 1976.

———. *New Paths in Muslim Evangelism: Evangelical Approaches to Contextualization*. Grand Rapids: Baker, 1980.

Paton, William. *World Community*. London: Student Christian Movement Press, 1938.

Peck, Malcolm C. "Saudi Arabia, Islamic Traditionalism and Modernization." In *Change and the Muslim World*, edited by Philip H. Stoddard, David C. Cuthell, and Margaret W. Sullivan, pp. 137–43. Syracuse, N.Y.: Syracuse University Press, 1981.

Peters, Rudolph. *Jihad in Mediaeval and Modern Islam*. Leiden: Brill, 1977.

Pickthall, Mohammed Marmaduke. *The Cultural Side of Islam*. Delhi: Islamic Book Trust, 1982.

———. *The Meaning of the Glorious Koran*. London: New American Library, 1953.

Pillsbury, Barbara L. K. "Islam, 'Even Unto China'." In *Change and the Muslim World*, edited by Philip H. Stoddard, David C. Cuthell, and Margaret W. Sullivan, pp. 107–44. Syracuse, N.Y.: Syracuse University Press, 1981.

"Qadianis—Non-Muslim."*Arabia*, June 1984, pp. 72–73.

Qazi, M. A. *A Concise Dictionary of Islamic Terms*. Chicago: Kazi, 1979.

Rahman, Fazlur. *Islam*. 2d ed. Chicago: University of Chicago Press, 1979.

Ramadan, Said. *Islam and Nationalism*. Takoma Park, Md.: Crescent, n.d.

Ramey, Robert Frank. "The Soteriology of Islam." Thesis presented to the Department of Theology, Dallas Theological Seminary, 1959.

Rashid, Mian Abdur. *Islam in the Indo-Pakistan Sub-Continent*. Lahore: National Book Foundation, 1977.

Rasjidi, Mohammad. "Unity and Diversity in Islam." In *Islam: The Straight Path*, edited by Kenneth W. Morgan, pp. 403–30. New York: Ronald Press, 1958.

Rauf, Mohammed A. *A Brief History of Islam*. Kuala Lumpur: Oxford University Press, 1964.

Reichelt, Karl Ludvig. *Religion in Chinese Garment*. Translated by Joseph Tetlie. London: Lutterworth, 1951.

Richey, Russell E., ed. *Denominationalism*. Nashville: Abingdon, 1977.

Rifkin, Jeremy, and Nicanor Perlas. *Algeny*. New York: Viking, 1983.

Rixhon, Gerard. "The Philippines." *The Muslim World*, vol. 56, no. 4 (October 1966), pp. 307–11.

Sadler, Albert W. "Visit to a Chishti Qawwali." *The Muslim World*, vol. 53, no. 4 (1963), pp. 287–92.

Sailer, T. H. P. *The Muslim Faces the Future*. New York: Missionary Education Movement of the U.S. and Canada, 1926.

Samuel, Vinay, and Chris Sugden, eds. *Sharing Jesus in the Two Thirds World*. Bangalore: Partnership in Mission—Asia, 1983.

Sarason, Seymour B. *The Psychological Sense of Community: Prospects for a Community Psychology*. San Francisco: Jossey-Bass, 1977.

Saunders, John J., ed. *The Muslim World on the Eve of Europe's Expansion*. Englewood Cliffs, N.J.: Prentice-Hall, 1966.

Sayegh, Fayez A. *Arab Unity: Hope and Fulfillment.* New York: Devin-Adair, 1958.

Schaeffer, Francis A. *The Church at the End of the Twentieth Century.* Downers Grove: Inter-Varsity, 1970.

Schanz, John P. *A Theology of Community.* Washington, D.C.: University Press of America, 1977.

Schimmel, Annemarie. *Mystical Dimensions of Islam.* Chapel Hill: University of North Carolina Press, 1975.

Schlorff, Samuel P., ed. *Discipleship in Islamic Society.* Upper Darby, Penn.: North Africa Mission, 1981.

Shaltout, Mahmud. "Islamic Beliefs and Code of Laws." In *Islam: The Straight Path,* edited by Kenneth W. Morgan, pp. 87–143. New York: Ronald Press, 1958.

Shedd, Russell Philip. *Man in Community: A Study of Saint Paul's Application of Old Testament and Early Jewish Concepts of Human Solidarity.* Grand Rapids: Eerdmans, 1964.

Shedd, William Ambrose. *Islam and the Oriental Churches: Their Historical Relations.* New York: Presbyterian Board of Publication, 1904.

Siddiqi, Mazheruddin. "Muslim Culture in Pakistan and India." In *Islam: The Straight Path,* edited by Kenneth W. Morgan, pp. 296–343. New York: Ronald Press, 1958.

Smith, Timothy L. "Congregation, State and Denomination: The Forming of the American Religious Structure." In *Denominationalism,* edited by Russell E. Richey, pp. 47–67. Nashville: Abingdon, 1977.

Smith, Wilfred Cantwell. *Islam in Modern History.* Princeton: Princeton University Press, 1957.

————. *On Understanding Islam.* The Hague: Mouton, 1981.

Snyder, Howard A. "The Church as Community: Subculture or Counterculture?" *Christianity Today,* 8 April 1983, pp. 28–32.

————. *The Community of the King.* Downers Grove: Inter-Varsity, 1977.

————. *The Problem of Wine Skins: Church Structure in a Technological Age.* Downers Grove: Inter-Varsity, 1975.

Stanton, H. U. Weitbrecht. *The Teaching of the Quran.* London: S.P.C.K., 1969.

Stewart, Desmond. *The Arab World.* New York: Time-Life Books, 1962.

Stoddard, Philip H., David C. Cuthell, and Margaret W. Sullivan, eds.

Change and the Muslim World. Syracuse, N.Y.: Syracuse University Press, 1981.

Stokes, Anson Phelps, and Leo Pfeffer. *Church and State in the United States.* New York: Harper and Row, 1950.

Swartz, Merlin L., ed. *Studies on Islam.* New York: Oxford University Press, 1981.

Ting, Dawood C. M. "Islamic Culture in China." In *Islam: The Straight Path,* edited by Kenneth W. Morgan, pp. 344–74. New York: Ronald Press, 1958.

Toffler, Alvin. *The Third Wave.* New York: Morrow, 1980.

Towns, Elmer L. *Is the Day of the Denomination Dead?* Nashville: Nelson, 1973.

Trimingham, J. Spencer. *The Sufi Orders in Islam.* London: Oxford University Press, 1971.

Uris, Leon. *The Haj.* London: Andre Deutsch, 1984.

Van Donzel, E., B. Lewis, and Ch. Pellat. *The Encyclopedia of Islam, New Edition.* Leiden: Brill, 1978.

Van Halsema, Thea B. *This Was John Calvin.* 1959. Grand Rapids: Baker, 1981.

Voll, John Obert. *Islam: Continuity and Change in the Modern World.* Boulder: Westview, 1982.

Von Grunebaum, G. E. *Modern Islam: The Search for Cultural Identity.* New York: Vintage, 1962.

———. *Muhammadan Festivals.* London: Curzon, 1951.

Waddy, Charis. *The Muslim Mind.* London: Longman Group, 1976.

Wagemaker, Herbert, Jr. *A Special Kind of Belonging: The Christian Community.* Waco: Word, 1978.

Watt, W. Montgomery. *Islam and the Integration of Society.* Great Britain: Northwestern University Press, 1961.

———. *Muhammad at Mecca.* Oxford: Clarendon, 1953.

———. *Muhammad at Medina.* Oxford: Clarendon, 1956.

———. *What Is Islam?* New York: Longman Group, 1968.

Weekes, Richard V., ed. *Muslim Peoples: A World Ethnographic Survey.* Westport, Conn.: Greenwood, 1978.

Werning, Waldo J. *The Radical Nature of Christianity.* Pasadena, Calif.: Mandate, 1975.

Wherry, E. M. *Islam and Christianity in India and the Far East.* New York: Revell, 1907.

Wilber, Donald N. *Pakistan.* New Haven: Hraf, 1964.

Williams, John Alden. *Islam*. New York: Braziller, 1963.

Williams, John Alden, ed. *Islam*. New York: Washington Square, 1961.

Williams, L. F. Rushbrook, ed. *Sufi Studies: East and West*. New York: Dutton, 1974.

Youssef, Michael. "Theology and Methodology for Muslim Evangelism in Egypt." M.A. thesis. Pasadena, Calif.: Fuller Theological Seminary, 1978.

Zimmerman, Carl C. *The Changing Community*. New York: Harper and Brothers, 1938.

Zwemer, Samuel M. *Heirs of the Prophets*. Chicago: Moody, 1946.

———. "Is Allah God?" *World Vision*, April 1967, pp. 7, 22.

———. *Islam: A Challenge to Faith*. New York: Student Volunteer Movement for Foreign Missions, 1907.

———. *The Law of Apostasy in Islam*. London: Marshall Brothers, 1924.

———. *The Moslem Christ*. New York: American Tract Society, 1912.

———. *A Moslem Seeker after God*. New York: Revell, 1920.

Index of Subjects

Index of Scripture

Index of Quranic References